T0320140

Restructuring Eastern Europe

To my parents

Restructuring Eastern Europe

The Microeconomics of the Transition Process

Edited by

Soumitra Sharma

Associate Dean and Professor of Economics, University of Zagreb, Croatia

Edward Elgar
Cheltenham, UK • Lyme, US

Published by
Edward Elgar Publishing Limited
8 Lansdown Place
Cheltenham
Glos GL50 2HU
UK

Edward Elgar Publishing Company
1 Pinnacle Hill Road
Lyme
NH 03768
US

A catalogue record for this book
is available from the British Library

ISBN 1 85898 576 5

Printed and bound in Great Britain by
Biddles Limited, Guildford and King's Lynn

Contents

Figures

Tables

Contributors

Will Bartlett, *Reader at the School for Policy Studies, University of Bristol (England).*

Milford Bateman, *Senior Research Fellow and Head of the Local Economic Development in Transition Economies Unit (LEDTEU) in the School of Languages and European Studies, University of Wolverhampton (England).*

Vladimír Benáček, *Research Fellow at Center for Economic Research and Graduate Education, Charls University and Economics Institute of the Czech Academy of Sciences of the Czech Republic, Prague (The Czech Republic).*

Aleksandar Bogunović, *Professor of Economics at the Faculty of Economics, University of Zagreb (Croatia).*

Shkelqim Cani, *Member of Parliament of Albania, Tirana (Albania).*

Bob Donnorummo, *Deputy Director Center for Russian and East European Studies, University of Pittsburgh, PA (USA).*

Ivo Družić, *Associate Professor of Economics at the Faculty of Economics, University of Zagreb (Croatia).*

David Dyker, *Fellow at the Science Policy Research Unit, University of Sussex, Brighton (England).*

Marin Aleksandrov Marinov, *Professor of Marketing at the Technical University, Sofia (Bulgaria). Currently Visiting Professor at School of Business, University of Colorado at Colorado Springs, COL (USA).*

Alexei Petrov, *Research Fellow at Center for Economic Research and Graduate Education, Charls University and Economics Institute of the Czech Academy of Sciences of the Czech Republic, Prague (The Czech Republic).*

Slavo Radošević, *Fellow at the Science Policy Research Unit, University of Sussex, Brighton (England).*

Soumitra Sharma, *Professor of Economics and Associate Dean of the Faculty of Economics, University of Zagreb (Croatia).*

Dmitri Shemetilo, *Research Fellow at Center for Economic Research and Graduate Education, Charls University and Economics Institute of the Czech Academy of Sciences of the Czech Republic, Prague (The Czech Republic).*

Pere Sikavica, *Professor of Management at the Faculty of Economics, University of Zagreb (Croatia).*

Marko Škreb, *Governor, National Bank of Croatia, Zagreb (Croatia).*

Jennifer Steedman, *Research Scholar, CERT, Economics Department, Heriot-Watt University, Riccarton, Edinburgh (Scotland).*

Janko Tintor, *Professor of Economics at the Faculty of Economics, University of Zagreb (Croatia).*

Jan Toporowski, *Reader in Economics, South Bank University, London (England).*

Introduction

Bob Donnorummo

Many of the transition countries have achieved considerable progress with macro-economic stabilization and reform, and the fruits of their effort to transform their economies are increasingly visible. Clearly, the transition process is working. (IMF, *World Economic Outlook*, Washington, DC, May, 1996)

This optimistic and promising observation by the IMF experts needs careful analysis, as lately many questions are being raised. The questions commonly being asked concern the role of the state in economic transitions occurring in Eastern Europe, the difference between the post-1989 transition period and other periods of great change in modern Eastern Europe, and what the developments in this transition process tell us about the type of market economy unfolding in Eastern Europe.

Our analysis relates the developments taking place in most of these countries, but the focus remains on the south-eastern and Vishygrad countries. By providing three general observations, we may identify the guiding philosophy of this ongoing process.

- In terms of economic progress, the transformation from state-owned command economies to privately owned market economies has been successful, although some countries have made more progress than others.
- Those countries which swallowed their bad-tasting medicine early and in large doses have been more successful than those which have attempted to implement a more gradual approach.
- In those countries where the state's direct involvement in the economy has been limited, one finds stronger and more potentially enduring economic development.

Should the state tightly control the transition process or limit its role to establishing helpful policies and institutions, as well as being an enforcer of abuses? While this analysis prefers the latter as a matter of principle, the issue is too broad to be answered by one definitive answer for the entire region. Each country faces specific and unique conditions and challenges, hence the latitude for the positive as well as negative roles for a particular state are wide-ranging. The view presented here is that, while efficient, predictable and attentive central and local governments are certainly positive factors, their role is sometimes overrated. The critical task for the states was (or in some cases, is) to quickly create policies and mechanisms conducive to privatization, liberalize prices and construct a legal and financial infrastructure appropriate for the establishment of a market economy. After making this radical break with the past, the role played by political institutions and leaders remains very important, but other, non-political, determining variables must also be highlighted.

THE ROLE OF THE STATE

The role of the state and political leadership in economic development is a complex and fundamental issue which defies simplification. If, for example, one extols the virtues of actions of leaders who at the very early stages of the transition process implemented a more radical approach and considers them to be more clever than those who did not, since their economics have in general fared better and appear to have established an enduring base for continued progress, one would be forced to acknowledge that there are two problems associated with this causal relationship. First, the GDP data for 1995 show that two countries whose political leaders implemented a gradual approach, the Slovak Republic and Romania, grew faster than Poland and the Czech Republic which took the fast track to the transition. Second, in 1989 there were many pre-existing determining conditions over which political leaders had little or no control.

One of the most important variables determining the speed and depth of the changes to be implemented, that is, a gradual and less fundamental versus a rapid and more radical approach, was the economic situation confronting the new leadership in 1989 (Slay, 1994, pp. 31–42). The immediate post-1989 governments of Eastern Europe had to assess the relative saliency of the existing inflation rates, the size of the foreign debt and the number of market mechanisms already in place in the former socialist economy. Also the existing structure of the economy was an important variable. In part, those countries which had stronger economies in 1989, the Czech Republic and Hungary, had more of a cushion in facing the structural problems.

There were also a range of critical non-economic factors such as the presence of a large national minority who might object to the austerity measures inherently associated with the more radical approach since they might view this approach as the spiteful handiwork of the ruling majority nationality. For example, the ethnically homogeneous nature of the Polish society allowed its leaders to implement austerity measures with less fear of backlash than would have been the case in the more heterogeneous societies of Romania, Bulgaria or Ukraine. Furthermore, conditions in a society which suffered extraordinarily acute material and psychological hardships under the preceding communist regime, such as Romania, may cause the austerity of a more radical approach to be politically unacceptable.

In addition, policy decisions had to consider such matters as the impact of the absence of trusted mediating institutions such as independent courts or police forces, and legal and financial infrastructures supportive of a market economy. Yet, given the experiences of the former Yugoslavia, as well as Georgia, Armenia, Azerbaijan and Tajikistan, one would have to note that the above-mentioned factors are reduced to comparative insignificance if there is an outbreak of nationalistically inspired collective violence. Then the determination of policy choices places state security above economic development, and the options presented to the leadership narrow considerably. This has been the experience of Croatia before 1996, for example.

Hence the selection of one set of policies and procedures as opposed to another is the result of a wide variety of economic and political factors. Cultural values and historical experiences also play a determining role, as do the presence or absence of dissatisfied and angry minorities, and the existing international atmosphere which in itself sets limits to the options afforded the political leaders of countries in transition. Having noted that there is not one correct path, the data on macroeconomic growth in the 1990s suggest that those countries which moved rapidly to implement price liberalization, private ownership (and, more slowly, restructuring of the economy) and began to erect the financial, legal and other institutions of a market economy, have been rewarded.[1] The two countries which were the first to take the fast-track plunge, Poland in 1990 and Czechoslovakia in 1991, have demonstrated superior economic growth during 1994–96. It is held that there is a causal connection between their policies which were designed to make a swift and fundamental transformation, and the economic success they are at present experiencing, as well as their economic outlook for the rest of the decade. They are outperforming the other countries of the region, most notably Hungary, which did not commit itself to fundamental change until 1994. However, a longer time span on a variety of comparative data is required, and there are short-termed exceptions to this proposed causal relationship. In 1995, the Slovak Republic and Romania, countries which have not moved as radically as Poland and the Czech Republic in transforming their economies, had superior rates of GDP growth: 7.4 per cent for the Slovak Republic and a surprising 6.9 per cent for Romania.[2] As with all data of a short-term nature, one should not overreact. The economies of the Slovak Republic and Romania are in large part determined by the results of a few large enterprises which are quite capable of exaggerating short-term trends.

The absence of a clear verdict on how to transform these economies most effectively is not surprising. The fact that many scholars were not able to put this transition in proper perspective in the first three or four years of the process is understandable, given that it is a unique revolution and as such at first unable to provide effective theoretical guides. It is not difficult to find books or articles written in 1992, 1993 or 1994 by thoughtful people who were doubtful about the possibility of a successful transition. The early years of the transition produced some dramatically negative numbers on the decline in industrial production and GDP, with exceedingly sharp drops of 40 to 50 per cent being the norm. For example, one of Europe's fastest growing economies in 1994 and 1995, Poland, had been experiencing serious problems since 1978 and faced very steep industrial and GDP declines in 1990, 1991 and 1992 (Kierzkowski *et al.*, 1994). One example of extreme pessimism concerning the changes is a publication resulting from a conference held in 1993 whose opening chapter notes that, 'in less than two years the enthusiasm and optimism for the transition ... turned into disappointment and distrust. What went wrong?' (Akyuz, 1994, p.3). The response to this rhetorical question is that, given the revolutionary nature of the transition, surprisingly little has gone wrong, at least in terms of the economic developments. By far the most serious problems have been caused by the surfacing of bitter nationalistic antagonisms and military conflicts which prevent one from labelling the transformations an unqualified success.

On the admittedly somewhat rarefied level of macroeconomics, the transformations have experienced a very promising start. Granted that the depression-like figures posted in Eastern Europe between 1989 and 1993 caused a great deal of individual pain and suffering, and that the baselines for judging future growth rates were lowered considerably, cannot be overlooked that, excluding the five countries of the former Yugoslavia, these economies grew at a 3.4 per cent rate in 1994 and 4.0 per cent in 1995.[3] The outlook for the next several years remains positive, and Russia, which began its path to radical transformation in 1992, may also improve its economy in 1997.

A corollary of this generally positive assessment is that the fear of significant social disruptions and the perceived dangers associated with the return of former communists to political power by voters who have experienced acute material deprivations and a loss of economic security during the transition have been played down. There are analysts who focus on the populace's pain and suffering, which is justified in that it is undeniably part of the process. Some imply that impending social upheavals will derail the entire transition. One cannot disprove something which has not yet happened and, since 1989, Eastern Europe has not experienced major social upheavals.

Perhaps there will be serious disruptions in the future, yet collective violence caused by the surfacing of nationalistic antagonisms is a much more likely candidate to derail a particular transformation, not the serious and admittedly potentially dangerous gap between rich and poor.

Nonetheless, this approach to developments in the region runs the risk of being callously glib. There is little doubt that the economic transition has been joyless for much of the population, and that only a minority have as yet benefited.[4] This is significant since it enhances the potential for disruptive phenomena such as strikes or large-scale protests, as well as a tendency to vote the initial reformers out of office. Yet it is held that social unrest (as opposed to nationalistic violence) has not been significant in the eastern half of the European continent in the 1990s, something that cannot be said for some countries in the west, and that this threat remains only a potentiality, not a reality. Secondly, while it is true that the original reformers, with the exceptions of Klaus in the Czech Republic and Berisha in Albania,[5] have been voted out of office, their replacements have not indicated that they will derail the transition process.

There is no doubt that many people in Eastern Europe are frustrated by their lack of job security,[6] high prices and inflation which has been extremely difficult for pensioners, but they have not taken to the streets in protest. In fact, there were more serious political and economic explosions in the pre-1989 regimes. Widening income gaps, poor health conditions and a host of other justified complaints require the close attention of the governments in the region, as well as the understanding of the International Monetary Fund. While there is often good reason to question the wisdom of the relative lack of a more assertive state policy, especially in the area of social policy (Orenstein, 1996, pp. 16–20), the solutions are not to be found in the previous system which itself had a failed social policy. Furthermore, contrary to the views of some politicians and analysts, there does not seem to be a clear causal link between the speed at which a country implemented its transition and the severity of the deprivations experienced by its populace. A comparison of Hungary with either the Czech Republic or Poland will demonstrate this point.[7]

It could be argued that of all the countries of Eastern Europe, Hungary, which had significantly tinkered with the socialist command economy from 1968 by introducing numerous market mechanisms, was the most advantageously poised to take advantage of the post-1989 transition. However, the conservative leadership of the Hungarian Democratic Forum between 1990 and 1994 decided not to implement radical and deep reforms, hoping to spare its citizens the pain associated with a more radical approach. It is held that this has not been the case.

A glance at the recent rates of GDP growth show that the Czech Republic and Poland grew two to three times faster than Hungary in 1994 and 1995, and that superior growth is scheduled to continue in 1996.[8] It is true that before 1994 Hungary's consumer price index rose less sharply than Poland's, but its increase was higher than in the Czech Republic.[9] Also Hungary did not experience the steep GDP declines of either Poland or Hungary in the 1990–94 period, with 20 per cent as opposed to almost 50 per cent. Yet the real wages of Hungarians, while better in 1990–91, were weaker in 1993–5, with a 10 to 12 per cent decline in 1995.[10] Furthermore, Hungary's agricultural output declined more noticeably,[11] and by 1995 it was forced to institute austerity programmes, which had been implemented earlier in the other two countries, helping it begin the process of shrinking its 1994 budget deficit of US$3.9 billion (7 per cent of GDP). Ironically, the gradualist approach was essentially abandoned by the former communists who were voted into power in May 1994 (Szilagyi,1995, pp. 62–6).

Hungary's failure to implement deep and fundamental changes in its policies of providing state subsidies resulted in a gross domestic public debt, which was 4 per cent relative to GDP in 1990, ballooning to about 25 per cent in 1993.[12] In 1995, expenditure on social welfare programmes, especially health and pensions, was almost 30 per cent of GDP, surpassed in Europe only by Sweden, a much wealthier country.[13]

Poland took a different path to transition when it instituted the more radical Balcerowicz Plan in January 1990. It freed prices, limited the growth of wages, tightened credit, and many firms were declared bankrupt and not subsidized by the state. In many cases these firms were purchased by their workers and management. Predictably prices skyrocketed, jobs were lost and unemployment shot up to 17 per cent (Mroziewicz, 1996, pp. 26–7).

The Czech Republic initiated its radical transition policies in January 1991. Privatization occurred via the voucher system, as opposed to Poland's privatization through liquidation. However, the Czech model was, and remains, more a controlled system where the state played a more active role in both social policy and its indirect control of privatized firms via state-owned banks which own investment firms which in turn had purchased 73 per cent of the vouchers, which were then converted into shares of companies placed on the stock exchange. The state provided a safety net using wage controls, subsidies for rent, utilities, transport and so on, as well as devaluing the currency and maintaining fixed exchange rates for the koruna,[14] which were relaxed only in October 1995.

The Czech model of guiding and regulating can be discerned from data on changes in the Czech workforce. Between 1987 and 1994 the total workforce declined by almost 1.9 million jobs (36 per cent), including a 58.7 per cent drop in agricultural employment, a 58.8 per cent loss in wholesale and retail jobs and, most critically, a 36.6 per cent loss in jobs in heavy industry.[15] Yet unemployment was only 3.2 per cent at the end of 1994, and a scant 2.9 per cent at the end of 1995 (Munich and Sorm, 1996, pp. 21–5). There were substantial job gains in construction and trade. Employment was also secured in the sizeable underground economy and in servicing the huge influx of tourists. Additional jobs (66 000) were found in financial services which grew by 275 per cent. The state was also a factor, with 61 000 jobs in public administration, a 51.2 per cent increase on the 1987 level.[16]

There is a debate as to whether the low unemployment rate is caused by a growing economy whose newly emerging private sector is absorbing jobs lost elsewhere or is the result of an economy where there has been too little restructuring and too many protected jobs (Munich and Sorm, 1996). Whatever the reason, the developments in the Czech Republic demonstrate the need for a perspective that extends beyond the policy decisions taken by the political leadership and considers the impact of the existing structure of its economy. This might be best illustrated by a comparison with the Slovak Republic.

Since 1990, the rate of unemployment in the Slovak Republic has been consistently much higher than in the Czech Republic. In 1994, the rate was about 14 per cent, as compared to only about 3.5 per cent for the Czech Republic (Fisher, 1994, pp. 58–65), and at the end of 1995 the rates were 13.1 per cent and 2.9 per cent, respectively. The fact that the Slovak economy was much more dependent on the production of heavy, non-consumer goods (steel, armaments and so on) was an important structural variable contributing to high employment.[17] Given their economic structure, the political leadership of the Slovak Republic was reluctant to travel the same path as the Czech Republic. The party in power since the January 1993 formation of the country (save for eight months in 1994), led by Mecair, has shown a marked distrust of a transition process that is not closely controlled by the state. The leadership presumably concluded that the suffering connected with the rapid and full commitment to market forces would be too severe for the people of the republic.[18] The presence of a few giant heavy industrial concerns dominating the Slovak GDP and labour force was an important part of the decision-making process which caused the state to take greater control over privatization.

As one commentator noted, 'the government thinks concentration [of ownership] and state intervention are the keys to success'.[19] While this remark was made sarcastically, it should be noted that the Slovak Republic's export-driven economy grew impressively in both 1994 and 1995. Its 7.4 per cent GDP growth rate in 1995 is a notable exception to the general rule that those countries which made a comparatively tentative commitment to the market have been outperformed by those who made a stronger commitment. Yet this trend has not stood the test of time, and there is no shortage of analysts who hold that the Slovak Republic's distinctive approach to privatization will prove disadvantageous in the long run. While over two-thirds of the Slovak economy has now been privatized, there are concerns that selling firms to the politically faithful at low prices on the margin and further reductions granted for reinvestments, does not add sufficient capital to the economy (Green, 1996, pp. 27–8).

While this approach had the advantage of avoiding the highly leveraged buy-outs witnessed in the Czech Republic, it contained other problems such as the relative absence of capital for technological improvements, which possibly lowers the competitiveness of the Slovak Republic's exports in the longer run. In general, the Slovak Republic's 'cronyism' runs the considerable risk of making decisions in opposition to market efficiency.

In contrast to the Slovak Republic's decision to cancel the second round of voucher privatization in favour of a rather vague plan to reward the populace with bonds redeemable after five years,[20] the Czech Republic intensified its voucher privatization by placing additional companies on the stock exchange to be purchased by individuals, and especially investment funds, which hold three-quarters of the vouchers. The Czech voucher privatization allowed the public to purchase vouchers for US$35 (100 koruna) which could then be applied to shares of firms later to be listed on the stock exchange, or sold to intermediaries such as investment firms. Hence the Czech Republic provided for the rapid privatization of its economy. Hungary took a different route. It had a head start in small-scale privatization, and also took advantage of the availability of foreign direct investments.[21]

Poland's privatization by liquidation and the more recent establishment of 15 national investment funds to manage over 500 formerly state-owned enterprises, the Czech Republic's voucher privatization, and Hungary's 'organic' small-scale privatization combined with foreign investments have all moved to rapidly privatize their economies. Indeed, during 1990–96 most of the economies of Eastern Europe have become, or are in the process of becoming, mostly private (Done and Robinson, 1995). The exceptions in 1995 remain Yugoslavia, Belarus and some of the Central Asian countries. While acknowledging this remarkable achievement, it is now appropriate for analysts to shift their focus from privatization to other issues, such as corporate control and governance. As Frydman and Rapaczynski have insightfully stated, 'the purpose of privatisation ... is not to transfer title, but to initiate a restructuring of enterprises and a rationalisation of the East European economies'(Frydman and Rapaczynski, 1994, p. 17). The seminal ideas of Frydman and Rapaczynski skilfully advance the position that the state has a central and positive role to play in the transition process. They see the real dangers of unbridled spontaneous development as being the 'capture of control by various special interests (especially labour and management)...and the subordination of economic to political concerns. ... The standard fear is that the cost of the transition may be so high that the process will be thwarted by political obstacles and the popular resistance that faces the still fragile democratic institutions' (Frydman and Rapaczynski, ibid., pp. 4, 46). Armed with this wise counsel, they focused their analysis on concepts that extend beyond privatization, and demonstrated the need for the transition process to provide for a rational functioning of the region's economies, most definitely including the need for accountable and rational corporate governance.[22] Hence Frydman and Rapaczynski are critical of a transition that is at the mercy of spontaneous forces and favour a positive and necessary role for the state.

While Frydman and Rapaczynski are correct in stating that privatization alone is not a sufficient factor for a successful transition, and that accountable and rational corporate governance is critical, one should not forget that privatization itself is essential; it is what most fundamentally distinguishes the communist from the capitalist system. While accepting the warning signals raised by Frydman and Rapaczynski, it should be underscored that those countries which rapidly moved to privatize their economies, no matter how chaotic the process, made the correct decision. The reasons for not moving rapidly towards privatization and deep structural change range from the populace's and leadership's distrust and fear of the consequences of what is perceived as largely uncontrollable market forces to the concern that privatization and austere economic policies could lead to disruptive social unrest. Both are legitimate concerns, but it should be noted that there are also risks in not moving swiftly to transform command economies, in that the absence of growth (à la Bulgaria) can also lead to frustrations which might seek destabilizing outlets.

The case of Ukraine is instructive. The previous leadership of President Kravchuk prominently waved the yellow and blue flag of Ukraine, but neglected economic reform. While Kravchuk's government should receive much credit for avoiding serious internal and external conflicts with its Russian citizens and with Russia, the economic results were disastrous. Since 1994, the new government of Kuchma has adopted a more pragmatic approach in addressing Ukraine's fundamental economic problems. The results concerning ongoing privatization and restructuring efforts are far from clear,[23] and the obstacles to successful economic transition in Ukraine are formidable, yet the way out of their difficulties is not to maintain tight state control and to proceed at a glacier-like pace toward privatization.

Developments in Ukraine argue for rejecting those who point to the absence of strong governmental controls over the transition process as a sign of weakness.[24] There is nothing inherently wrong with guiding the process, as is the case in the Czech Republic, or with state ownership coexisting with private ownership, or with strict regulations placed upon the market-place. However, the key element for success is for the state to create the conditions, politically, mentally and institutionally, for free-flowing economic activity (within acceptable parameters) and to allow forces which it does not completely control to develop the economy. Unless this is done, there can be various degrees of intrusion by the state into the economy.[25]

Poland is an example of a country with a weak and chaotic government, but a growing economy. It has had seven governments since 1989, yet its economy grew by 5 per cent in 1994 and 6.5 per cent in 1995 (Nolan, 1995). This is not to suggest that political chaos is the best formula for economic success during the transition process; only that the presence of strong state control is neither virtuous nor necessary. If nationalistic conflicts can be avoided and a helpful international atmosphere maintained, and if the leadership establishes positive conditions for economic growth, the chances for a successful transition are greatly enhanced regardless of the powers of the central state. In January 1993, *The Economist* got it right when it stated that Poland's neighbours 'should draw lessons from its experience. Not, though, because Polish reform worked perfectly. It did not. On the contrary, Poland provides an excellent example of how reform works when politicians are weak. [While weak], the central government did decide on and create the basic macroeconomic conditions for investment and growth'.[26]

At the other extreme, as late as 1993 it was stated that the 'decline in output has also been less drastic in countries where the state did not really loosen its grip on the economy, e.g. Belarus and Kazakhstan'(Akyuz, 1994, p. 4). With the advantage of hindsight, it is held that Belarus and Kazakhstan are examples of how not to implement a successful transformation. The transition process in Kazakhstan unfortunately demonstrates how a resource-rich country which did not enthusiastically embrace private ownership, for a variety of complex reasons, or establish an open democratic decision making structure has gone from being viewed as a country with strong possibilities for foreign investment to one in which Chevron and Unilever have reduced their level of investment. Chevron slashed its investment in the huge Tengiz oil fields by 90 per cent in 1995, from US$500 million to US$50 million.[27] Much of this had to do with the inability to construct pipelines to reliably transport oil out of Kazakhstan without a veto from Russia,[28] but there were also concerns about the safety of investments which are vulnerable to the decisions of a few strong political leaders and the absence of a legal infrastructure supporting the private sector. In March 1995, President Nazarbayev dissolved the Parliament and was declared the country's leader until 2000.[29] Similar developments have taken place in Uzbekistan and Turkmenistan.[30] A more effective pattern for a successful economic transition out of communism is one that provides more freedom for an emerging private sector.

This perspective which stresses reduced governmental control is not meant to advance the notion that inequities, injustices and outright corruption do not exist, and that all goes along well without state intervention. It should be noted, however, that, until a more effective structure evolves, some inequity is part and parcel of a system based upon private ownership and market relationships. In 1989 (or 1991 in the former Soviet Union), the choice was made to focus on efficiency as opposed to equality (Hewett, 1988) and the ramifications of that decision are now becoming reality.

One of these injustices is the unseemly and distasteful power of organized crime throughout the region. It has become a major focal point for much of the electronic and print media. It is an important issue, and it has negative moral, social, political and economic ramifications, yet it is not the only story to be told. Aslund, correctly notes that greater focus should be placed on official corruption and the relationship between criminals and political and corporate leaders, rather than on the admittedly more colourful and dramatic exploits of organized crime.[31] All societies would be better served without unfair advantages for a privileged corrupt few, and forceful attempts must be made to eliminate organized crime. However, by itself, it should not derail the transition.

THE CURRENT AND THE PAST TRANSITIONS

It is held that the years 1918, 1945 and 1989 were the most pivotal years for Eastern Europe in this century. The most important difference distinguishing each of these periods was the international atmosphere in the years following World War I, World War II and 1989. The years following 1918 and 1945 were ones of conflict between various European countries, and the global atmosphere was dominated by division and distrust. After World War I, there were continued conflicts between European countries, and the global situation after World War II was dominated by the Cold War confrontations between the USA, Western Europe and the Soviet Union, together with its East European 'allies'. The revolutionary developments of 1989 and 1991 are unfolding within the context of an expanding Europe Union (EU) and the absence of a bipolar Cold War between NATO and the Warsaw Pact. However, the countries of the former Yugoslavia and five countries in the former Soviet Union have experienced serious outbreaks of destabilizing national-istic conflict. The war in Bosnia–Herzegovina, Yugoslavia and Croatia casts a large and ominous shadow over the entire region and the UN embargo against Yugoslavia and the Greek embargo against Macedonia FRY were exceptions to policies of free trade.

Yet on the whole, the post-1989 years have been ones of international political and economic cooperation. This has provided important advantages which were not enjoyed by Eastern European countries after the two world wars. A brief comparison of Poland's international situation in 1918 and 1989 is illuminating. After World War I, Poland's relations with its Ukrainian, Lithuanian and Czech neighbours were tense, and it fought a war against the embryonic Soviet state in 1919 and 1920. In both 1918 and 1989, Poland suffered from the collapse of its important eastern markets, Russia and the Soviet Union (Dabrowski, 1991). Yet after 1989 Poland and other East European countries were able to shift much of their foreign trade to Western and Central Europe. As early as 1992, the then Czechoslovakia had reversed its trading patterns, switching the majority of its trade from the Soviet Union and Eastern Europe to Western Europe.[32] Today, even with continuing attempts to expand trade amongst the four Vishygrad countries by eliminating tariffs and quotas before the end of the century, Poland and Hungary conduct over two-thirds of their trade with Central and Western European countries where consumers and businesses have enough resources to provide viable markets for these export-driven economies. These countries cannot and should not ignore their eastern markets, but their export-led growth depends on their ability to sell to the west.[33]

However, in the 1920s, Poland's ability to shift its trade from the east to the west was severely hindered by its poor relations with its neighbours. While today the cross-border shopping of Germans in Poland exceeds US$3 billion annually, and by the end of 1995 Germany had invested almost US$ 700 million in Poland, the situation in 1925 was very different. In 1925, Germany instituted an embargo against the import of Polish coal, which was Poland's leading export and about half of which was purchased by Germany. The German government stated that the cause of the embargo was the poor treatment of ethnic Germans within Poland (Rothschild, 1966). The division between Eastern and Western Europe in the post-World War II era prevented the region from benefiting from international aid, investment and trade with the west. The post-1948 economies of Eastern Europe were not allowed to accept help from the Marshall Plan and their trade was largely limited to inter-bloc activities. However, in the 1990s, there is comparatively little political, military and economic division within Europe. Instead of embargo, Japan, the USA and Western Europe, through the European Bank for Reconstruction and Development (EBRD), the International Monetary Fund (IMF) and the World Bank, are providing modest, but timely aid (Bjork, 1995, pp. 89–124). Instead of political and military divisions between the eastern and western halves of Europe, there is brisk foreign trade and investment, as well as plans to include Eastern Europe in the EU and NATO.

As of mid-1995, the foreign direct investment (FDI) stock, that is, exclusive of portfolio investments in bonds and the region's stock markets, was over US$26 billion. While this accumulation over a period of seven years pales in comparison with the amounts invested in China, and is less than what is invested directly into another emerging market area, Latin America, it is nonetheless an important part of the transition process. In Hungary, which has received US$10.7 of this FDI stock, foreign companies account for about 10 per cent of its GDP and over half of its exports.[34] There is a debate about positive and negative long-term effects of FDI from developed western and Asian countries, but many believe that it is responsible for upgrading the region's technology, making its exports competitive in the west, and that it has forced restructuring and provided a needed element of management expertise. But regardless of one's view of the desirability of FDIs, they do place these economies within the sphere of the global economy and this is very different from the situation in the post-1945 era.

Eastern Europe has 'returned to Europe'. One speaks of when the non-warring countries of Eastern Europe will enter the EU, not whether they will join. There is the probability that Poland, Hungary, the Czech Republic and possibly the Slovak Republic, Slovenia, Estonia, Lithuania and Latvia will be members of the EU within the next decade, and that other Eastern European countries will follow. Although many of the existing forecasts as to when these countries will become full (as opposed to associate) members of the EU tend to err in selecting a date which is perhaps too early, there is little doubt that they will eventually become members. In 1993, the Copenhagen agreement committed the EU to eastward expansion, but considerable obstacles to rapid entry remain. More will be known after the EU's evaluation of the expansion possibilities, but it should be noted that the EU must also deal with problems from its southern neighbours and should not be expected to focus exclusively on its eastern boarders.

The countries of Eastern Europe are poor agricultural exporting countries and this poses problems for the EU. The Eastern European economies are far behind most EU countries in terms of per capita GDP. Even Hungary, which is wealthier than most Eastern European countries, has a per capita GDP which is only 35.7 per cent of the EU average.[35] If Poland continued to enjoy strong economic growth for the next 15 years, by 2010 its per capita GDP would still be lower than that of one of the EU's poorest countries, Spain.[36] The EU faces a formidable challenge in integrating these poor, debtor countries for whom agriculture is an important export – about 20 per cent for Hungary.[37] While agriculture comprises less than 10 per cent of the GDP of the Vishygrad countries (and only 3.1 per cent in the Czech republic), the Romanian and Albanian economies are heavily dependent on agriculture. The EU already has a sizeable surplus of agriculture goods and would not welcome more of these products brought onto its markets. Also the farms of Eastern Europe are small and inefficient, as demonstrated by the fact that 29 per cent of the Polish people live on farms which in turn contribute only 6.1 per cent to its GDP.[38] Abiding by EU rules limiting state subsidies to farms would place many of these farms in a difficult situation. Furthermore, while estimates of the cost to the EU via its Structural Fund and Common Agricultural Policy (CAP) vary widely, it will most certainly represent a steep increase.

The road to EU membership will not be smooth, but the pattern of EU expansion is well established: from six countries in 1958, to 15 in 1995, and perhaps 18 or 20 by 2005.[39] There will be temporary setbacks, and the expectations of the Eastern Europeans will outpace reality. Thousands of integrative legal and administrative regulations will have to be implemented. The amount of aid to be provided by the Structural Fund and the CAP, and the existing EU trade barriers to agricultural products, textiles and steel from the east will be formidable obstacles. Yet the EU's restrictive trade policies, especially on textiles, steel and agricultural products, have been relaxed and modified since 1991, when the countries of Eastern Europe started becoming associate members. On the whole, administrative problems are solvable, and the trade issues are sometimes blown out of proportion since so few of the EU's imports are from Eastern Europe.[40]

This discussion of EU expansion eastwards is reflective of the principal difference between the international atmosphere of the 1990s and that which followed the other two years of drastic change in Eastern Europe in the twentieth century, 1918 and 1945. While not perfect, the impact of the transnational relations of the 1990s is politically and economically positive for the countries of Eastern Europe. The exception is the former Yugoslavia, where the situation is too fluid to allow for more than speculation.

THE TYPE OF UNFOLDING MARKET ECONOMY

This is a subject which is enormously interesting, but at the same time not nearly as important as is often thought. The issue of the type of economic system being established in Eastern Europe and the former Soviet Union is usually raised in the context of the ways in which these transforming economies will differ from those currently classified as capitalist. Given the large number of country-specific determining variables, the powerful legacy of 44 (or 74) years of communism, as well as the genuinely revolutionary nature of the process begun in 1989 (or 1991), one should not be surprised if these economies fail to conform neatly to any system now in existence.

The political and economic transformations in Eastern Europe and the former Soviet Union are unique. They defy exact comparisons. In an attempt to underscore the exceptionally wide lens needed to pursue the subject, a few selective, and by no means comprehensive, issues will be noted. One important element of the transition process is the relative lack of progress in restructuring the agricultural sector in Eastern Europe and the former Soviet Union. For example, the fact that only 5 per cent of the arable land of Russia is privatized is an important and troubling development, yet it receives little attention (Sigel, 1995, pp. 15–18). The fact that the region's transition did not start with agriculture, as in China, and the fact that for most countries in the region it included the development of genuine democratic institutions, unlike China, are potent determining variables. The Asian model has focused on both private and state ownership, while Eastern Europe has tended to concentrate more on the emerging private sector.[41] Selected comparisons to the experiences in Asia add breadth and depth to the debate between the more gradual, agriculture-led approach preferred in China or Vietnam, as opposed to what many label a more radical, industry-led approach of Eastern Europe and the former Soviet Union.

There are many important questions concerning the process of privatization and restructuring in Eastern Europe which can be answered only by the test of time. For example, privatization in the Czech Republic has been justifiably considered successful, but the Czech variant has its own special features which are sometimes at odds with the commonly accepted, or perhaps 'mythologized', concepts of 'normal' ownership patterns in a capitalist economy. The Czech variant should be viewed as uniquely Czech, not a form of hybrid capitalism. The Czech system provided investment funds with a great deal of power and wealth. These investment funds purchased almost 73 per cent of the vouchers held by individual Czech citizens, and were thus able to dominate the purchasing of shares on the Czech stock market. Yet six of the top ten Czech investment funds in 1995 were owned by state banks. Are they then private companies, and what are the rules of corporate governance? To whom do the investment funds owe their loyalty: the bank, the firm they partially purchased, or the fund itself? (Coffee, 1994, pp. 25–33; King, 1995, pp. 24–6). The situation in Russia, where banks have loaned the government money in return for a percentage of the ownership of troubled state enterprises, also raises many questions concerning the type of capitalism unfolding in that country.[42]

There are few certainties, but it seems clear that the role played by the state will be greater than in the USA, where the model is one of more open competition and limited state intrusion. Yet asking if the model for the region will resemble the economies of Western Europe, or of Japan, where the state bureaucracy and the large companies are closely intertwined, is in essence unfair and somewhat misguided. It presumes that there are several accepted models for economic growth in a capitalist system, and that anything that deviates from one of those models is less than workable. Given the uniqueness of the revolutionary events of 1989 and 1991, the powerful legacy of the region's communist past and its specific cultural and historical traditions,

Eastern Europe is going to establish its own brand of capitalism, and attempts to categorize it are not productive exercises.

The problem for the region is not what form of capitalism should be their role model, but whether there is sufficient political resolve to make a firm, strong and enduring commitment to a privately owned market economy. The other key ingredients for achieving a successful transition are the avoidance of the violence associated with nationalistic conflicts, and the continued presence of a cooperative international atmosphere. Given what has already transpired since the transition process started, there are grounds for optimism.

NOTES

1. This trend is clear from a variety of sources. See, for example, _Transition Report 1995: Investment and Enterprise Development,_ London: EBRD. National growth charts for 1994–6 are presented in Done and Robinson, 'EBRD Praises 'Fast-track' Countries', _Financial Times,_ 2 November 1995, p. 2. Also see the _World Development Report, 1996,_ Washington, DC: The World Bank.
2. See 'Slovak Republic', _Financial Times Survey,_ 20 December 1995, and 'Romania', _Financial Times Survey,_ 9 July 1996.
3. See 'Deutsche Bank Research Review', in _Central European Economic Review,_ July/ August 1995, p. 6; and _Economic Survey of Europe in 1994–1995,_ Geneva: United Nations' Secretariat of the Economic Commission for Europe, 1995, p. 72, put the figure at 3.7 per cent for 1994, and other studies show even higher totals.
4. See _Economic Survey of Europe in 1994–1995,_ pp. 97 and 103 for tables on increases in consumer price indexes and drops in real wages.
5. For the narrow victory of Klaus' party in the May/June, 1996 elections in the Czech Republic, see Pehe, 'Election Result in Surprise Stalemate', _Transition,_ **2,** 28 June 1995, pp. 36–7. For the Albanian elections, see Schmidt, 'Election Fraud Sparks Protests', _Transition,_ **2,** 28 June 1996, pp. 38–9. Also see Boland, 'Poverty Fatigue Stalks Czech Politics', _Financial Times,_ 18 October 1995, p. 2.
6. See _Economic Survey of Europe in 1994–1995,_ p. 113 for increased unemployment rates.
7. It should be noted that the division between the countries included in the 'radical' as opposed to the 'gradual' camp is somewhat arbitrary. For example, while the UN Secretariat of the Economic Commission for Europe (1995) would agree on the benefits of a more radical approach to the transition, it would also place Hungary in the camp of the radical reformers. It stated that 'Hungary, Poland, Slovenia have all adopted [the] radical approach to reform' (_Economic Survey of Europe in 1994–95,_ p. 73) and have thus provided a healthy foundation for transition.
8. _Economic Survey of Europe in 1994–1995,_ p. 72.
9. Ibid., p. 97.
10. Ibid., p. 103. For 1995, see Beck, 'Focus on Hungary: Taking Stock', _Central European Economic Review,_ March 1996, p. 15.
11. Ibid., p. 138.
12. _Economic Trends in Eastern Europe,_ Budapest: Kopint-Datorg Economic Research, Vol. 3, No. 3, 1994, p. 172.
13. See Marsh, 'Search for New Cuts as Hungary Court Rules on Austerity Package', _Financial Times,_ 4 July 1995, p. 2; 'Hungarian Coalition Left Exposed', _Financial Times,_ 21 September 1995, p. 3; also Robinson and Marsh, 'Hungary Revived by Tough Medicine', _Financial Times,_ 31 October 1995, p. 3. See 'Hungary', _Financial Times Survey,_ 21

November 1995; 'Hungary Survey: The Next Step', *Business Central Europe*, December 1995/January 1996, pp. 35–46.

14. Boland, 'Koruna Ready to Enter Uncharted Seas', *Financial Times*, 20 June 1995, p. 2; 'Czechs Take Plunge on Koruna Convertibility', *Financial Times*, 28 September 1995, p. 3; and Cook, 'Czech Balancing Act', *Central European Economic Review*, March 1996, p. 18.

15. Czech Statistical Office, 1995.

16. Ibid.

17. 'Slovak Republic', *Financial Times Survey,* 16 December 1994, and 'Slovak Republic', *Financial Times Survey,* 20 December 1995.

18. Boland, 'Meciar Slows Slovak March Towards Market', *Financial Times,* 14 July 1995, p. 3; also 'Internal Battles Mar Slovak Credibility', *Financial Times*, 9 August 1995, p. 2; and Fisher, ibid., pp. 44–9.

19. Boland, 'Slovak Privatization U-Turn Shocks Funds', *Financial Times,* 9 June 1995, p. 2; and King, 'Slovak Republic Plans to Make Changes in Privatization', *Wall Street Journal – Europe*, 9–10 June 1995, p. 4.

20. Boland, 'Slovak Republic's Investors in a Gloomy Mood', *Financial Times*, 28 August 1995, p. 17.

21. *Economic Survey of Europe in 1994–1995*, p. 151. Also see 'Thinking Global: Foreign Investment Survey', *Business Central Europe*, April 1996, pp. 39–55 for an update.

22. For a brief discussion of their concepts concerning corporate governance, see 'Eastern Europe's Capitalism, Who's Boss Now?', *The Economist*, 20 May 1995, pp. 65–7.

23. Kaminski, 'Red Directors Block the Path', *Financial Times*, 30 August 1995, p. 12; Perlez, 'Ukraine Sells Its Companies, But Buyers Are Few', *The New York Times*, 2 November 1995, pp. A-1 and A-7.

24. It should be noted that this is not a rejection of the ideas of Frydman and Rapaczynski, which do not favour strong governmental control. They view the state as important and necessary, but not as a dominating or suffocating factor in the transition process.

25. For further discussion and an alternative view, see Nolan (1995).

26. 'Poland's Economic Reforms', *The Economist*, 23 January 1993, p. 23.

27. Holden and Pastor, 'Chevron Slashes Outlays for Kazakhstan Oil Fields', *The Wall Street Journal,* 13 February 1995, p. A-3; Bahree, 'Caspian Oil Resources Are Starting to Look Much Less Promising', *The Wall Street Journal – Europe*, 10–11 November 1995, pp. A-1 and A-6.

28. Levine, 'Stakes Its Claim in Central Asia', *Financial Times,* 4 May 1995, p. 4; 'U.S. and Russia at Odds Over Caspian Oil', *The New York Times*, 4 October 1995, p. C-2; and Levine and Clark, 'Compromise Deal Today Over Caspian Oil Route', *Financial Times*, 9 October 1995, p. 2.

29. Thornhill, 'Kazakh Deputies Fall Victim in Reform Battle', *Financial Times*, 17 March 1995, p. 7.

30. Stanley, 'Ex-Communist Rules Turkmenistan Like a Sultan', *The New York Times*, 23 November 1995, p. A-3.

31. Aslund, 'Russian Sleaze Factor', *The New York Times*, 11 July 1995, p. A-11.

32. In 1928, only 27 per cent of Czechoslovakia's foreign trade was with former CMEA (Council for Mutual Economic Assistance) nations, but in 1985 inter-CMEA trade accounted for 55.3 per cent of its total foreign trade. By the first quarter of 1992, CMEA trade was reduced to 21.8 per cent. Conversely, Czechoslovakia's trade with EU and EFTA (European Free Trade Association) nations was 60 per cent in 1982, but only 23.6 per cent in 1985, and back up to 61.1 per cent in the first quarter of 1992 (*Privatization Newsletter of Czechoslovakia*, no. 7, June 1992, 8). For annual changes in foreign trade by world region between 1992 and 1994, see *Economic Survey of Europe in 1994–1995*, p. 124.

33. See 'Pipe Dreams', *Business Central Europe*, October 1995, pp. 9–11, 14.

34. See 'Thinking Global: Foreign Investment Survey', *Business Central Europe,* April 1996, pp. 39–55.

35. Marsh, 'Hungary Knocks Hard on EU Door', *Financial Times*, 19 July 1995, p. 2.

36. Bobinski, 'Poles Await the Starting Gun to Begin Race for EU Entry', *Financial Times*, 10 July 1995, p. 3.
37. Marsh, 'Hungary Knocks Hard on EU Door'.
38. Harding, 'Poland May Find the CAP a Tight Fit', *Financial Times*, 13 March 1995, p. 25.
39. Robinson, 'East Europe Impatient for Seat at the Top Table', *Financial Times*, 9 December 1994, p. 2.
40. In 1992, less than 2 per cent of the EU's imports came from the Vishygrad countries (see Galinos, 'Central Europe and the EU: Prospects for Closer Integration', *RFE/RL Research Report*, **3**, (29), 1994, pp. 19–25).
41. Rana and Dowling, 'East Europeans Could Learn from Asian Patience', *International Herald Tribune*, 22 October 1993, p. 6.
42. For political aspects of the bank's loans for share concept, see Banerjee, 'Russian Communists Exploit Loan Flap', *The Wall Street Journal*, 14 February 1996, p. A-10. For the larger picture, see Aslund (1995).

REFERENCES

Akyuz, Y. (1994), 'Reform and Crisis in the Transition Economies,' in *Privatization in the Transition Process: Recent Experiences in Eastern Europe*, New York: United Nations.

Aslund, A. (1995), How Russia Became A Market Economy, Washington, DC: Brookings Institution.

Bjork, J. (1995), 'The Uses of Conditionality: Poland and the IMF', *East European Quarterly*, **XXIX**, (1), 89–124.

Coffee, J.C. (1994), 'Investment Privatization Funds: The Czech Experience', in *Corporate Governance in Central Europe and Russia*, Washington, DC: Transition Economics Division, World Bank.

Dabrowski, P. (1991) 'East European Trade', Parts I–III, *RFE/RL Research Report*, (40), 28–37; **2**, (41), 28–36; (42), 18.

Done, K. and A. Robinson (1992), '"EBRD" Praises "Fast-Track" Countries', *Financial Times*, 2 November 1992, p. 2.

Fisher, S. (1994), 'The Slovak Economy: Signs of Recovery', *RFE/RL Research Report*, **3**, (33), 58–65.

Frydman, R. and A. Rapaczynski (1994), *Privatization in Eastern Europe: Is the State Withering Away?*, London: Central European University Press.

Green, P. (1996), 'Monopoly Capitalism', *Business Central Europe*, **6**, (32), 27–8.

Hewett, E. (1988), *Reforming the Soviet Economy: Equality Versus Efficiency*, Washington, DC: Brookings Institution.

Kierzkowski, H., E. Phelps and G. Zoega (1994), 'Mechanisms of Economic Collapse and Growth in Eastern Europe', *Discussion Paper No.10*, Warsaw: Polish Policy Research Group.

King, N. (1995), 'Can Anything Tame the Fund Monsters?', *Central European Economic Review*, **3**, (5), 24–6.

Mroziewicz, D. (1996), 'Polish Economic Reform Marked by High Unemployment', *Transition*, **2**, 26–7.

Munich, D. and V. Sorm (1996), 'The Czech Republic as a Low-Unemployment Oasis', *Transition*, **2**, 21–5.

Nolan, P. (1995), *China's Rise, Russia's Fall*, London: Macmillan.

Orenstein, M. (1996), 'The Failure of Neo-Liberal Social Policy in Central Europe', *Transition*, **2**, 16–20.

Rothschild, J. (1966), *Coup d'Etat*, New York: Columbia University Press.
Sigel, T. (1995), 'The Dismally Slow Pace of Agricultural Reform', *Transition*, **1**, (8), 15–18.
Slay, B. (1994), 'Rapid Versus Gradual Economic Transition', *RFE/RL Research Report*, **3**, (31), 31–42.
Szilagyi, Z. (1995), 'A Year of Economic Controversy', *Transition*, **1**, 62–6.
IMF (1996), *World Economic Outlook*, Washington, DC: May.
World Bank (1996), *World Development Report*, Washington, DC

1. Major issues in restructuring and transition in Eastern Europe[1]

Soumitra Sharma

Processes of 'restructuring' and 'transition', which are taking place in economies around the world, are loaded with confusion in terms of concept, policy and achieved results. It is becoming difficult to understand and foresee precisely their future course. To add to the confusion, in the minds of scholars, advisers, policy makers and, finally, the people in the countries involved, a growing mountain of literature on the subject (often conflicting in arguments) is appearing too fast to cope with.[2]

To tackle the problem we begin by defining the two terms. While by restructuring we understand providing a new structure, rebuilding or changing from within the already existing one, transition would mean passing from one set of circumstances to another. In the above sense, in economics, both these terms are often studied, independently of each other, both from macro and micro aspects.

To us, restructuring and transition are two sides to the same coin, and if it is a question of sequencing the two, it is an 'egg and hen' dilemma. Although opinions differ, the majority of experts feel that stabilization should precede structural transformation. To this aim, the early announcement of systematic measures, such as a quick move towards privatization and demonopolization, are desirable (Nuti, 1991; Jeffries, 1993). In the context of events, socio-political changes and the economic processes in the countries involved, transition and restructuring can be interpreted as follows. Restructuring, seen from the macroeconomic point of view, refers to governmental measures adopted at national level for making general structural changes, so as to create a market economy. These include measures such as launching a privatization programme, setting up a market environment, developing a social safety net and so on.[3] In a microeconomic sense, it can be used very broadly to refer to actions taken in order to change the existing structure of the enterprise along five dimensions: general business philosophy, internal organization, employment, growth of output and increase/decrease in investment. Transition, on the other hand, is basically treated as a macroeconomic category. In this sense, the list of activities which governments must undertake in countries attempting transition to a market economy is staggering. These, according to Clague, consist of three main categories of action (Clague, 1992, p. 5):

1. activities related to creating a new set of rules, such as setting up a legal infrastructure for the private sector, devising a new tax system, devising rules for the new financial sector, determining ownership rights and enacting foreign exchange regulations;
2. tasks related to macroeconomic management, such as reforming prices, creating a safety net, stabilizing the economy; and
3. tasks related to privatization, such as small-scale and large-scale privatization, financial reforms, and so on.

Multilateral institutions look at the process as a series of broad-based, painful, systemic and determined reforms at macro and micro levels. In their opinion, this process of change is likely to release a complex course of destruction, adaptation and creation. The core of these reforms in transitional economies is the liberalizing of prices, the market and new business entry, and the implementing of programmes to regain or to preserve the stability of the general price level. Thus, while liberalization, stabilization and globalization represent the key macro aspects, changing property rights and enterprise reforms are microeconomic tasks (The World Bank, 1996).

From the microeconomic point of view, according to some economists, the governments of transitional economies must adopt at least the following measures (Hare, 1991, p. 3):

*   the abolition of centralized material balancing and supply planning, a plan breakdown to enterprise level;
*   an end to central control over marketing, output, enterprise output profiles, and managerial and other appointments; the reinstatement of profit as the sole criterion of an enterprise's performance;
*   relaxation of most control over prices; the decentralization of wage settlements; a more uniform tax/subsidy reform and the abolition of most subsidies on production and consumption;
*   granting enterprises the right to make their own investment decision, to engage in foreign trade; the creation of new financial institutions;
*   the introduction of legal reforms so as to facilitate the creation of western-type companies, clarification of property rights and ensuring their marketability, strengthening of laws related to contracts, and provision for bankruptcy and liquidation of businesses running on loss;
*   the liberalization of imports of supplies;
*   the extensive privatization of the state or cooperative sector; and

- the enactment of laws/institution to regulate monopoly and competition.

Although this is a lengthy list, the author considers them 'probably the minimum that has to be done'.

TRANSITION

The failures of the socialist economic system and ultimately the collapse of communist political power in the former Soviet Union in 1989, after the Gorbachov reforms (*'glasnost'* and *'perestroika'*) had failed,[4] set in motion a process of change which embraced practically all the countries of Central and Eastern Europe in the 1990s. This process is popularly known as 'transition'. This process of transition first began in the two PHARE (Pologne, Hongrie, Assistance à la Reconstruction Economique) countries, namely, Poland and Hungary. In 1990 it was extended to Bulgaria, Czechoslovakia, Romania, former Yugoslavia, and to Albania in 1992.

From the very beginning, there was a strong political desire in Poland and Hungary to move towards a market economy. Foreign advisers were also very enthusiastic in suggesting a variety of policies to do just that. Poland, being the first experimental site for transition policies, was joined in the mission by those policy makers, experts and multilateral institutions who thought that shock therapy was needed immediately to stop hyperinflation, to cure the budget deficit and to initiate structural reforms. Thus the so-called 'big-bang' model was introduced in January 1990. Similar policy models were later devised for other countries. It was expected that these measures would restore external and internal balance in the countries.

Immediately, a debate over the manner of transition, its consequences and the future of such policies started. Experts were sharply divided and two lines of thinking developed. The first was supported by the Cambridge, Massachusetts economists who were the first to call this 'big bang' or 'shock therapy' (Dornbusch, 1993; Williamson, 1991, 1994; Sachs and Lipton, 1991, 1992; Winiecki, 1993). They recommended launching a rapid all-out programme, undertaking as many as reforms possible in the shortest possible time. The all-out approach aims to replace central planning with rudiments of a market economy in a single thrust of reforms. These include rapid price and trade liberalization, accompanied by a determined programme to establish price stability and a quick move towards current account convertibility; the immediate opening of the market to entry by new private businesses; and initiating a wide range of changes such as the privatization of state-owned companies, the demonopolization of industry and the reform of accounting standards, the tax system, the legal system, the financial sector, and the civil services.

An alternative road on the journey to transition was also devised very early, primarily by Hungarian economists, and was identified as the 'gradualist' or 'evolutionary' approach (Kornai, 1986, 1990, 1992; Koves, 1992; Abel and Bonin, 1992). This approach aims to change the planned economy into a market one by partial and phased reforms. This model begins with the idea of coexistence of plan and market for at least some time to come and favours step-by-step reforms, starting with selected localized experiments, which are to be expanded later as the projected success emerges. This strategy relies on there being a large scope for reaping large productivity gains from pilot reforms. These, in turn, raise income and build momentum for a more diffi-cult phase that follows. The gradualists believe that shock therapy cannot be used in the case of structural reforms and that benefits of the same can be achieved at lesser social costs. They further claim that gradualism can sustain the reforms over an extended period and include side-effects, such as liberal-izing the economy selectively.

It must be noted, however, that each path offers its own distinctive patterns of risk and rewards. But hardly any country that embarked on the transition train was in any position to choose between the two because the existing economic and political circumstances dictated the path. The objectives of transitional policy, at least in the beginning, were vaguely defined. The long-term objective of transition, it was claimed, is to build a thriving market capable of delivering long-term growth in living standards. Thus the short-term objectives are subservient to the long-term objective, and these are stabilization, liberalization and economic growth.

Stabilization, Liberalization and Economic Growth

The governments of Central and East European countries have frequently devised their stabilization programmes in consultations with the IMF. This stabilization policy package usually consisted of the following measures: price liberalization, balancing the budget, a restrictive monetary policy and foreign trade liberalization. Among structural measures often adopted were privatization, financial sector reforms and social measures. Marie Lavigne considers the introduction of political reforms, the choice of transition con-cept ('big bang' versus 'gradualism'), policies of price liberalization, demonopolization and privatization, the introduction of banking and financial reforms, the setting up of capital markets, the devising of a social protection system and the opting for an outward orientation of the economy to be the 'building blocks' of a stabilization policy (Lavigne, 1995, pp. 122–5).

Inflation and unemployment are the two most serious problems which every economy has to face. In most of the transitional economies there was already hyperinflation and disguised unemployment. It was for these very reasons that stabilization programmes were designed for these countries in the first place. In the process of transition the stabilization policy is generally considered complementary to the policy of liberalization. Policies of containing inflation and imposing hard budget constraints on firms are necessary for the growth of a market economy and for the restructuring of firms, but the interaction between macroeconomic policies and other reforms, including liberalization, is greatly affected by initial conditions (The World Bank, 1996, p. 34).

Inflation in Central and East European countries had a certain pattern.[5] In the early stages of liberalization there was an early release of the monetary overhang that had accumulated under the earlier system. In the years that followed, inflation was followed by abolition of subsidies to the firms and the degree of freedom in product pricing. In the latest phase of transition inflation became dependent upon the exchange rate policy and capital flows. Experience in transition economies shows that in the latest phase inflation was significantly reduced under both regimes, namely fixed exchange rates (Croatia, the Czech Republic, Estonia, Hungary, Poland and the Slovak Republic) and flexible arrangements (Albania and Slovenia). The situation was greatly eased in all these countries by the inflow of foreign capital.

On the employment front, at the start of the transition policy there were some serious doubts about the ability of the labour force to adjust to the stabilization and restructuring policy. The labour market responded by introducing changes in wage level and structure, changing sectoral and regional employment patterns, and adjustment through unemployment. It was observed that, in the transition period, unemployment in the state sector increased sharply. In Croatia, the Czech Republic, Hungary and Slovenia, there is a continuous labour shedding. As opposed to such trends in the state sector, private-sector employment expanded strongly in the Czech Republic, Poland and Hungary. Also long-term and youth unemployment has increased rapidly everywhere. Finally, labour adjustments are yet to take place.

The planned economies were autarchic. Economies had suffered chronic shortages. There was the seller's market which discouraged any improvement in quality. State-owned firms lacked property rights that spur work and profit earned in market economies. Firms had little reason to use inputs efficiently and strong incentives to hoard both labour and raw materials. Many firms added negative value – at world prices the costs of their input would have exceeded the value of their output. The combination of dominant heavy industry, low energy prices and wasteful use of inputs caused energy intensity to rise and had a severe environmental impact. Liberalization exposed firms to customer demand, the profit motive and competition, and it allowed relative prices to adjust in line with true scarcities.

Liberalization usually means eliminating price control and relaxing trade protection. The speed and scope of free market reforms have varied greatly in transition economies. The liberalization index, which is an aggregate indicator of the combined duration and intensity of liberalization, for the period 1989–95, shows a medium exposure of each country.[6]

Experience in transitional economies has thus far shown that both extensive liberalization and determined stabilization have been vital for improved economic performance (McKinnon, 1991). While liberalization led to the freeing of prices, trade and business entry from state control, stabilization has meant reduced inflation and contained domestic and external imbalances. The two are linked together and must be adopted as early as possible.

Without going into a lengthy discussion on the issue, it can be stated that, with regard to economic growth, measured in terms of output and growth rates, there was initially a sharp decline in output and thus growth rates were negative. Allowing for statistical deficiency in reporting, an average estimated fall in output was recorded at around 16 per cent (The World Bank, 1996, pp. 172–3). But the growth rates in 1994 and 1995 had much improved.

Social Relief

What matters in society is the people and their standard of living. In all manifestos, constitutions and political and economic proclamations, the long-term objective put forward is raising the incomes and standard of living of the people. This is also true of the proclaimed transition policy. How transition has affected the life of the people in these countries remains to be thoroughly studied. Without going into discussion on this point, it must be stated that the transitional policy has definitely affected the life of the people in these countries. The process has been painful in general. With a fall in output, a reduction of employment, a decline in wages, an increase in disparities in the distribution of wealth of incomes and curtailment of social benefits, the people generally have felt the pinch. The fact remains that in Central and East European countries few people have gained from the policy and poverty has increased. It is only to be hoped that, with the reversal of negative growth, an upward trend may begin in the coming years.[7]

Open Economy

The watchword of world economy today is globalization. Globalization is supposed to be one of the objectives of transition policy. Transition economies are trying hard to enter the world system. After being closed to the outside world for so long, they are finding it fairly difficult to enter, but they stand to gain quickly from international integration. The economic benefits of moving into the world market are the benefits of internal market liberalization. Capital, goods and technology cross borders in response to demand and supply. Integration into the world system also helps to fuel a faster growth of income and productivity, and to increase the volume of trade. In this respect, progress so far has been slow and we have yet to see positive results.

RESTRUCTURING

In the 1990s, transitional economies of Eastern Europe companies have essentially been faced by various aspects of enterprise restructuring, such as basic incentives,[8] corporate governance, financial system reforms, privatization and physical restructuring. Economists believe that the main building block of restructuring is privatization, which means creating a 'greenfield' private sector (setting up new companies) and changing formerly state-owned enterprises through (a) small-scale (primarily the service sector, construction and housing) and (b) large-scale (industrial and service enterprises) privatization.

An intensive and thorough analysis of the restructuring process has been conducted and a collection of case studies of over 450 enterprises in the Czech Republic, Hungary, Poland, Russia and the Slovak Republic has been compiled (Carlin *et al.*, 1995). Some of the notable findings in the survey are as follows:

1. Not all restructuring being carried out in these countries can be seen as contributing to the creation of a competitive market economy. It is theoretically possible for an enterprise to find itself in post-macro transition, that is, a competitive market.
2. Since the real power in any enterprise lies with its manager(s), the manager is constrained by two options: to restructure, which entails a cost to the enterprise (and not only to the employees who lose their jobs) in the current period and an uncertain pay-off in the future; or to maintain the status quo, which is painless now but entails a cost with certainty in the future. The manager's incentive to restructure is augmented by the hardening of budget constraints which can be seen as increasing the penalty on passive behaviour (for example, by bringing forward the date of closure of the enterprise).
3. Three broad patterns of restructuring have been observed: some enterprises have actively participated in restructuring, with the aim of becoming consistent with the development of a competitive market; others have shown minimal organizational and behavioural changes; a third group consists of those who have recorded active behaviour, but it is not clear how far this is consistent with furthering market economy reforms.

Under the socialist economic system the core philosophy of functioning of any business firm was different from that of a firm in a market economy in the sense that the socialist firm was considered as a symbol of workers' rights (and not duties), the source of political power and a unit of production of goods and services so as to meet the state-determined planned objectives. Such a concept of the firm determined its general business philosophy, which can be defined as that of self-reliance, of self-sufficiency, of production for the sake of some undefined higher social objectives and not for profit and market, of conducting business under conditions of virtual monopoly and state protection. Restructuring, in the first place, means changing the attitude of the people in the government, in the emerging market institutions and above all of the company employees. In a word, the whole value structure system of conducting business requires change.

In general, prior to the transition period, the companies in East European countries were faced by inconsistent objectives, such as the creation of more jobs, which will help in the regional development of the country, to meet the centrally set output, marketing and distribution targets, to achieve a pre-set goal for sales through arbitrarily planned prices, to provide a social safety-net to a larger section of the society, and so forth. Accordingly, an important step forward in restructuring and transition had been to remove these peripheral goals and to allow companies to operate on the principle of maximization of efficient and profitable production and sale on the market.

Corporate governance, that is company management, is a key issue in the restructuring process of companies. It is rather difficult to introduce competent governance in all companies. There are two aspects to the task. First, it could be achieved in a variety of ways, such as setting higher educational, technological, experience and performance standards for executive jobs; ensuring better salaries, rewards and benefits for competent mangers; attracting foreign ownership and thus management, and so on. Second, until the process of privatization and change of ownership is completed, the government should, at least temporarily, appoint competent persons whose attitude is identical to that of those managing privately owned companies and who would uphold the performance criteria. These corporate executives should be allowed to operate free of political and bureaucratic meddling, and should only be instructed as to the 'do nots'.

The Financial Reforms

Under the previous system, the company managers hardly ever needed to pay heed to the financial losses of their enterprises. Therefore a successful restructuring of companies requires a change in the attitude of managers and workers alike. They should be made to understand that their employment with the company need no longer be permanent and that the company's very existence depends upon its market performance, and that continued losses mean going out of business and liquidation of assets.

A reformed banking system can play a very significant role here, because banks have the power to grant or deny loans. As a matter of policy, banks must not loan funds to those companies whose financial performance over a given period of time does not conform to the basic economic criteria of productivity and profits. In all the socialist states, banks were not banks in the real sense of the word, but served as institutions of financial transactions between the state, companies and citizens. Consequently, if the process of company restructuring needs to take place prior to the reforming of banks, it is clear that a more judicious judgement on denials or grants of funds to the companies is required. The creation of holding companies which administer the assets of restructuring companies has been found to be a suitable solution, but the dangers of the creation of a new political power structure, and political manoeuvring and influence have been demonstrated. The critical point, however, remains the restriction of governmental influence in holding companies. The reform of the banking system, among other things, would necessarily mean that banks, as company creditors, will have to be allowed to make their own decisions concerning the writing off of bad loans without risking their own financial viability. This could perhaps be done by allowing a restructuring agency (or a holding company) to buy off the bad loans of the banks, which will ultimately have to be written off by the government.

Extensive empirical evidence from Central and Eastern European countries suggests that shrinking subsidies, rigorous financial discipline and profit-oriented incentives have made a significant difference. These have inevitably resulted in labour shedding or a fall in real wages, or even some combination of the two.[9] Furthermore, two other cushions – bank loans on easy terms and arrears on payments due to government for taxes, duties and social security – have been removed by some governments. All this has boosted efficiency.

Privatization

Economists more or less unanimously agree that most of the decisions concerning restructuring should be made by the companies themselves. This necessarily implies that the privatization of ownership is a vital element in this process. It has to be implemented on a wide scale, even though there are many who argue that it is impossible to carry out privatization without a market. It must be emphasized however, that the actual process of privatization will be a major driving force in creating an active market in company shares. Privatization can be done either on or off the market. While privatization on the market implies floatation of company shares on the stock market and their sale and purchase, the latter includes measures such as the voucher system (as attempted in the Czech Republic) or free distribution of shares among all company employees, the sale of state enterprises, and so on. Either way, sooner or later, these measures are going to create a share market. While the voucher system has yielded the quickest results, a widespread distribution of property rights is also likely to create an effective market. As far as the selling of state enterprises is concerned, what in fact is happening is that governments are often unwilling to sell profitable concerns as these serve as a source of income which meets their running expenditure. On the other hand, they are unable to dispose of loss-incurring companies.

An argument against privatization through giving away property rights is that the allocation of shares, it is claimed, is likely to be socially unfair. But this could possibly be corrected, to a certain extent, by introducing a system of quotas of shares to certain sections of the population, such as employees and lower-income groups. At the same time, it is also argued that such unfairness may be a very small price to pay for the beginning of a process that will ultimately lead to efficient and profitable production.

In Croatia, Hungary and Slovenia the popular argument is that the process of restructuring and privatization must go hand-in-hand. Theses countries claim that many of the preliminaries for market transition were achieved in the 1970s and 1980s. Lately, inflation has been brought under control, trade and price liberalization is already well under way, financial discipline on companies is kept tight through monetary policy and the legal framework for creating an efficient market system is being strengthened. However, many problems at the company level remain to be dealt with.

In countries such as Hungary, Poland and former Yugoslavia the ownership status of companies has been ambiguous from the beginning of the transformation process. It had to be resolved first, prior to the restructuring process. Apart from this, many of these enterprises were burdened by huge losses. Formal bankruptcy procedures have, in many cases, provided a spur for the restructuring of companies in transitional economies, but it has been difficult for their governments to handle a legal and financial situation in which between one-third and one-half of all the companies have been operating with heavy losses.

Perhaps one of the most debatable points in the privatization process is the assets valuation procedure. The book value of assets of the companies in the transitional economies has been far from accurate owing to an inadequate system of accounting. Accordingly, prior to the privatization of companies, an expertise by foreign auditors, often expensive, but nonetheless helpful, was essential. Lately, however, some serious questions are being raised in many countries regarding the appropriateness of the sale of state or communal assets to the private sector at low prices. Restructuring agencies, bureaucrats and politicians are often accused of collusion with the private sector and of deliberate low asset pricing and sale for personal gains. This has been rendered even more difficult where the initial sale of the company was at a low price and the same company was sold again at a substantially higher price after job cuts. It is argued that a company's valuation and price are two separate questions and that, while the former is subject to future cash flows, the latter is determined by supply and demand, but, somehow, the reality of privatization in Eastern Europe so far remains that price is more important than the objective value of assets.

Physical Restructuring

Following the general advice of the World Bank, some countries, such as Croatia and Slovenia, have established separate agencies for restructuring small and large enterprises. A special programme has been developed for the largest loss makers, a number of centres for small business initiatives have been set up to provide advice, incubator facilities and franchising arrangements to encourage the emergence and growth of new and existing small companies. Splitting larger enterprises into smaller companies according to their activities in the first phase and privatizing them in the later is another way in which restructuring has mostly been done so far.

Physical restructuring of companies is an important element in the restructuring process of companies. In physical terms, it is very difficult to handle the large number of companies, practically in all the transitional economies, which need restructuring in a uniform way. It seems logical that in the case of smaller companies it is convenient to provide some general mechanism, financial and technical support, and leave them free to restructure themselves; but in the case of large companies or conglomerates, it might be useful to divide the companies into smaller units which are easy to manage, privatize, control and restructure financially. Only the profitable units should be allowed to operate and the remainder should be liquidated. In the absence of a proper social safety net, however, the political risks in such cases remain high because of massive job losses and the socioeconomic problem of absorption of the unemployed people. Thus the restructuring process in larger enterprises might be painful and sometimes subject to long legal and political battle. Letting people know the direct and indirect costs of keeping such enterprises alive, using policy levers and subsidies by the government may alleviate some of such pressure.

Many firms are operating without effective owners; information and legal systems have not yet adapted to market mechanisms; private firms have trouble getting bank credit; the government finds it difficult to tax emerging sectors to make up for lost revenues from declining ones.

To sum up, it can be said that liberalization, stabilization, privatization, company restructuring and the provision of social relief are vital to transition, but not enough to create a flourishing market economy. Early gains of the process need to be cashed in on by creating a congenial climate for good institutional performance and a skilled and adaptable labour force – capable of integration within a global economy.[10]

NOTES

1. In this volume the term 'Eastern Europe' refers to the following countries: Albania, Bulgaria, Croatia, Czech Republic, Hungary, Macedonia FRY, Poland, Romania, Slovak Republic and Slovenia.
2. Just to illustrate the points we refer to the Bibliographical Note added to the *World Development Report 1996*, Washington, DC: Oxford University Press for the World Bank, pp. 148–70.
3. Sometimes the question is posed as to what distinguishes transition from earlier reforms in these countries, as these countries have a long history of reforms. The difference is seen in that it involves far-reaching systemic changes.
4. Earlier attempts at partial reforms in communist countries failed to raise efficiency, productivity and growth largely because they were too limited to affect incentives. For example, in the USSR, the *perestroika* itself involved little reform and was followed by measures to boost investment in the face of shrinking resources. The result was inflation and foreign indebtedness rather than higher productivity. Wages rose more than prices. The existence of subsidies along with greater autonomy in state-owned enterprises increased the fiscal deficit.
5. The essence of the inflation story in most Central and Eastern European countries and newly independent states is that free market reforms first turned high repressed inflation into high open inflation, and then further liberalization and tight financial policies brought the inflation down by containing persistent domestic subsidy pressures (The World Bank, 1996, p. 35).
6. Hungary and China began liberalizing gradually in the 1960s and the late 1970s, respectively. Vietnam accelerated its liberalization in 1989 after partial reforms failed to raise growth rates or to stabilize the economy sufficiently. Poland liberalized with a 'big bang' in January 1990. Soon after that, Albania, the Baltic countries, the Czech Republic, the Slovak Republic and the Kyrgyz Republic followed this model of comprehensive liberalization. Bulgaria initially did the same, in 1992, but soon reversed the reform. In Romania price reforms advanced fitfully but liberalization has recently been accelerated.
7. For a detailed analysis of this issue, see *World Development Report 1996*, Chapter IV.
8. The *World Development Report 1996* (p. 44) observes that a change in basic incentives for the managers of enterprises is an important factor that lies at the heart of transition.
9. For example, the largest 150–200 firms in the Czech Republic, Hungary and Poland reduced their work force by 32, 47 and 33 per cent, respectively, between 1989 and 1993, as their sales fell by 40–60 per cent (The World Bank, 1996, p. 45).
10. See part two of the *World Development Report 1996* for an elaborate discussion.

REFERENCES

Abel, I. and J.P. Bonin (1992), *The 'Big Bang' versus 'Slow but Steady': A Comparison of the Hungarian and the Polish Transformation*, London: Centre for Economic Policy Research.

Carlin,W., J. van Reenen and T. Wolfe (1995), 'Enterprise Restructuring in Early Transition: The Case Study Evidence from Central and Eastern Europe', *Economics of Transition*, **3**, (4), 427–58.

Clague, C. (1992), 'The Journey to a Market Economy', in C. Clague and G.C. Rausser (eds), *The Emergence of Market Economics in Eastern Europe,* Oxford: Blackwell, pp. 1–24.

Dornbusch, R. (1993), *Stabilisation, Debt and Reform*, Englewood Cliffs, NJ: Prentice-Hall.

Hare, P.G. (1991), 'Eastern Europe: The Transition to A Market Economy', *The Royal Bank of Scotland Review*, 3–16.

Jeffries, I. (1993), *Socialist Economies and the Transition to the Market: A Guide*, London/New York: Routledge.

Kornai, J. (1986), 'The Hungarian Reform Process: Visions, Hopes, and Reality', *Journal of Economic Literature*, (24), 1687–1737.

Kornai, J. (1990), *The Road to a Free Economy*, New York: W.W. Norton.

Kornai, J. (1992), *The Socialist System: The Political Economy of Communism*, Princeton, NJ: Princeton University Press.

Koves, A. (1992), 'Shock Therapy versus Gradual Change: Economic Problems and Policies in Central and Eastern Europe 1989–1991', *Acta Oeconomica*, **44**, (1–2), 13–36.

Lavigne, M. (1995), *The Economics of Transition: From Socialist Economy to Market Economy*, New York: St Martin's Press.

McKinnon, R.I. (1991), *The Order of Economic Liberalization: Financial Control in the Transition to Market Economy*, Baltimore, MD: Johns Hopkins University Press.

Nuti, M. (1991), 'Stabilization and Reform Sequencing in the Reform of Central and East Europe', in S. Commander (ed.), *Managing Inflation in Socialist Economies in Transition*, Washington, DC: EDI, World Bank, pp. 155–74.

Sachs J. and D. Lipton (1991), '"Shock Therapy" and Real Incomes', *Financial Times*, 29 January.

Sachs, J. and D. Lipton (1992), 'Privatisation in Eastern Europe: A Case of Poland', in Soumitra Sharma (ed.), *Development Policy*, London: Macmillan.

Williamson, J. (1991), *The Economic Opening of Eastern Europe*, Washington, DC: Institute for International Economics.

Williamson, J. (1994), *The Political Economy of Policy Reform*, Washington, DC: Institute for International Economics.

Winiecki, J. (1993), '"Heterodox" Stabilization in Eastern Europe', *Working Paper No. 8*, London: EBRD.

Economic Commission for Europe (1990–91, 1991–92, 1992–93), *Economic Survey of Europe*, New York: Economic Commission for Europe.

World Bank, *World Development Report 1996*, Washington, DC.

2. Industrial restructuring and supply chain development in Eastern Europe

Milford Bateman

In all of the Eastern European economies, the collapse of the various planning systems precipitated a serious fall in output very early on in the transition from communism to capitalism. One particular feature of the transition was responsible for much of this fall in output: the disruption to the supply chains and inter-enterprise linkages which were built up by the planners in communist Eastern Europe, and their ongoing replacement by those which better reflect the new realities of the market economy, private ownership and the opening up to the outside world.[1] Most enterprises have been thrown into confusion by these abrupt changes and new imperatives, and it quickly became apparent that the reconstitution and construction of market-driven supply chains would be one of the most pressing tasks for them, and for the economic reform process as a whole.

There was also another factor which underlined the critical importance of reconstructing supply chains in Eastern Europe. It is becoming apparent that it is the nature and extent of the supply chain which is one of the key determinants of enterprise success, and therefore also of national and regional economic success. Local and regional supply chains have been well documented as associated with economic success in Germany and Italy (Pyke and Sengenberger, 1992), though most spectacularly in Japan (Friedman, 1988; Asanuma, 1989; Nishiguchi, 1994). Indeed, Japanese supply chain management techniques have become the basis for much of the corporate restructuring which has taken place in the western economies (Porter, 1990; Lewis, 1995). Western enterprises are increasingly attempting to match the quality and cost standards achieved by their Japanese competitors through actively managing and supporting their supply chain. These new methods are a refutation of the aggressive corporate philosophy of the 1980s, which was to bully and browbeat suppliers into financial and other concessions. Sophisticated supply chains also played a critically important role in the economic success of the East Asian economies (Cheng and Gereffi, 1994; Meyanathan, 1994) and they are also becoming a feature of industrial development in less developed countries (LDCs) (Lall, 1980; Mead, 1984; Kaplinsky, 1994).

In view of the success of the regions just noted, it is not surprising that an increasing number of policy programmes have been established which aim to develop and strengthen the operations of supply chains, and thereby the regions in which they operate. This has been the case in the EU as a whole, where Brussels has implemented a wide range of supportive policy measures as part of its regional development plans (Van Kooij, 1991), and in some individual member states, such as in the UK, where the Department of Trade and Industry (DTI) has sponsored Regional Supply Networks which aim to strengthen the cooperation between local large and small enterprises (DTI, 1995). Also important are the enormous number of support programmes for small enterprises in all the member states, which act so as to increase and strengthen small and medium sized enterprises (SMEs) and their ability to integrate into supply chains centred around neighbouring larger firms. Japanese central and regional authorities are also very active in strengthening supply chains and in providing substantial support for the small firm population (MITI, 1995). These government programmes are in addition to the programmes implemented by the larger Japanese enterprises themselves, which are wide-ranging and well-funded (Kagami, 1995). East Asia has followed the Japanese model and also implemented a great many support programmes to develop indigenous supply chains, especially making use of foreign investments (Meyanathan, 1995).

The question for the transition economies of Eastern Europe is therefore one, not just of reconstructing old supply chains, but of attempting to develop supply chains which replicate the highly efficient production systems in many of the western economies. In this chapter we will consider the role of supply chain development in the Eastern European economies as an aspect of the broader industrial restructuring taking place.

THEORETICAL ISSUES

We can first briefly sketch out a number of developments, beginning with the work of Marshall (1890). Marshall was one of the first to point to the existence of communities of small and large industrial firms, and the emergence of supply chains in a locality, with his concept of the Industrial District. The Industrial District described by Marshall was essentially a cluster of smaller firms engaged in roughly the same operations and supplying a handful of larger firms producing a final product. The development of local supply chains allowed for the realization of a number of agglomeration economies of scale, and gave rise to a supporting tissue of institutions which underpinned the competitiveness of the region as a whole. The smaller firms were better placed to win orders outside the region because their relationship with local larger firms encouraged greater productive efficiency on their part. For example, it gave them the advantage of high levels of regular work, and thus the motivation to continually invest in product- and process-specific machinery, equipment and training.

This early focus upon the value of small firm–large firm cooperation was lost in the face of the rise of the giant corporation in the 20th century, especially after World War II. Until the 1980s, the conventional wisdom was that the relationship between small and large firms was necessarily one-sided and exploitative: the large firm kept the small firm at arm's length and was able to force it to accept whatever margins and other conditions it deemed to be appropriate for it to realize maximum profitability. Large firms sought competitive advantage by using small firms to reduce labour costs, externalize risk, absorb demand fluctuations and circumvent a variety of government legislation. This exploitative scenario was held to be one of the reasons for the rapid growth in small firms in Western Europe in the 1980s, especially in the UK, as large firms increasingly moved production over to lower cost subcontractors and hived off non-core units from the parent firm (Shutt and Whittington, 1987). This feature, moreover, was given even greater visibility by the cost-cutting element evidenced in many of the privatization programmes in the western economies, which saw small firms as eager recipients of the range of local government services work previously undertaken by a more expensive, unionized labour force.

The advent of the flexible specialization thesis in the 1980s overturned many of the previous assumptions equating small firms to exploitation and assigned a more proactive role for the small firm in economic development. The rediscovery of Marshallian Industrial Districts, first in Italy, but then in many other Western European economies, indicated that regions had the capacity to develop their own successful economic trajectories at least partly independent of multinational capital and corporations (Piore and Sabel, 1984). Networks of small firms were identified in areas of Italy (Emilia-Romagna) and Germany (Baden-Württemberg) characterized as offering generally well paid employment, through being able to take full advantage of new production technologies and shifting demand patterns in order to cooperate with the large firm to their mutual advantage. Smaller firms were identified which could take advantage of their inherent flexibility, innovativeness and creativity in order to move into markets where lowest cost was not the defining competitive attribute. They were able to integrate into several subcontracting networks at the same time, working within a vertical supply chain with a large firm and within a horizontal network with other smaller firms. There was a high rate of investment in product- and process-specific technologies.

Small firms began to be seen as both equal partners with the large firm and a key enabling feature in the production system (Pyke, 1992). Large firms were increasingly turning to smaller firms in order to integrate them into a comprehensive and complex production process which saw the production line evolve into a network of individual enterprises bound up into one unit, a supply chain. The success of the supply chain depended upon all the participants and their ability to cooperate in bringing products through to the market. In addition, further weight was given to the value to regional and local supply chains of the tissue of supportive institutions arising in the surrounding geographical space, because it appeared that the quantity and quality of local institutions – the degree of institutional thickness – correlated well to the degree of regional economic success (Amin and Thrift, 1994).

The Japanese economy provides probably the most powerful example of large firm–small firm partnerships and the potential on offer from active supply chain development. The Japanese industrial system after World War II developed along what we could call traditional capitalist lines, with large companies attempting to use smaller suppliers as a source of cheap components and as a way of externalizing risk. The government was also keen to see large firms recover and develop low-cost operations, and implemented a number of supportive industrial and financial policies. But the key event took place when the government embarked upon a policy of mass entry of small enterprises, as a way of building up a political power base of rural and urban entrepreneurs. This saw the number of small enterprises in Japan rapidly rise over the next two decades. These policies lasted until the 1960s, when attitudinal changes and government regulations began to alter the industrial structure in two ways. First, there emerged a more equal distribution of power between large and small firms as the former realized increasingly that a more involved partnership with their suppliers was more conducive to efficiency than the old 'hands-off' way of simply demanding the lowest possible prices (Friedman, 1988). Second, the state at all levels began to intervene and regulate to support the development of supply chains as a whole, rather than individual firms, thus strengthening the partnership element between the large and small firm and making it more likely that the supply chain was operating to the benefit of both sides (MITI, 1995).

The above models of supply chain development indicate that the concept of inter-enterprise cooperation has a relatively long history and, moreover, has become firmly associated with regional and national economic success. For this reason governments in the reforming Eastern European economies are increasingly looking towards supply chains and other inter-enterprise links where they see the potential to incorporate them into their own industrial policies.

SUPPLY CHAINS IN PRE-TRANSITION EASTERN EUROPE

Typically, East European enterprises were highly vertically integrated, with as many stages of the production process as possible brought together in giant factories. This was in order to reap economies of scale and to minimize the coordination and administrative intervention required to oversee the production process. This integration process included most of the intermediate inputs which went into the final product, but in some cases included raw materials. Even capital goods were produced in-house whenever possible, in so-called secondary machine building workshops (Dmitrieva, 1996). Thus the most striking feature of the communist industrial system, given this vast amount of in-house production, was how little they actually required supply chains. Enterprises were like cathedrals in the desert.

The model for this structure can be found in the industrial history of many western countries, especially in the USA, where industrial development in the early part of this century was based upon the mass-production techniques pioneered by the Ford Motor Company. Many now see these techniques as historically specific: suited to an age when low-cost production was imperative, achieved through standardized products and mass markets. However, this production paradigm became increasingly redundant when the pace of technology began to change rapidly, when consumer tastes became more differentiated, and when disposable incomes began to increase so that low-cost production was no longer critical (Piore and Sabel, 1984). Although the industrial structure in the western economies evolved over the years to reflect these changes in business parameters, the Eastern European industrial structure remained firmly wedded to the early, and increasingly inefficient, model.

In spite of the very large amount of in-house production, basic supply chains nevertheless evolved under communism. There were sometimes intermediate inputs which required altogether different production processes, or needed geographically specific factors of production, or else were simply manufactured elsewhere because of political priorities, especially the desire to maintain reasonably equitable regional development. Where these supply chains differed from their western equivalents lay in the fact that most intermediate inputs were generally ordered via the various central planning bodies, instead of by direct contact with subcontracting firms. The planning authorities saw direct inter-enterprise contact as unnecessary, mainly because it was their job to plan an enterprise's intermediate product line and they had to instruct it to produce the required amount for the entire economy (or for the entire CMEA demand in some enterprises).

In addition, some local networks of suppliers were encouraged to develop and specialize. In the former Soviet Union there was a form of intense networking in the shape of the military/industrial 'closed cities'. Here 'hot-house' conditions were created using local supply chains in order to develop the products and technologies to be able to compete in the arms race. However, the cost of this to the economy was enormous (OECD, 1994). In former Czechoslovakia, small private-sector firms were quite heavily involved in subcontracting to supply inputs to local state firms (Swanson and Webster, 1992). Perhaps the most far-reaching development of small suppliers was in the case of those economies where communism had evolved into a decentralized, market-oriented system, such as in Hungary and former Yugoslavia. Here there was much more freedom for inter-enterprise contact and for large enterprises to order and negotiate over intermediate inputs directly. In Hungary there was experimentation with various forms of subcontracting as part of a package of reform measures in the 1980s (Neumann, 1993) and the rapidly expanding small enterprise sector after 1989 was noted for its extensive linkages with the state sector (Webster, 1992). In former Yugoslavia enterprises were for a long time able to take the lead in establishing new, independent production units to satisfy their requirements for certain intermediate inputs, a process which became one of the major sources of new entry in the economy (Sacks, 1983; Bateman, 1987).

However, supply chains in pre-reform Eastern Europe remained under-developed and extremely inefficient in relation to their western equivalents. They were bound up within the planning systems, which inevitably meant they would be inflexible and slow. This was recognized in the 1960s and 1970s, but particularly so in the 1980s, when the western economies began vastly to improve their own supply chains thanks to the introduction of systems of JIT (Just-in-time) and other Japanese-inspired innovations. The overall inefficiency led to the use of unofficial middlemen or fixers when disruptions to the supply chain were threatening to close down final production in the large enterprises. In the former Soviet Union such fixers were known as *tolkachi* and they became a major feature of industrial life (Nove, 1986).

Moreover, enterprises designated as producers of intermediate inputs tended to be large enterprises also, and they generally had to cover a wide range of inputs. This mass-production of inputs inevitably meant poor quality. For example, in the former Soviet Union almost the entire oil and gas industry's equipment requirements were produced by one giant plant, Glavneftemash, located in Baku, Azerbaijan. Having to produce numerous equipment lines, it was unable to specialize in the production of any one line. Thus the standards and specifications were usually poor and inefficiencies abounded.

Finally, enterprises at the start of the supply chain were often considered less important than those at the end, the giant flagship enterprises producing the final goods.[2] As a consequence, they were generally allocated comparatively fewer investment resources in the plans and could therefore not invest in the machinery and technology. The flow of intermediate products through the supply chain was therefore of a very poor standard, with the result that the final product was inevitably also of poor quality.

BARRIERS TO SUPPLY CHAIN DEVELOPMENT IN EASTERN EUROPE

Three related barriers to supply chain development are apparent in Eastern Europe today. First, there is the continuing absence of an infrastructure of potential small firm suppliers. The relative absence of small firms was one of the main structural weaknesses in the economic systems of the communist economies throughout Eastern Europe. This was the so-called 'socialist black hole' (Petrin and Vahčić, 1989). Small firms were not promoted under communism for a number of reasons: they did not reap economies of scale, they were associated with backward technology, ideologically they were suspect since they were associated with the private sector, and it was difficult to incorporate large numbers of small firms into the planning mechanism. The result is that large enterprises which may now actively want to develop a supply chain have to work with very few potential small enterprise partners, especially small manufacturing enterprises.

The second problem relates to the wider disintegration of supply chains in the wake of the collapse of communism. The rapid decommissioning of the planning systems in Eastern Europe left many large enterprises unaware of the identity of both their suppliers and customers, let alone their specific business needs and requirements Re-establishing the old supply chains is taking time. After further evaluation, many are not considered appropriate because relative cost and price changes since the ending of state controls have made many suppliers and customers no longer cost-effective. For the states of the former Yugoslavia, and the former Soviet Union, re-establishing the old supply chains now involves international links, many of which, for a variety of reasons, are proving difficult to re-establish. There are problems with different currencies, tariffs, transport and so on.

The third problem relates to the development of trust between large and smaller firms, which is a crucial element in facilitating the operations of a supply chain. In many parts of Eastern Europe the old social fabric and business relationships have broken down under the weight of change, misunderstanding, increasing criminality and the settling of old scores. This is particularly the case in the least liberal of the former communist states. In the former Soviet Union many larger firms refuse to cooperate with smaller private firms because of suspicions that they are all linked to the burgeoning organized crime. In some cases, large firms simply misunderstand the market economy and insist that, if there is any profit to be made by smaller firms, then it can just as easily by reaped by the larger firm producing in-house, and so refuse to deal with smaller firms.

DEVELOPING SUPPLY CHAINS IN TRANSITIONAL ECONOMIES

It is clear that support for key inter-enterprise linkages and supply chains should be incorporated into the reform policies in Eastern Europe. We now outline what we believe are the key issues to consider in shaping a support policy.

Increasing the Numbers of Small Manufacturing Firms

As we have noted above, the rapid development of supply chains in Eastern Europe is effectively predicated upon there being a critical mass of small and medium-sized enterprises (SMEs), especially manufacturing SMEs. This critical mass is vital because the dynamic processes of industrial clustering, and vertically and horizontally integrating the production process, will not otherwise begin. Where supply chains have developed most impressively – northern Italy, Japan and in East Asia – the key environmental factor behind the emergence of such links was a pull factor in the shape of a very large population of small enterprises, brought about through extremely high rates of entry (and high rates of exit too, however). The constant recombination of ideas, experience, technical skills, and machinery and equipment, which characterizes a rapidly changing and expanding small enterprise environment, inevitably increases the depth and variety of services small manufacturing enterprises can provide in a supply chain. Against this propitious background, search costs incurred by the large enterprise are minimized. The large enterprise can go on to develop relationships with the most suitable small enterprises, it can test and reject newcomers, it can make use of local innovations and it can recruit specialized labour easily. The overall result of this dynamic process is to propel the supply chains towards efficiency, flexibility and innovation.

Policies to support small enterprise development in Eastern Europe rapidly emerged after the collapse of communism, and a strongly entrepreneurial business culture began to emerge alongside the prevailing bureaucratic–administrative business culture, though more so in Central Europe than in countries further east (Bateman, 1996). Consequently, there has been a surge in small enterprises throughout Eastern Europe (EBRD, 1995). However, in spite of this massive increase in numbers, the depth of the change taking place is not so impressive: by far the bulk of small enterprises which have become established since the collapse of communism are in the fields of trade, import–export and services.[3] These are valuable sectors in many senses, but they are less than ideal when we are considering supply chain development involving the manufacturing sector. Therefore the first aim of current policy support in most parts of Eastern Europe should be to continue to increase the number and variety of smaller manufacturing firms in order to achieve critical mass as soon as possible. This approach we can term the quantity approach (Bateman, 1993). In practice this approach would favour smaller packages of support – subsidies, grants, advice and so on – for a larger number of potential new start manufacturing enterprises, as well as support for institutions which in turn support the various sectors of manufacturing small enterprises. While there are obvious dead-weight and displacement losses, and perhaps other problems related to this approach (Bateman, 1993), these may be more than offset by the externalities generated by the hot-house atmosphere.

Moreover, there are real problems with the policy alternative to the quantity approach – the quality/selectivity approach. This approach is represented by those policies emerging in the Western European economies which seek to assist those small firms already operating with some degree of success with the potential to grow rapidly. Such policies have emerged within the context of the Western European economies for sound economic reasons (Storey and Johnson, 1987; Storey, 1992), but there are several reasons why this approach should remain 'on hold' in Eastern Europe for some time. The first point has been noted and is obvious enough: there remains a serious absence of small manufacturing enterprises, which is a serious structural distortion that can only really be rectified in the foreseeable future by massive new entry. Second, the quality/selectivity approach is really the work of the venture capital institution, where the key aim is the achievement of a high success rate and maximum financial payback from the businesses supported. Government policy to support small enterprises should differ from this approach because it should take into account the wider economic and social externalities: otherwise government support for small enterprise development represents nothing more than one additional source of start-up finance. Third, the quality/selectivity approach is very likely to lead to the creation of a small number of monopolistic/rent seeking producers which tend to have a comparatively minor impact on competition, the industrial structure and production efficiency (Bateman, 1993, 1995; Schmitz, 1993; Schmitz and Musyck, 1994; Schmitz and Furlong, 1995).

Obtaining Large-firm Support for Small-firm Development

The discussion above indicates that large enterprises very much require the presence of large numbers of small enterprises with which to cooperate selectively in building an efficient supply chain. In some instances, there may be deficiencies in the population of small enterprises, and large enterprises may take the lead in establishing those which would be most suitable to them. In the western economies, given the vast population of small enterprises, the motive for assisting in small enterprise development is less because of the subcontracting services they can provide, and more because it is good corporate public relations. In the 1980s, many of the largest enterprises were restructuring and shedding jobs, a feature which they, as well as the local community, found unpalatable. It led to the growth of many support services for potential entrepreneurs being financed by the large enterprise sector (OECD, 1986). In other areas, in East Asia for example, and increasingly in the EU countries too, the motive for supporting local enterprise development is to buy favour with local and central government, particularly in the case of incoming multinationals who seek a favourable business environment for their operations (see the various chapters in Meyanathan, 1994). Whatever the motive, it is difficult to underestimate the importance of core demand to new enterprise development and to regional economic development as a whole. Too many regions have tried to generate local supply chains as a way of kick-starting economic development, but most have failed because they did not have both demand and supply conditions present. In general, because they were depressed areas they tended to have only the supply-side feature – surplus trained labour, financial assistance from central government, ample free business space, and so on.

In Eastern Europe there is much more of a direct commercial motive for large enterprises to assist in the establishment of new small enterprises, because there remain many gaps in the supply chain which could be filled by local small enterprises, were they to exist. In this situation the larger firm should be given every encouragement to support the development of locally based small enterprises. For example, they could offer subcontracting work to potential new starts. The establishment phase is the most vulnerable period for a small enterprise and this core demand would go a great way towards providing a rapid financial return, as well as being a useful form of leverage to obtain support from other institutions. Central and local government and other support bodies should plan to work with this process of small enterprise creation. As in the west, they can make it conditional upon the large enterprise receiving favourable treatment. Many of the largest multinationals investing in Eastern Europe, especially the big motor vehicle manufacturers, have been granted numerous regulatory concessions in return for undertaking to move quickly to a high percentage of local content using local small enterprises. In other examples, the large enterprise wishes to integrate into the local community and develop a good corporate profile, and so is willing to support local small enterprises as a way of supporting the local community within which it must operate.

One method of large enterprise support for small enterprise development arises because of the fact that the large enterprise sector remains heavily overmanned, yet employees are loath to leave their existing job because it very often implies abandoning a variety of social and state benefits. At the same time, the legacy of the business culture under communism is that large firms are reluctant to force employees into redundancy. These factors have given rise to numerous voluntary redundancy programmes, which allow for a wage to continue to be paid to an employee who establishes a new private business, and which are often in an area where the large firm is having difficulty in sourcing. This type of redundancy–small firm creation programme offers considerable advantages in terms of kick-starting the development of specifically local supply chains. First, residual loyalty to the parent business is tapped into, as employees will generally remain keen to retain links with their old employer for sentimental, as well as commercial, reasons. Second, the new business is fully cognizant of the operating procedures, specifications and business culture of the parent business, thus minimizing the chances of cultural and systems mismatch. Third, the new business has a degree of loyalty towards and understanding of, not just the parent firm, but also the locality. Fourth, the new business has familiarity and connections with local institutions and capacities. Such programmes are a feature of labour market policies in many parts of Eastern Europe. In Macedonia FRY over 15 000 workers have taken advantage of the programme (Bartlett and Bateman, 1996). In Croatia, a similar programme came into being in the early 1990s (Bateman, 1996).

Building of Trust

The rebuilding of trust relationships in the emerging business cultures in Eastern Europe will take some time, but it is an essential prerequisite for the development of inter-enterprise linkages and effective supply chains. In less advanced business environments, for example in the former Soviet Union, the main requirement is for tougher government legislation and sanctions against law-breaking firms (Bruno, 1996). The example of a corrupt bureaucracy acts against building trust in business life. It may also be necessary to establish new training procedures for the bureaucracy and better conditions of service. The example of the French Grande Ecole may be useful to follow.

In some cases the old system of connections may actually be harnessed to the development of supply chains. In East Asian development the trust between economic actors is greatly underpinned by the various family, community and ethnic ties, and this reduces transaction costs to a minimum and maximizes information exchange (Kagami, 1995). This process is happening already in parts of Eastern Europe. In Croatia, for example, the connections (*veza*) are proving a useful background to the establishment and successful operation of simple supply chain relationships (Bartlett and Bateman, 1996) and in Kazakhstan probably the most vibrant business communities are those of the ethnic Koreans and Germans (Taylor, 1996).

Facilitating Technology Transfer and Development

Supply chains in the western economies involve an element of technology diffusion down the supply chain, as the larger enterprise attempts to improve the performance of the chain by upgrading the technological profile of its constituents. Moreover, the growth in flexible technologies and reduction of minimum efficient scale means that smaller enterprises are now ideally suited to providing high-quality inputs. However, in many cases the larger enterprise is assumed to have the scale of operations and resources to acquire and develop new technologies which the smaller ones simply do not have, and it is important that this filter through into the supply chain. This form of technology transfer is especially common in Japanese supply chains (Nishiguchi, 1994). It clearly improves the performance of the supply chain as a whole, and the standard of inputs flowing through to the larger enterprise, as well as improving the technological capability of constituent small enterprises in the supply chain. Perhaps the most obvious example of an enormous technological potential which could and should be passed on to the enterprise sector is in Russia, where the military/industrial system took the lead in developing many advanced technologies thanks to massive resource transfers from the state.

There is also an element of upward technology transfer as smaller enterprises are encouraged to upgrade their production techniques, possibly with the financial assistance of the larger enterprise, and the improved intermediate product is passed up the supply chain, or on to the larger enterprise to be incorporated into the final product. It makes sense for smaller enterprises to purchase product-specific technology since their position within the supply chain has reduced some of the inherent risk of customers switching suppliers. Alternatively, the smaller enterprise may tap into purpose-built technology transfer mechanisms, such as the Steinbeis Foundations in Baden-Württemberg (see Pyke, 1994) or the technology demonstration centres and SME schools in Japan (Kagami, 1995), the fruits of which also (and are meant to) pass upwards. This requires a financial commitment to the regional infrastructure and the vision to coordinate various local technological actors, such as universities, research institutes and the like. It also requires patience and a longer-term perspective, since such measures do not always produce results quickly.

Supply chain development has a multifaceted appeal for policy makers. For a start, the precariousness of many larger enterprises throughout the Eastern European transition economies deserves the attention of policy makers. These problems are, as we have seen, partly related to the collapse of supply chains established under communism. Accordingly, in order to provide for a more efficient and competitive large enterprise sector a major feature of industrial restructuring policy must include the promotion and strengthening of regional and local supply chains. Moreover, efficient supply chains are associated with successful small-firm sector and regional development outcomes, as in Japan and parts of Western Europe. Where smaller firms cooperate with each other and with larger firms they give rise to a supporting tissue of institutions, the overall affect of which is to generate significant economies of agglomeration and a small-firm sector which has the capacity to compete internationally. Therefore attention to supply chain formation and development should feature as a key aspect of regional policy as well.

We have outlined some of the key issues which deserve further analysis if the promotion of regional and local supply chains is to have real meaning in Eastern Europe. At present, the bulk of aid and investment flowing into the region is being directed towards individual firms, generally larger firms. We would argue that more needs to be directed towards supply chain building, if the economic health of the larger enterprises is to be considered and regional development imperatives are to be addressed.

NOTES

1. Supply chains involve vertically integrated networks of regionally and locally based small and large firms, linked together through undertaking different stages of the production process. Supply chains involve more than the simple purchase of inputs in a 'hands-off' fashion, instead representing a definite flow or production line which is shared between firms, generally passing from the smallest firm up to the largest.
2. However, this was also the situation in the western economies, until the Japanese experience indicated that the entire supply chain was as important as the final product.
3. Most worryingly, manufacturing enterprises established before the collapse of communism are moving back into trade (OECD, 1994).

REFERENCES

Amin, A. and N. Thrift (eds) (1994), *Globalization, Institutions and Regional Development in Europe*, Oxford: Oxford University Press.

Asanuma, B. (1989), 'Manufacturer–Supply Relationships in Japan and the Concept of Relation-Specific Skill', *Journal of the Japanese and International Economies*, **3**, 1–30.

Bartlett, W. and M. Bateman (1995), 'Development of the Small Firm Sector in Macedonia FRY', unpublished mimeo.

Bartlett, W. and M. Bateman (1996), 'The Business Culture in Croatia and Slovenia', in M. Bateman (ed.), *Business Cultures in Eastern Europe*, Oxford: Butterworth-Heinemann.

Bateman, M. (1987), 'Local Economic Strategies: Local Employment Promotion and Support in the Yugoslav Economy', *Working Paper No. 8*, Department of Economics, University of Bradford.

Bateman, M. (1993), 'Policies for Small Firm Sector Development in Post-communist Economies: The Case of Russia', paper presented at the Roundtable on Economic Transition in Southern Europe, Skopje (Macedonia FRY), 27–8 April.

Bateman, M. (1995), 'Industrial Restructuring and Local SME Development: The Case for a "Hands On" Approach', in Z. Frohlich, S. Maleković, J. Padjen, M. Polić and S. Švaljek (eds), *Industrial Restructuring and Its Impact on Regional Development*, Zagreb: Croatian Section of the Regional Science Association.

Bateman, M. (ed.) (1996), *Business Cultures in Eastern Europe*, Oxford: Butterworth-Heinemann.

Bruno, M. (1996), 'The Business Culture in Russia', in M. Bateman (ed.), *Business Cultures in Eastern Europe*, Oxford: Butterworth-Heinemann.

Cheng, L. and G. Gereffi (1994), 'The Informal Economy in East Asian Development', *International Journal of Urban and Regional Research*, **18**, (2).

Department of Trade and Industry (1995), various publications, London: DTI.

Dmitrieva, O. (1996), *Regional Development: The USSR And After*, London: UCL Press Ltd.

EBRD (1995), *Transition Report*, London.

Friedman, D. (1988), *The Misunderstood Miracle: Industrial Development and Political Change in Japan*, Ithaca, NY: Cornell University Press.

Kagami, M. (1995), 'Strategies for Competitiveness in Production – An East Asian Approach', *Small Enterprise Development*, **6**, (1).

Kaplinsky, R. (1994), *Easternisation: The Spread of Japanese Management Techniques to Developing Countries*, Ilford: Frank Cass.

Lall, S. (1980), 'Vertical Inter-Firm Linkages in LDCs: An Empirical Study', *Oxford Bulletin of Economics and Statistics*, **42**, (3), 203–26.

Lewis, J. (1995), *The Connected Corporation,* New York: The Free Press.

Marshall, A. (1890), *Principles of Economics*, London: Macmillan.

Mead, D. (1984) 'Of Contracts and Sub-contracts: Small Firms in Vertically Disintegrated Production/Distribution Systems in LDCs', *World Development,* **12**, (11/12), 1095–1106.

Meyanathan, S. (ed.) (1994), *Industrial Structures and the Development of Small and Medium Enterprise Linkages: Examples from East Asia*, Washington, DC: EDI, World Bank.

MITI (1995), *Outline of Small and Medium Enterprises Policies of the Japanese*

Government, Tokyo: Small and Medium Enterprise Agency, Ministry of International Trade and Industry.

Neumann, L. (1993), 'Decentralization and Privatization in Hungary: Towards Supplier Networks?', in G. Grabher (ed.), *The Embedded Firm: On the Socioeconomics of Industrial Networks*, London: Routledge.

Nishiguchi, T. (1994), *Strategic Industrial Sourcing: The Japanese Advantage*, Oxford: Oxford University Press.

Nove, A. (1986), *The Soviet Economic System*, Winchester, Mass.: Allen & Unwin.

OECD (1986), *The Role of Large Firms in Local Job Creation*, Paris.

OECD (1994), *Science, Technology and Innovation Policies: Federation of Russia*, 2 vols, Paris.

Petrin, T. and A. Vahčić (1989), 'Financial Systems for Restructuring the Yugoslav Economy', in C. Kessides, T. King, M. Nuti and C. Sokil (eds), *Financial Reforms in Socialist Economies*, Florence: EDI, World Bank/European University Institute.

Piore, M. and C. Sabel (1984), *The Second Industrial Divide: Possibilities for Prosperity*, New York: Basic Books.

Porter, M. (1990), *The Competitive Advantage of Nations*, London: Macmillan.

Pyke, F. (1992), *Industrial Development Through Small Firm Cooperation*, Geneva: International Institute for Labour Studies.

Pyke, F. (1994), *Small Firms, Technical Services and Inter-firm Cooperation*, Geneva: International Institute for Labour Studies.

Pyke, F. and W. Sengenberger (1992), *Industrial Districts and Local Economic Regeneration*, Geneva: International Institute for Labour Studies.

Sacks, S. (1983), *Self-Management and Efficiency: Large Corporations in Yugoslavia*, London: Allen & Unwin.

Schmitz, H. (1993), 'Small Firms and Flexible Specialisation in Developing Countries', in B. Spath (ed.), *Small Firms and Development in Latin America*, Geneva: International Institute for Labour Studies.

Schmitz, H. and D. Furlong (1995), *Growth Constraints of Small-Scale Industry and Policy Options for Government*, Brighton: Institute of Development Studies, University of Sussex.

Schmitz, H. and B. Musyck (1994), 'Industrial Districts in Europe: Policy Lessons for Developing Countries', *World Development*, **22**, (6).

Shutt, J. and R. Whittington (1987), 'Fragmentation Strategies and the Rise of Small Units', *Regional Studies*, **21**, (1).

Storey, D. (1992), 'Should We Abandon the Support to Start-up Businesses?', mimeo, University of Warwick: SME Centre.

Storey, D. and S. Johnson (1987), *Job Generation and Labour Market Change*.

Swanson, D. and L. Webster (1992), *Private Sector Manufacturing in The Czech and Slovak Federal Republic: A Survey of Firms*, Washington, DC: Industry and Energy Department, World Bank.

Taylor, M. (1996), 'The Business Culture in Kazakhstan', in M. Bateman (ed.), *Business Cultures in Eastern Europe*, Oxford: Butterworth-Heinemann.

Van Kooij, E. (1991), 'Japanese Subcontracting at the Crossroads', *Small Business Economics*, **3**, 145–54.

Webster, L. (1992), *Private Sector Manufacturing in Hungary: A Survey of Firms*, Washington, DC: Industry and Energy Department, World Bank.

3.   Corporate governance and decision making: a case study

Pere Sikavica

'The issue [of corporate governance and decision making] has existed for as long as there have been social institutions; yet until two decades ago, the term corporate governance had not been coined' (Kay and Silberston, 1995). The term has become popular in the context of transitional economies of the Central and Eastern European countries. Much of the concern with corporate governance (company management) – a concern which is a largely Anglo-American model – arises from the tension between this model and the practical reality of how large corporations operate today all over the world.

An additional key objective in all transitional settings is long-term institution building. Privatization has spurred the development of market institutions, but mass privatization has not been able to produce the best company owners in this short period. It is believed that it might lead to better corporate governance in the long run if it promotes the development of capital markets and intermediary monitoring institutions for the economy as a whole.

What is effective governance? The primary economic rationale behind privatization is to create a class of owners who are motivated to use resources efficiently. But changes in ownership will not change managerial behaviour if new owners lack the power, incentives and capability to monitor managers and ensure that they act in the interest of the firm. Owners must also have the right to change managers to effect deep restructuring. For small firms, such corporate governance is simple as mostly the owners are managers themselves. It is in medium and large-sized firms that the separation of owners and managers creates a need for monitoring. Direct supervision by shareholders is one way of doing this. Another is to sell shares when performance is weak and the falling share prices discipline the managers. In the early stages of transition, direct monitoring is important for capital markets and the managerial class is not sufficiently developed to exert strong competitive pressure on managers (The World Bank, 1996, p. 52). A sad fact of the transition process is that newly privatized enterprises may fail to restructure because of inappropriate corporate governance.

With the above considerations in mind, this chapter tries to study the actual behaviour of large and medium-sized companies and their managers in an emerging transitional economy – Croatia. An extensive survey of the functioning of corporate management in Croatian companies was undertaken by a survey including 67 questions grouped into the following nine categories: basic data concerning the manager; main functions of the management and the manager; delegation of authority and responsibility in managing; levels of management; knowledge, skills and qualifications which managers must possess; styles of governing; how a manager organizes his/her time; systems in managing; and the company's decision making. The survey included 24 companies and was based on a statistically defined relevant sample, from all parts of Croatia. The companies belong to following fields: industry and mining (17), water-power engineering (1), construction (1), transport and communication (1), trade (1), tourism (1), utilities (1) and financial, technical and business services (1). Out of a total of 66 809 employees working in the companies included in this survey, most (85.7 per cent) are employed in industry and mining (41.8 per cent), and transport and communications (43.9 per cent). The remaining 14.3 per cent of the employees work in other fields.

Since the functioning of management as well as the behaviour of managers differ in small and large companies, a sample selection of companies was made bearing this difference in mind. Out of 24 companies included in the survey, two companies employed between 101 and 200 employees; five employed between 201 and 500 employees; nine employed between 501 and 1000 employees; three employed between 1000 and 2000 employees; four employed between 1001 and 5000 employees and one company employed between 20 001 and 30 000 employees (the post and telecommunication company employs around 29 500 people).

The number of answers received is equally important for the validity of the results of the survey. Out of 313 questionnaires distributed to managers at all levels in 24 companies, 231 responded (74 per cent). The number is fairly satisfactory since the poll was anonymous.

MANAGEMENT AND DECISION MAKING

Although the basic principles of management have been known for a long time, modern management is a phenomenon typical of the 20th century. Management itself represents a significant innovation. It has effectively revolutionized the manner of conducting business over the last hundred years to such an extent that a managerial revolution is spoken of with much justification, in the same way as one speaks of the automobile and telecommunication revolutions which have changed lifestyles the world over (Drucker, quoted in Lessem, 1989, p. 73).

Despite the existence of numerous schools of thought within management theory, there are still no consistent theories that might be implemented in practice. Closest to this goal is the theory of contingency, which stresses the importance of the real situation in which the manager finds himself, regardless of the place of operation. For this very reason, management as a concept, besides having a scientific dimension, contains elements of both art and skill. This is the main reason why management cannot be completely learnt, still less copied (Koontz and Weihrich, 1990, p. 504; Derek *et al.*, 1989, p. 393).

The success of companies at the present time is a result of effective management more than ever before. One-half of new businesses fold during the first two years of operation and around 70 per cent of all new businesses disappear within the first five years. In most of these cases, over 90 per cent, the reason for failure is ineffective management (Gordon *et al.*, 1990, p. 3).

Although the main task of managers, such as planning, organizing, personnel development, leadership and control, are familiar to every manager, an open challenge is still posed by the manner in which general managerial expertise should be integrated into a unified theory (Koontz and Weihrich, 1990, p. 504). The reason for this lies in the fact that managerial work, unlike other tasks, is somewhat indefinite, unclear and nebulous, and hence cannot be completely and precisely described and defined. This represents a challenge to every manager, allowing for freedom of action and creativity (Derek *et al.*, 1989, p. 27). Today, as always, one of the toughest problems of management is how best to utilize an organization's resources in a volatile, even turbulent, environment. In other words, an optimum combination of resources and their optimum utilization still remain one of the toughest problems modern management is faced with. The more complex the organization, the tougher these problems become.

An ideal organizational structure seems almost unattainable, particularly in such propulsive sectors as companies involved in developing and marketing state-of-the-art technologies, which operate within an environment that is not only complex but extremely volatile. The most that is required of management under such circumstances is to respond promptly to challenges coming from the environment. One of the most momentous tasks of the modern manager is to motivate his/her colleagues, which often depends on his/her personal charisma and other features (Gordon *et al.*, 1990, p. 6). For this particular reason, the same group of people are willing to follow a certain leader and not another. It is of utmost importance for every manager to have a profound understanding of his/her job and, even more important, to understand his/her subordinates or colleagues.

Successful managers can be differentiated from others according to three criteria. The first, according to authorities on the subject, is selecting the best coworkers, the second is finding ways to motivate them, while the third is giving them enough freedom to work in their own way. A few more characteristics can be added, such as full commitment to his/her work, a high level of self-confidence, lower organizational dependence and greater autonomy (Wriston, 1990, p. 80). Successful corporate governance depends upon efficient and speedy decision making. Decision making can be most briefly defined as choice or selection among several options. Decision making may seem relatively easy if it is based on the choice of one of the options. However, it is much more difficult to select the right option or, in other words, to make the right decision. In the decision-making process it is not good to operate with either too few or too many options. With few options, there is little likelihood that the best decision will be made; with too many options, the decision-making process will be protracted unnecessarily. This means that, even in the process of generating options, one should have a sense of measure, so that there are neither too few nor too many possibilities to solving a problem.

Every decision-making process must provide answers to several important questions, such as the place for decision making, the time for decision making, the manner in which the decisions are made and the subject of decision making. One of the most difficult problems with which almost every decision maker is faced is the discrepancy between limitless wishes and limited possibilities in the decision-making process. Whenever the discrepancy between wishes and possibilities is great, decision making is more difficult and there is a greater danger of making a wrong decision. It is most difficult to make decisions in a situation where wishes are great and possibilities small, while it is easy to make decisions when the case is the other way round. The latter is desirable, while the former is reality.

Management and decision making are closely connected, in that decision making is the primary function of management (Duncan, 1989, p. 69). Indeed, decision making is not the only function of management, but it is present in all workplaces. Managerial decision accounts for most of managers' work. In the decision-making process, a successful manager has to be able to provide valid answers to three basic questions: (1) what is the problem to be solved by decision making; (2) what solutions are at my disposal to solve the problem; and (3) which is the best solution to the problem?

One of the difficulties in managerial decision making is evident when decisions are made under pressure of time and in crisis situations. In both cases there is a likelihood that a bad decision will be made. If you are pressed for time, you cannot evaluate all available options because you are under pressure and a decision must be made quickly, which in a way blocks you in your decision making. The same is true when a decision must be made in a crisis situation.

Since every decision is a mixture of intuition and rationality, we can talk about intuitive decision making, evaluation-based decision making and rational decision making. Such a sequence of decision making is hierarchical because, as a rule, operational decisions should be made intuitively, tactical decisions should be made on the basis of evaluation and strategic decisions should be made rationally. This is, however, a theoretical concept. In practice, it is not rare for the most important decisions to be made by intuition. The practice of both domestic and foreign companies abounds in examples of intuitive decisions on issues crucial to their future.

THE CASE OF CROATIA

The Managers

A survey conducted on various aspects of corporate governance in Croatian companies took into consideration factors such as sex, age, qualifications, type of work, level of management, and so on, making it possible for us to compare the data. Of the managers who participated in the survey, 85.6 per cent were men and 14.4 per cent were women. Evidently, men seem to be predominantly responsible for all the successes and failures in the Croatian economy, and women only have marginal responsibility. If we analyse the sex of managers, we find that out of 10 managers at all levels of management, with the exception of the mid-level, nine are men and only one is a woman, and that at the mid-level of management, out of 10 managers, eight are men and two are women.

Women's inferior position to their male colleagues is reflected in the fact that female managers at middle levels of management have twice as favourable a position compared to that of their colleagues at other levels of management leads us to conclude that, of all managerial functions, women as managers are second-best at the level just below the top. It must be noted, however, that the proportion of managerial functions between men and women is in no way better in other countries, although the role of female managers is growing fast in the world.

Another relevant element for measuring the success of managers in Croatian companies was their age. The largest number (29.9 per cent) at all levels of managing are in the age group 41–5. Over 60 per cent of all the managers are under 45 years of age, an extremely favourable fact. Managers in the 45–50 age group make up 19.9 per cent of all managers. Some 18.6 per cent of the managers fall within the 50–60 age group. If we analyse the age of managers at certain levels of management, we find similar results. The largest number of managers at the top, upper-middle and middle levels belong to the 41–5 age group. At the top level of management, 22.3 per cent of the managers are between 51 and 60 years of age. Evidently, the proportion of this age group is too high for top level of management. The largest age group of managers at middle level of management is 31–5 (60 per cent). At the lowest level, a sizeable number falls within the 46–50 age group (with 42.9 per cent of all the managers at that level). Thus these are people for whom the lowest level of management is the ceiling which they can reach in their career, unlike managers at middle level, who have the chance of getting promotion in time.

The educational background of managers covered by the survey seems to be fairly satisfactory, as 74.1 per cent of managers at all levels have university education, and 82.8 per cent of them possess an MA or a PhD while 17.8 per cent of all the managers have two-year college diplomas or some lower qualification. If we compare the qualifications of Croatian managers to their counterparts abroad, as far as formal education is concerned, there is hardly much difference.

One of the most important finding of our survey on corporate management in Croatian companies concerns the level of management at which a particular executive is working. Of those who responded to the survey, 52.8 per cent are managers at the highest level (company directors, deputy directors, assistant directors and managers of units directly subordinated to them); 29.7 per cent are at middle level closer to the top level; 12.2 per cent are at middle level; 2.2 per cent are managers at middle level but closer to lower managing levels and 3.1 per cent are managers at the lowest level of management (foremen, supervisors and so on). From the structure of those surveyed we may also conclude that as many as 82.5 per cent of managers fit into the category of top managers and upper-middle managers.

Delegation of Power and Managing Responsibilities

The process of growth and development of a company, its product diversification and divisionalization of organizational structure should follow a decentralization process of management which is in turn closely related to the process of delegating power and responsibility (Mescon *et al.*, 1985, p. 282). In large companies, delegation of power and responsibility is a *condicio sine qua non* for successful management. It is necessary for the survival and functioning of any form of organization, since it is impossible for one person to have total authority in decision making. Difficulties arise in this process, either because of the inability of superiors to transfer power and responsibility to their subordinates or because of the fact that subordinates are not ready to accept them.

The following conclusions can be drawn from the survey conducted. As many as 62.1 per cent of the managers always delegated their power and responsibility to their associates, and only 3 per cent never did. An additional 34.9 per cent of them claimed that they sometimes did, and at other times did not, delegate. According to other questions to which managers responded, two-thirds of the managers at all levels had a tendency to delegate power. In conclusion, Croatian managers see the importance of the factor because of its effectiveness in governance. Results are as shown in Table 3.1.

Table 3.1   Delegation of power and responsibilities at particular levels of management (in percentages)

Tendency	Level of management				
	High	Upper-middle	Middle	Lower-middle	Lowest
To delegate	66.1	60.3	60.7	40.0	28.6
Not to delegate	1.7	2.9	0.0	0.0	42.9
Only sometimes	32.2	36.8	39.3	60.0	28.5

Source: Computed from the survey.

As far as delegation of duties is concerned, the task of achieving a balance between authority and responsibility is also important. Such a balance is expected to be achieved at all levels of management. But, according to the results of the survey, only 73.8 per cent of the managers find it exists, and 23.6 per cent fail to notice it. This means that managers at higher levels have greater authority than responsibility at the expense of lower levels of management. Only 2.6 per cent of the managers have greater authority than responsibility. The further we go down the ladder, the more managers find their responsibilities to be greater than their authority.

A very large number of managers, some 81.6 per cent, find difficulties in delegating authority and responsibility owing to the fact that subordinates are not ready to accept the delegated authority. Naturally, only 5.4 per cent of the managers find themselves responsible for hindering the delegating process, while 12.8 per cent of the managers consider both sides to be guilty.

The most important reason for a manager's unwillingness to delegate authority and the responsibility to his/her associates is the fact that, as shown by the survey, firstly, they feel that they do a job better and secondly, there is an aversion towards risk in delegating (17.8 per cent). The existence of distrust among their subordinates ranks third and, finally, there is undeveloped and insufficient communication between the manager and his/her subordinates and associates.

When asked why they are not ready to accept delegated authority and responsibility, 71.2 per cent of both subordinates and associates answered that they considered it easier to ask their superiors for solutions to the problem rather than solve it by themselves. This answer corresponds with the most frequent way managers see the same problem (71.2 per cent, as against 67.8 per cent), which means that managers really are not guilty of unwillingness to delegate. The same answer applies to the second important problem: lack of information, and sporadic communication between the chief executive and his associates (10.4 per cent).

If the issue is the desire to delegate, considering the age pattern, it is interesting to note that the youngest and the oldest managers are the most unwilling people to delegate. The reason for it lies in the self-confidence of younger managers, who think they can do everything best by themselves, while, older managers feel that, since they have been through 'everything' they know exactly how to do what is expected of them. The former do not want to miss any chance, while the latter say that they have regretted delegating authority many times in their managerial career. The same reasons for unwillingness to delegate to their associates are common to all levels of management.

Style of Governance

In theory as well as in the practice of management leadership, there are several ways or styles of governance which lie between the two extremes of autocracy and democracy. In addition, some other methods have also been developed. In an autocracy-based style of managing, unlimited power of decision making is concentrated in the hands of one person. A democracy-based style of managing is characterized by the involvement of subordinates in the process of decision making. Each of the styles of managing suits a certain situation and each has its advantages and disadvantages. In some cases, the autocratic style can be advantageous, but as a rule in managing, especially in contemporary business conditions, it is not desirable.

Croatian corporate bosses see themselves as autocrats in only 2.6 per cent of cases, while their associates see them as autocrats in 13.8 per cent of cases, which is not much of a cause for concern. This percentage would be higher if more managers from the lower levels of management had participated in the survey. This explains the low percentage of autocratic managers in the top and higher levels, which were not evaluated.

The managers see themselves as democratic leaders in 40.3 per cent of cases, whereas their associates see them as such in 31.7 per cent of cases.

There is a high percentage of managers who state that their style of managing is 'somewhere between autocratic and democratic' (57.1 per cent), an opinion supported by 54.6 per cent of their associates. As a high percentage of managers run companies in a style somewhere between autocracy and democracy, this should really be seen more as an autocratic style, rather than a democratic. This is because a very small number of people at lower levels of management were covered by the survey. They are the ones who should verify the statements of higher levels of management. The data on how managers of a particular level see themselves or how their associates see them are shown in Tables 3.2. and 3.3.

Table 3.2   Managers' evaluation of own style of leadership (in percentages)

Style of leadership	Level of management				
	High	Upper-middle	Middle	Lower-middle	Lowest
Autocratic	4.2	0.0	3.6	0.0	0.0
Democratic	35.5	40.3	60.7	40.0	57.1
In between	60.3	59.7	35.7	60.0	42.9

Source: Computed from the survey.

Table 3.3   Evaluation of style of leadership of superiors (in percentages)

Style of leadership	Level of management				
	High	Upper-middle	Middle	Lower-middle	Lowest
Autocratic	13.7	9.1	14.3	60.0	28.6
Democratic	34.9	30.3	25.0	20.0	28.6
In between	51.4	60.6	60.7	20.0	42.8

Source: Computed from the survey.

The survey further shows that a large number of managers often confront their subordinates with problems and solicit their suggestions while making decisions (44.3 per cent). At times they make decisions together with their associates (29.1 per cent) and sometimes they present decisions to their employees for discussion (19.6 per cent). This appears to indicate that managers try to be democratic, but this is denied by the subordinate executives at lower levels.

To a certain extent, the way managers address their subordinates illus-
trates the style of managing: while 88.6 per cent of the managers think that
their superiors address them in a manner which encourages readiness to
understand and solve the problem, in 11.4 per cent of cases their superiors
are seen as addressing them in a manner which makes them adopt a defen-
sive attitude.

Decision Making Within the Company

Perhaps the most important part of every manager's duty is making decisions
and communicating with the subordinates. In view of the hierarchy of levels,
certain kinds of decisions are made at each level of management. Thus it is
necessary to set up a clear-cut division of decisions to be made at each level
within a company. In large part, strategic decisions will have to be made by
the management at the top, tactical decisions by middle-management, while
administrative and routine decisions are made by lower level management.
This kind of relationship is also visible in the degree of authority managers
have, as well as in the size of their salaries.

Only 14.1 per cent of the total number of decisions made by managers are
strategic, 19.4 per cent tactical, 44.9 per cent operational, and 21.4 per cent
are routine decisions. With such a high percentage of highest level of governance represented in our sample, the percentage of operational and routine
decisions being made is too high (66.3 per cent). This points to the fact that
higher levels of management in Croatia do not deal with 'real' issues. Such a
high percentage of operational and routine decision making also shows that
higher level management tends not to delegate authority.

At the highest level of management, strategic decisions make up to 18.6
per cent of all decisions made at that level, while only 7 per cent of strategic
decisions are made at the lowest level of management. The number of strategic decisions made at the top level is rather small and it is even more
disturbing to note that strategic decisions are made even at the lowest levels
of management.

The highest level of management makes very few routine decisions: 19.2
per cent of the total number of decisions made at that level. At the same time,
lowest level managers make 40.7 per cent of the routine decisions. The
structure of decisions made at the top level is also unfavourable for managers
at that level, since they make 61.7 per cent of the operational and routine
decisions. Bearing in mind the knowledge, abilities and the position of that
level within the enterprise, the top level is too highly paid to be preoccupied
with matters of lesser importance.

All decisions made within a company could be classified as programmed
and unprogrammed. Programmed decisions are generally used to solve

routine problems and are based on previously set criteria of decision making and are mostly used in recurring situations.

According to our survey, 52.2 per cent of the total number of decisions made are programmed, and 47.8 per cent unprogrammed. This ratio between programmed and unprogrammed decisions is unfavourable for the structure of management in the sample, since 82.5 per cent of the managers belong to higher and top levels, who are expected to make more unprogrammed and fewer programmed decisions. The results are presented in Table 3.4.

Table 3.4   Programmed and unprogrammed decisions (in percentages)

Decisions	Level of management				
	High	Upper-middle	Middle	Lower-middle	Lowest
Programmed	49.7	53.6	55.0	56.0	70.7
Unprogrammed	50.3	46.4	45.0	44.0	29.3

Source: Computed from the survey.

Every decision within a company is a combination of intuition, evaluation and rationality. The sequence in the decision-making process follows a hierarchy, in the sense that operational decisions should be made intuitively, tactical ones should be based on evaluations and strategic decisions should be based on rationality. Moreover, this is only a theoretical concept. There are certainly cases of intuitive strategic decision making. Croatian managers seem to make 19.3 per cent of decisions intuitively, 35.2 per cent are based on estimates and 45.7 per cent are based on rationality.

Decisions in every company are made in varying conditions related to certainty, risk and uncertainty. According to our survey, 53.6 per cent of decisions are made in conditions of certainty, 26.4 per cent in those of risk and 19.8 under uncertainty. We feel that such a high percentage of decisions made in conditions of certainty in Croatian companies is not a very reliable result for the survey, but the smaller percentage of decisions made in conditions of uncertainty corresponds to a small percentage of strategic decisions (14.1 per cent), since, in general, strategic decisions are made in conditions of uncertainty.

According to the results of the survey, in the opinion of Croatian corporate managers, there are three important factors that determine the quality of decision making:[1] competent and professional willingness to make decisions (87.4 per cent); good and objective information available to those who make decisions (81.7 per cent); and responsibility for decisions (69.6 per cent). Very similar answers were obtained at other levels of management.

According to our survey, the methods managers most often use are system analysis, operational research and simulation. It is important to add that the distribution of answers regarding methods used in decision making is questionable, since 66.3 per cent of all decisions made are operational and routine. When making such decisions, there is hardly any need for sophisticated methods such as system analysis, operational research or simulation.

The last question in the questionnaire that managers in our sample had to answer was how they evaluate their own role in and influence on the decision making process within their company. Only 8.1 per cent of the managers stated that they have a very strong influence, while 32.1 per cent said that their influence was significant. This result is significant in view of the fact that 82.5 per cent of the executives belonged to top levels of governance. While some 46.8 per cent of the managers classified their influence on decision making within their company as average or small, only 2.3 per cent believe they have no influence at all. The surprising fact is that 8.6 per cent of the managers were not even able to evaluate their own influence on the process of decision making within their own company.

To sum up, Croatian company bosses have yet to learn to behave like modern corporate executives and to make use of expertise in the field of corporate governance in the world. As far as the internal structure of a company is concerned, contrary to recent trends in modern theory and practice of company organization, as well as to transitional policies in Central and East European countries, there is a strong tendancy towards a split of existing enterprises into smaller companies. Since 1990, Croatian companies have taken a different course: large consolidated (holding) companies have been created. This contradicts the intentions of those who strongly believe in transition policy, because it hinders competition and creates monopolies. Fortunately, new company laws provide an opportunity to reverse this trend. What needs to be done is for rules of strict internal financial discipline to be set within sections of a single company and for the responsibility to be fixed at definite points.

Another problem which Croatian company management faces is that theory and practice of management are often applied overenthusiastically, resulting in cases of extremely regressive processes. It seems that scant attention is being paid to the available expertise in management science, so that in certain cases we relapse into the pioneering stage of management.

Questions arise with regard to management: which experience should be applied when, where and how? To approach these questions we must mention that, first and foremost, Croatian corporate executives must learn from those from whom something can be learned, but should apply only such management practices which best fit the environment of our companies. Another important fact to be noted is that it is impossible mechanically to copy and apply the management practice of others.

In Croatian companies, a worrisome yet increasingly popular trend must be highlighted in particular: the centralization of management and leadership accompanied by the corresponding marginalization of all other employees. This should not be taken as a rule. If this trend becomes pervasive, surely our management practice is in danger of dropping below the attained expertise level in the modern world. Decentralization is a natural process resulting from a company's growth and expansion, from its diversification and departmentalization.

Another phenomenon noticed in Croatian companies is the crisis of middle managers which is a result of the assumption of authority by top management and the marginalization of middle management in the decision-making process. Only when responsibility points are fixed, internal financial discipline becomes the criterion, and profit earning becomes the aim of every enterprise, will middle management regain its dignity and an equilibrium between authority and responsibility be established.

NOTE

1. The total exceeds 100 as the people surveyed were allowed to respond to more than one answer in the questionnaire.

REFERENCES

Derek, T., J. Weightman and J. Kristy (1989), *Effective Management: People and Organization*, New York: Prentice-Hall.

Duncan, N.J. (1989), *Great Ideas in Management*, San Francisco/ London: Jossey–Bass.

Gordon, J.R., R.W. Mondy, A. Sharplin and S.R. Preruaux (1990), *Management and Organizational Behavior*, Boston, Mass.: Allwyn and Bacon.

Kay, J. and A. Silberston (1995), 'Corporate Governance', *National Institute Economic Review*, (153).

Koontz, H. and H. Weihrich (1990), *Essentials of Management*, 5th edn, New York: McGraw-Hill.

Lessem, R. (1989), Global Management Principles, New York: Prentice-Hall.

Mescon, M., M. Albert and F. Khedouri (1985), *Management*, New York: Harper & Row.

Wriston, W.B. (1990), 'The State of American Management', *Harvard Business Review*, January–February.

World Bank (1996), *World Development Report 1996*, Washington, DC.

4. Entrepreneurship in the turbulent environment of Eastern Europe

Marin Aleksandrov Marinov

Economists consider four major strategies for entrepreneurial development: capital strategy, nucleus strategy, evolutionary strategy and privatization of state-owned companies (Brunner, 1993). The application of a certain strategic approach depends on the current conditions of the economy and governmental attitude and goals for development of entrepreneurship. This way of analysing entrepreneurship focuses on the macroeconomic and political conditions for new venture creation. It considers the state as entrepreneur, without concentrating on the entrepreneurial characteristics and requirements of the individual entrepreneur and entrepreneurial support system. The entrepreneur is the key player in the successful start-up of any business. He is the one that, through realizing market opportunities based on motivation, drive and ability, mobilizes resources for such a purpose. Therefore creating conditions for individual entrepreneurial activities could be the basis for the effective implementation of a certain macroeconomic entrepreneurial strategy encompassing focuses on the development of businesses with present comparative advantages, creating islands of excellence and reducing the state ownership and control of the productive assets of the economy.

The transfer of ownership from state to private is the crucial issue of the transition from a centrally planned to a market-led economy. The practical achievements in this field, however, are unsatisfactory and disappointing in the global context of Eastern Europe. Some of the main reasons for these can be found in the approaches to change of ownership and the respective development of entrepreneurial system.

This chapter discusses the existence of the key elements needed for the success of entrepreneurial ventures in the context of the market-led economic transition in Eastern Europe. We concentrate on the needs and characteristics of entrepreneurship in the transitional post-communist economies, followed by an analysis of models for successful entrepreneurship and their applicability to the situation in Eastern Europe. Through analysis of entrepreneurial environmental prospects some features of the new small business ventures and their relationship with the existing environment of state-owned companies are defined. Finally, the goals of entrepreneurship in transition are discussed and key factors for entrepreneurial development evaluated.

TRANSITION, OWNERSHIP AND ENTREPRENEURSHIP

Dubravčić (1995) considers the change of ownership of economic assets as a part of a global entrepreneurial system that includes risk-taking and profit-seeking agents, as well as help in their entrepreneurial efforts from a business support structure, basically from a financial market structure.

When the communist economic system of central planning was introduced in the countries of Eastern Europe, their entrepreneurial and business support systems were totally destroyed. One of the major tasks of the transitional period is their restoration. The successful implementation of this process will depend upon the creation, development and availability of all absolutely essential elements of the entrepreneurial system. According to the communist ideology, the capitalist economic system has two basic evils. Entrepreneurship, based on the private form of ownership of productive assets and free market mechanism, is the prime evil as the communist ideology states that economic realities are exclusively the outcome of social forces. The secondary evil is the functioning of the market. The historic role of the proletarian revolution was thus the total destruction of private ownership and complete liquidation of market forces as regulators of the economy. Consequently, as the most important feature of the evils described above, entrepreneurship was totally eliminated from social life with the victory of the proletarian revolution. Global state ownership and central planning became the core features of the communist economic system. All private business support institutions were abolished.

Attempts to revitalize the artificial communist economic system were made in all former communist countries with different levels of liberalism. They aimed at the creation of economic incentives for the labour entrepreneurs, but under severe governmental control and constraints. Reconstruction of the entrepreneurial pre-communist system was neither meant nor achieved by those initiatives. The types of entrepreneurship related to the needs of small business creation and development in mature transitional economies, having the characteristics described in Table 4.1., were non-existent in the centrally planned communist economies of Eastern Europe.

The types of entrepreneurship shown in Table 4.1. can be domestic or foreign. As a result of the systematic destruction under communist rule, domestic entrepreneurship (productive and financial) in Eastern Europe is now in very poor shape and cannot fully benefit from the availability of

Table 4.1. Characteristics and requirements of entrepreneurial types in Eastern Europe

Type of entrepreneurship	Features of entrepreneurship	Level of innovation	Degree of risk taking	Level of profit
Productive (owners of small business are often also managers)	Develop from successful single proprietorship by hiring additional work force. Financial markets supply funds from savers to provide productive entrepreneurs with capital.	Important	Very important	Very important
Financial	Savers who choose among a variety of opportunities differing according to their attitudes to risk taking and eagerness to make a bigger fortune.	Important	Very important	Very important
Productive managerial	Deciding on education and employment opportunities and acting in direction of creating and improving position in the enterprise. Risk and awards are related to career development and income increase and not to the amount and value of assets.	Very important	Important	Very important
Financial managerial (managers in the financial institutions)	Agents acting as intermediaries of financial markets offering investment opportunities for savers and funds to productive entrepreneurs for creation and development of enterprises.	Important	Important	Important

Source: Marinov, *Gospodarstvo u tranziciji*, Zagreb: Economics Faculty (1995).

44

existing opportunities. The rudimentary financial markets, as the main business support institutions, cannot provide the necessary help for entrepreneurship in Eastern Europe. Foreign entrepreneurship, predominantly financial, does not fully exploit the emerging opportunities in the region because of political and economic instability, lack of legal guarantees for investment, high and, in some countries, out of control inflation. The strong positions of the former *nomenklatura*, socialist (former communist) governments in many Eastern European countries and the existence of very powerful organized crime, which also influences the revival of entrepreneurship, raise additional barriers to entry of foreign productive entrepreneurs. The financial business support structure mainly consists of state-owned institutions. Because of the poor economic conditions in Eastern European countries, internal investment funds are very scarce, which limits the performance of domestic financial managerial entrepreneurship. Therefore financial managerial entrepreneurship is mainly foreign, through investment funds and international financial institutions.

MODELS FOR SUCCESSFUL ENTREPRENEURSHIP

Cooper (1989) suggests that there are three major groups of factors influencing the success of entrepreneurial ventures:

1. antecedent influences upon the entrepreneur, including the many aspects of his background which affect his motivations, his perceptions, and his skills and knowledge;
2. incubator organization – the organization for which the entrepreneur had previously been working, whose characteristics influence the location and the nature of the new firms, as well as the likelihood of spin-off;
3. various environmental factors, which make the climate more or less favourable to the starting of a new firm.

Cooper's model is appropriate for analysing the entrepreneurial activities in Eastern Europe, as it takes into consideration a broad range of factors influencing entrepreneurs' decisions. Its applicability is limited by the fact that little is known about the actual characteristics and measurability of the variables (Birley, 1989). It is hard to estimate the relative significance of each group and specific factor as the model does not contain relative prioritizing of factors. Customer orientation is included, but insufficiently emphasized.

Burns (1989) defines broadly the elements of success for small business entrepreneurship: the entrepreneur, the product/service idea, and good governance. Burns' model is customer-centred and concentrated on the individual as entrepreneur and on creating a style for management excellence. Good governance through directing all the resources of the business towards satisfying customer needs is the mechanism by which the entrepreneur can turn a product/service idea into a successful business. This model is based on the assumption that there is always a 'disturbance event' in the owner-manager's life throughout the creation and growth of a business. Apart from these individual related disturbances, any business is influenced by external environmental factors which are not incorporated in Burns' model. As the macroenvironmental factors in Eastern Europe are of crucial importance for entrepreneurial success, the analysis of their influence, if included in the model, would make it more appropriate for evaluating the factors for entrepreneurial success in the region.

Hatton and Raymond (1994) have developed a conceptual model for examining congruence in a small business setting. They stress that the model has to be applicable both to the entrepreneurial, or start-up, phase as well as to the ongoing administrative management of a small business. Three concentric aspects of a business are presented in this model: (1) variables describing the environment and strategy of the business; (2) organizational tasks and technologies; and (3) individual and organizational structure variables. A business is considered effective if the six organizational variables are simultaneously congruent. The authors describe the interactions between variables in the same layer, such as environment and strategy, as more critical than the interactions between other pairs of variables. However, it is most appropriate to match macro variables with other macro variables and micro with micro variables before determining congruent relationships across layers or boundaries.

Using the model of Hatton and Raymond for the overall evaluation of entrepreneurship in Eastern Europe, the variables of which it consists are characterized, as required by the model analysis, with measurable dimensions. The variable environment represents all internal and external factors actively or potentially relevant in making business decisions. The variable strategy is regarded as a pattern in a continuous stream of decisions, past and future, that is expressed in two aspects: it guides the progressing adaptation to and influence on the environment of a business, and forms its internal policies and procedures (Miles and Snow, 1978; Mintzberg, 1978). Task and technology are conceptually almost inseparable, as the task represents the objective of the business and the technology provides a detailed description of how this objective can be realized. The structure of a business includes the official organizational hierarchy and lines of communication, as well as the informal structure and actual lines of communication during the functioning of a business. The individual, a controversial variable, is analysed by Hatton and Raymond in the aspects of bureaucratic orientation and degree of strength needed for higher discipline.

In the analysis of the model developed by Hatton and Raymond, with the use of the information in Table 4.2, both entrepreneurial and administrative aspects of the organizational activities of a small business are considered. The original idea of the model is to give guidance for entrepreneurial decisions from the start-up of a small business, beginning with the analysis from the outermost layer and continuing towards the centre.

Table 4.2 Variable dimensions affecting entrepreneurship in Eastern Europe

Variables	Dimension	Predominant characteristic of dimension in Eastern Europe
External environment	Simple–complex Static–dynamic	Very complex Very dynamic, unsettled, turbulent
Internal environment	Simple–complex Static–dynamic	Very complex Very dynamic
Business strategy	Defenders–prospectors	Mostly prospectors for start-up businesses Mostly defenders in later phases
Task	Simple–complex Predictable–uncertain Interdependence: pooled–sequential–reciprocal	Complex to not very complex Mostly uncertain Reciprocal or sequential, rarely pooled
Technology	Mediated–long-linked–intensive	Mediated, rarely long-linked or intensive
Structure	Centralised–decentralised Organic–mechanical	Mostly decentralized Mostly organic, rarely mechanical
Individual	Bureaucratic orientation: high–low higher strength: higher–low	Mostly low, medium

Source: Marinov, *Gospodarstvo u tranziciji*, Zagreb: Economics Faculty.

The characteristics of the environment in Eastern Europe are assessed as very complex and dynamic. The reason for complexity, both for domestic and foreign entrepreneurs, is the fact that the macro environment lacks the necessary institutional business support infrastructure. For a domestic entrepreneur, crucial from the financial point of view can be the insignificant amount of domestic investment funds, and the supply of financial help provided by foreign investment funds or international financial institutions is far less than the existing demand. The dynamic characteristic of the macro environment is related to the processes of political and governmental instability in most of the countries (in most of Eastern European countries, governmental change occurs frequently and each government comes up with its own programme for restoration of the entrepreneurial system). This hampers the restoration process and causes changes in the legislation and institutional structure, delaying the appropriate re-establishment of the entrepreneurial system indispensable for market economies. The existing economic system also changes as a result of the processes of restructuring, change of ownership and liquidation of the state-owned enterprises which have existed for several decades. The availability of many niches in the markets creates good opportunities for the entrepreneurs in Eastern Europe. The problems, related to both macro and micro specifics of the environment, arise from the need for integration of the new start-up businesses in the existing economic structure, which itself has been undergoing considerable changes continuously since the beginning of the transition process.

Of fundamental importance for the entrepreneur, in general and especially in Eastern Europe, considering the characteristics of the environment, is the determining of the business characteristics so that they can match the environment and the market in the best possible way. The major problem with the market in Eastern Europe is a relatively small purchasing power of the individual and industrial customer there. High inflation results in high interest rates on loans, which in fact puts off many of the less enthusiastic and risk-averse entrepreneurs. Creating a strategy for a new venture comes after the analysis of all aspects of the environment. The niche strategy is very suitable for creating a small business where economies of scale cannot be exploited because of the market limitations for certain products or services and the theoretical optimal size is not achievable. The current economic structure in Eastern Europe affords opportunities to many industries to specialize on the basis of product/service and market to serve well-selected market segments. As when based on a well-developed niche strategy a small business start-up has better chances, most successful small businesses in Eastern Europe created during the transition period are *niche* enterprises. The specifics of the environmental characteristics define the entrepreneurs at the start-up as prospectors. The complexity of the environment; the absence of knowledge, experience and skills among the Eastern European entrepreneurs; the lack in most cases of efficient competition; the rudimentary and inexperienced financial markets; the insignificant amount of domestic investment capital; the high inflation and unemployment rates and the macroeconomic and political instability often turn the strategy of the entrepreneur from that of prospector to that of defender.

Data from the literature (see, for example, Arendarski and Mroczkowski, 1994; Bartlett, 1993; Marinov, 1993; Puchev, 1990) and our own experience in small business consulting show that the tasks of entrepreneurs in Eastern Europe can be described as having significant complexity related to the unfavourable and turbulent characteristics of the economic structures. The tasks are unpredictable, which is rarely due to the character of the business. The predominant interdependence of tasks' characteristics is sequential or reciprocal, rarely pooled.

The technology of small businesses in Eastern Europe, if viewed as the extent of computer technology used in an organization, could be described as relatively scarce, primitive if at all existing. Information technology is rarely to be found. If technology is defined as the application of knowledge to perform work, then it can be suggested that in Eastern Europe it is mostly mediated, rarely strategy-related or intensive. That creates competitive disadvantages for small businesses in Eastern Europe compared with western companies of the same type, in terms of product quality that corresponds to international standards, market and customer information gathering and handling, and information flow efficiency within the organizations.

The organizational structure of newly created small businesses in Eastern Europe is predominantly a decentralized system of hierarchy or a certain mixture of functional and decentralized form with low rigidity. Being organic organizations, small businesses in the region are in the form of mutual collaborations with few well-defined rules and procedures. That accounts for their potential for production and market flexibility, but the latter is restricted by the scarce financial resources and mainly domestic market operations. These businesses differ from the ones that come into existence as a result of the privatization and restructuring of the large, former state-owned companies where their structural characteristics tend to be more centralized and less flexible. Additionally, while in newly created small businesses the formal and informal structures are identical to a great extent, differences in this aspect are more common for the small businesses born from the break-up of former state-owned mega-businesses.

Entrepreneurs in Eastern Europe are mostly low in bureaucratic orientation and independent decision making. Their activities are mainly determined by the environmental constraints that are complex and restrictive in nature.

THE ENTREPRENEURIAL ENVIRONMENTAL SETTING IN EASTERN EUROPE

Small businesses start-ups in Eastern Europe appear in a setting still dominated by large firms. Many authors point out the importance of dependency between small and large firms (for example, Lee, 1993; Shutt and Whittington, 1986). The small businesses in Eastern Europe can be analysed from two main aspects: dependency upon large firms and type of relationship with large firms. As stated above, niche market small firms are typical of Eastern European entrepreneurship. As large firms in many Eastern European countries are still predominantly state-owned (for example, in Albania, Bulgaria, Poland, Romania and Ukraine) or recently privatized (for example, in the Czech and Slovak Republics, Hungary and Russia), in small start-up businesses entrepreneurs prefer to create niche market firms where, apart from the good market opportunities, the degree of dependency on large firms is insignificant and the actual relationships among the two types of firms are not close.

As low-cost small firms have close relations with large firms, they have limited potential for development and because of the economies of scale their chances of success in price competition with large firms are poor. Consequently, their number in Eastern European countries is small and their chances of survival and success are limited. Depending heavily on the large firms for their subcontract work, jobbing firms are also rare. An additional reason for this is the fact that the traditional markets of the large firms in Eastern Europe in most cases were totally destroyed with the liquidation of CMEA. The chances of getting contracts from large firms, therefore, are very much reduced. Some jobbing small firms, although very vulnerable as regards contract existence and cash flow, can be found in services.

Partnership small firms exist in Eastern Europe and their number is rapidly growing, but most of them, in order to be less vulnerable, operate independently of large firms. Small businesses dependent on large firms and having relatively close relations with them are rarely found in the region. The partnership small firms in the post-communist economies aim at achieving greater independence from the large state-owned or recently privatized companies that suffer great financial, production, marketing and employment difficulties in the transitional process. However, their relationships with big firms in the future, when the economic structures are developed and settled, are likely to expand.

GOALS OF ENTREPRENEURSHIP IN THE TRANSITION PROCESS

The experience to date in transitional reforms of post-communist economies in Eastern Europe indicates that 'macro stabilisation will be difficult to achieve … in the absence of an adequate micro adjustment' (Svejnar, 1991) and that institutional reforms and privatization are insufficient for efficient and effective economic restructuring without entrepreneurship (Acs and Audretsch, 1993) aiming at successful new venture creation.

Pre-transition comparative research in the economic structures of capitalist economies and planned communist economies identifies the existence of a hole in the latter economies (see, for example, Gibb, 1993; Petrin and Vahčić, 1989). The hole represents a remarkable absence of small firms in the economic structures of economies of Eastern Europe. Most severe is the lack of small to medium-sized firms with numbers of employees between 51 and 250. The characteristics of firm size distribution are inherited from the years of communist megalomaniacal economic development, characterized by severe restrictions on the development of small private businesses and lack of property rights guaranteeing such development.

The macroeconomic role of the entrepreneurs in Eastern Europe is, first, to increase the number of firms with up to 50 employees, mostly through creation of new private ventures, and second, to restructure large state-owned firms, thus forming new entities. While it is relatively easy to accomplish these tasks, the most difficult one seems to be to fill in the hole through creation of enterprises with between 51 and 250 employees. The latter firm size group is seen by Bannasch (1990) as the major route to small business development in the industrial and service sectors of Eastern European countries. Bannasch's suggestion is appropriate for the conditions in the region where the most significant obstacle to setting up new firms with 51–250 employees is the scarcity of financial resources, mostly among domestic entrepreneurs. On the basis of the entrepreneurial task in a macro sense, tasks on a micro level can be broadly defined. Their successful implementation can result in macro restructuring of the transitional economies in Eastern Europe. The entrepreneurial task on a micro level can be summarized as follows (Tyson *et al.*, 1994).

- Entrepreneurs have to play active roles and implement the processes of privatization and restructuring of state-owned companies. The realization of these tasks needs a broad range of activities. Entrepreneurs have to divide large firms into smaller, more efficiently functioning enterprises, giving better effects. Doing this could enable the scarce resources to be made available and utilized in a better way, reduce existing excessive diversification and create a better and more effective configuration of related businesses. In the meantime the entrepreneurs have to restructure and reorganize the smaller privatized firms in order to create an appropriate managerial network in the restructured enterprises, stimulate the development of managerial skills needed in a market economy, invent new incentive schemes, introduce total quality management, and make the reorganized companies innovative, flexible and globally oriented to the market.
- Entrepreneurs also have to start from scratch new modern small businesses that will contribute to filling in the gap. As Arzeni (1992)

shows, the average employment share of small firms in Eastern Europe is 3 per cent. It must be noted that in the 1980s, two utterly controversial processes took place in the market and centrally planned economies. While the small-firm share of employment in the developed western economies has recently increased considerably (see, for example, Duche and Savey, 1987; Storey and Johnson, 1987), the same had been decreasing until the start of transition in the former centrally planned economies (Carlsson, 1989).

● Entrepreneurs have to help the process of global change of the characteristics of the industrial structure of the economies of Eastern Europe. Such a shift must result in fundamental industrial restructuring, replacing the excessive dependence of the economies upon outdated heavy industries with more balanced industrial structures resulting from the development of industries where individual countries can gain comparative advantage. Through the exposure to new markets, the influence of market forces has already created conditions for such changes, as prices of goods have been permitted to reflect their actual supply on the world markets. The pricing policy, in the domestic markets, is faced by the restricted and very small purchasing power of the domestic customers. Entrepreneurs will have to find a good answer to this complication as well.

Regarding the operational activities needed for the start-up of a new venture or restructuring of an existing business, the principal entrepreneurial tasks at any stage are production/operations, finance and marketing (Arendarski and Mroczkowski, 1994).

Production/Operations

The environmental characteristics and their restrictions are the most important factors that determine the particular kind of business to pursue, especially if it is of a bigger size. In Eastern Europe as well as in western countries, previous experience and business contacts play a crucial role. This is especially true of businesses with international markets, trade and service companies. The recession in Eastern Europe is forcing more thought and creativity into the production/operations task. The start-up firms in manufacturing usually have to restrict their activities by applying low-cost, low-technology production processes because of the lack of sufficient capital and significant difficulties in obtaining modern equipment and technology. Some help in this aspect has been provided by foreign entrepreneurs, usually resulting in creation of international joint ventures.

Finance

Initial capital is needed for the establishment and early development of new ventures and often for the restructuring of existing businesses. Studies in numerous Eastern European countries have revealed the extreme significance of an individual's own capital for starting a business. Bank credits have had a very limited role, as has financial help through various foreign investment funds. New ventures are usually undercapitalized owing to the macroeconomic specifics accompanying recession (high inflation, high interest rates and constantly decreasing availability of domestic credit opportunities). The birth of new ventures means competition, which decreases competitors' chances of making a profit as competition keeps prices down despite the contrary effect of recession. The global evaluation of the financial task of the entrepreneur in Eastern Europe gives it a complicated and controversial connotation which significantly hampers its fulfilment.

Marketing

The recession of the 1990s in Eastern Europe has created a hard time for the new private companies since their pricing policy is severely restricted by their undercapitalized condition. The infrastructure in the region, which is underdeveloped and unsuitable for a market economy, has created many problems with distribution of products for most new private businesses. In some countries, such as Bulgaria, the wholesale and retail system are undergoing very significant changes and this process creates an additional burden for entrepreneurs. For many new private businesses, the most important customers are state-owned companies which, being bigger and stronger, enjoy strong bargaining power, especially when supply is provided on a highly competitive basis. This makes the respective small businesses substantially dependent on the condition of the public sector, which in most of these countries is poor or very poor. Such entrepreneurs have to cope with very sophisticated problems. Consequently, the worsening health of the state-owned companies can produce an equivalent result in otherwise healthy private firms. Being new and small, the established private businesses are generally of local importance, operating within the boundaries of a single town or a smaller part of it. In such cases the owners of the businesses often act as distributors and retailers (small firms run on a family basis in agriculture are good examples). International markets are usually regarded by small venture start-ups as a potential for the expansion of their markets, creating an international joint venture or seeking additional opportunities for technology transfer and sources of credit.

KEY FACTOR CHARACTERISTICS OF ENTREPRENEURIAL DEVELOPMENT

Taking as a basis for the analysis, the characteristics of the key factors for developing small business policy suggested by Haskins, the picture in Eastern Europe is shown in Table 4.3. The tradition of support for small firms was severely curtailed with the establishment of communist dictatorships in all Eastern European countries and consequently there was no means to promote and push forward the development of small firms, so that the past experience and traditions of entrepreneurship are nowadays difficult to resurrect and start functioning effectively and efficiently. The distribution of political power is a gradual process, as the gap between central planning and market-driven decentralization is still very big. The central governments resist radical change and delegation of authority to local governments as the old societal structures continue to be powerful. The monopolistic position of the industrial giants in Eastern Europe have been shaken in recent years through the processes of restructuring and privatization, but they still dominate the national output and have the highest contribution to GDP in almost all these countries. Consequently, small businesses and entrepreneurship in Eastern Europe have low economic power and are too vulnerable in the turbulent economic conditions.

Institution building to support the development of small business is a serious task and a big challenge that will take a lot of time. The existing network of private and restructured former public institutions is far from sufficient and adequate. The developed bank sector which is indispensable for a market economy is still emerging. There is little evidence of coherent local and regional strategies for small business development, and very little has been done in this regard at central government level.

Obviously, Eastern Europe has to resolve a very complicated and unprecedented task of transition from central planning to market orientation. Global economic restructuring is the most important precondition for the success of this transition. In the implementation of this extremely difficult task, entrepreneurship has a creative role of crucial importance. Although having to cope with many constantly changing problems, appearing as from some Pandora's box, entrepreneurs in Eastern Europe have achieved many successes. Privatization, restructuring of former state-owned companies, creation of new small business ventures and changing the whole industrial structure of the economy are processes that are in progress in the entire region. However, the bulk of the work related to transition has yet to be done. Entrepreneurs are supposed to be the main doers. An appropriate entrepreneurial system is in process of creation and development in many countries and it is to be hoped that others will follow their example. Eastern Europe awaits global revival, and entrepreneurship is one of its major aspects.

Table 4.3 Dimensions of the key factors for entrepreneurial development in Eastern Europe

Key factors in shaping small firm policy	Dimension of the factor in Eastern Europe
The length of tradition of support for small firms	None in the last 45 years at least
The relative distribution of political power between central, regional and local governments	At present unclear; historically very concentrated in the central governments
The strength of the existing small-firm sector	Mostly weak, financially dependable and insignificantly developed
The balance of industrial and political power between large industry and small business reflected in the small firm orientation	The cases are different in various countries, but mostly power still stays in large industries
The overall economic and social rationale for policy	Development of small private business is considered to be of significant importance in the economic restructuring of the countries in Eastern Europe, but processes of reconstruction are not well supported by national programmes for restructuring
The basic ideology of governments	The processes of restructuring have been slowed down with the forming of socialist governments in many Eastern European countries following the election victory of socialist (former communist) parties in the last elections

Source: Haskins *et al.* (1986).

ACKNOWLEDGEMENT

This chapter is based on the research conducted by the contributor under the research fellowship grant 94-349-F provided through the scheme of Action for Cooperation in the field of Economics (ACE) of the European Commission.

BIBLIOGRAPHY

Acs, Z.J. and D.B. Audretsch (eds) (1993), *Small Firms and Entrepreneurship: An East–West Perspective,* Cambridge: Cambridge University Press.

Arendarski, A. and T. Mroczkowski (1994), 'A Study of the Redevelopment of Private Enterprise in Poland: Conditions and Policies for Continuing Growth', *Journal of Small Business Management,* **32**, (3), 40–51.

Arzeni, S. (1992), 'Encouraging the Entrepreneur', *OECD Observer,* (179), February–March, 19–22.

Audretsch, D.B. (1991), 'The Role of Small Business in Restructuring Eastern Europe', *Fifth Workshop for Research in Entrepreneurship,* Vaxjo, Sweden.

Bannasch, H.G. (1990), 'The Role of Small Firms in East Germany', *Small Business Economics,* **2**, (4), 307–13.

Bartlett, W. (1993), 'Privatization and Small Firms in Bulgaria', *Working Paper 116,* University of Bristol: SAUS Publications.

Birley, S. (1989), 'The Start-up', in P. Burns and J. Dewhurst (eds), *Small Business and Entrepreneurship,* London: Macmillan, pp. 9–27.

Brunner, H.P. (1993), 'Entrepreneurship in Eastern Europe: Neither Magic nor Mirage. A Preliminary Investigation', *Journal of Economic Issues,* **XXVII**, (2), 505–13.

Burns, P. (1989), 'Strategies for Success and Routes to Failure', in P. Burns and J. Dewhurst (eds), *Small Business and Entrepreneurship,* London: Macmillan, pp. 33–59.

Carlsson, B. (1989), 'The Evolution of Manufacturing Technology and its Impact on Industrial Structure: An International Study', *Small Business Economics,* **1**, (1), 21–38.

Cooper, A.C. (1989), 'Strategic Management: New Ventures and Small Business', in B. Lloyd (ed.), *Entrepreneurship: Creating and Managing New Ventures,* Oxford: Pergamon Press, pp. 97–103.

Dubravčić, D. (1995), 'Entrepreneurial Aspects of Privatization in Transition Economies', *Europe–Asia Studies,* **47**, (2), pp. 305–16.

Duche, G. and S. Savey (1987), 'The Rising Importance of Small and Medium Sized Firms: Towards a New Industrial System?', in F.E. Hamilton (ed.), *Industrial Change in Advanced Economies,* London: McGraw-Hill.

Gibb, A. (1988), *Stimulating Entrepreneurship in New Business Development,* Geneva: International Labour Office.

Gibb, A. (1993), 'Small Business Development in Central and Eastern Europe – Opportunity for a Rethink?', *Journal of Business Venturing,* **8**, (6), 461–86.

Haskins G., A. Gibb and A. Hubert (1986), *A Guide to Small Business Assistance in Europe,* Aldershot: Gower.

Hatton L. and B. Raymond (1994), 'Developing Small Business Effectiveness in the Context of Congruence', *Journal of Small Business Management,* **32**, (3), 76–94.

Kupserberg, F. (1992), 'Bandits and Bureaucrats: The Role of Entrepreneurship in the Transition from Socialism to Capitalism', *Seventh Nordic Conference on Small Business,* Turku, Finland.

Lee, G. (1993), 'Entrepreneurship, Technology, Quality and Small Firm–Large Firm Relationships in Britain', paper presented at the Third Biennial High Technology Management Conference, 16–18 June, Boulder, Colorado, USA.

Marinov, M.A. (1993), 'Small Private Business in Bulgaria – Organisational and Marketing Characteristics', *Proceedings of the 23rd European Small Business Seminar: Small Business in International Markets,* 15–17 September, Belfast, Northern Ireland, Vol. 1, pp. 459–80.

Miles R.E. and C.C. Snow (1978), *Organisational Strategy, Structure and Process,* New York: McGraw-Hill.

Mintzberg, H. (1978), 'Strategy Making in Three Modes', *Academy of Management Review,* (16), 44–58.

Petrin T. and A. Vahčič (1989), 'Financial Systems for Restructuring the Yugoslav Economy', in C. Kessides, T. King, M. Nuti and C. Sokil (eds), *Financial Reforms in Socialist Economies,* Florence: EDI, World Bank/European University Institute, pp. 154–62.

Puchev, P. (1990), 'A Note on Government Policy and the New Entrepreneurship in Bulgaria', *Small Business Economics,* **2**, (1), 73–6.

Shutt, J. and R. Whittington (1986), 'Large Firm Strategies and the Rise of Small Units', in T. Faulkner *et al.* (eds), *Readings in Small Business,* Aldershot: Gower.

Storey, D. and S. Johnson (1987), *Job Creation and Labour Market Change,* London: Macmillan.

Svejnar, J. (1991), 'Microeconomic Issues in the Transition to a Market Economy', *Journal of Economic Perspectives,* **5**, (4), 123–38.

Tyson L., T. Petrin and H. Rogers (1994), 'Promoting Entrepreneurship in Eastern Europe', *Small Business Economics,* **6**, (3), 165–84.

5. Efficiency under restructuring from a microeconomic perspective

Vladimír Benáček, Dmitri Shemetilo and Alexei Petrov

The appreciation of the Czech macroeconomic miracle is often complemented by a disclaimer to the effect that the microeconomic adjustment has
not yet proceeded sufficiently, and especially in large firms (for example,
former state-owned enterprises undergoing privatization under the voucher
scheme) the process of restructuring is still in the beginning stages.[1] In this
chapter we consider the process of restructuring Czech textile and clothing
firms most harshly hit by liberalization of economy, and we try to show that
the tendency towards creating competitive market-oriented firms is very strong.

Let us first provide a short introduction to the situation in the Czech
industrial sector before 1995. According to the official data, real output
(GDP) in the Czech Republic was subject to a decline of 26 per cent during
1990–93, followed by a growth of 2 per cent in 1994. There was a reduction
of labour by 19 per cent in 1990–93; by 24 per cent in manufacturing. The
fundamental explanation for such a decline is the reaction to the loss of
artificially contrived demand.

However, the aggregate state of the economy cannot be considered separately from the developments in the firms. We analyse the efficiency of
production in a perfectly competitive framework and assume that each firm
has constant returns to scale technology $Y_i = A_i * f(K_i, L_i)$ (where Y is income, K
capital and L labour). We also assume that the function f is industry-specific,
coming from the fundamental properties of the technological process and
reflecting the degree of capital intensity of the industry. Thus all firms in a
given industry are described by the same function f, while the parameter A_i is
specific for every particular firm i of the industry and reflects its technical
abilities. Therefore every firm is fully described from a technological point of
view by the set $\{A_i, f\}$.

The path of a firm during transition which we suggest is shown in Figure
5.1.[2] In the beginning (1990–91) the demand shock caused a sharp fall in
production and the coefficient A in the production function sharply decreased.

Then firms started shedding labour (1991) but at a less intensive rate than that when production was falling. After that, production began to rise (1992–4) and the coefficient *A* increased; however, the sunk capital costs prevented unit *K* from suffering a large decrease comparable to the decrease in unit *L*. The producers in the manufacturing firms under transition may often find themselves trapped in a situation where a complete specificity of their capital makes them stay with the given capital endowment, which thus becomes a barrier to their exit. In an extreme case of completely sunk capital costs, all parts of the firm's capital can be completely immobile for any economically productive alternative uses. This is one explanation for capital hoarding in the firms most harshly hit by the loss of demand as a result of transition.

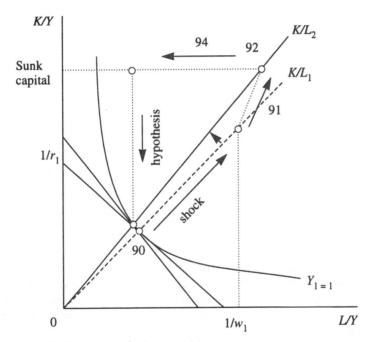

Figure 5.1   Path of a firm during transition

DEFINITION AND MEASUREMENT OF PRODUCTION EFFICIENCY

From a microeconomic point of view, the perfectly efficient firms minimize the unit costs and lie on the same ray, which we call the industrial optimal input mix. We regard inefficiency as deviations from the optimal input mix.[3]

Figure 5.2 presents both a perfectly efficient firm (at point X_e) and inefficient ones (at points X_a, X_b and X_c). The fact that the more efficient firm has a higher parameter A, as seen with firm X_b and firm X_a, means that this firm is located on a lower unit isoquant (labelled YY_1) and cost minimization requires the choice of inputs at the tangency point between the unit-value isocost line and the unit-value isoquant (point X_e).

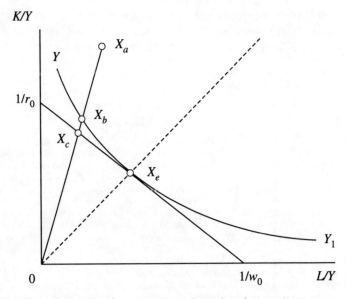

Figure 5.2   The relationship between the technical and cost efficiencies

We use two types of efficiencies, which is similar to the approach of Kopp and Diewert (1982). The first one, technical efficiency (E_T), relates to the technological constant A. E_T measures how far the unit isoquant is from the origin. A more technically efficient firm with a higher parameter A has a smaller E_T.

The second type of efficiency is allocative efficiency (E_A). An allocatively inefficient firm deviates from the optimal (cost-minimizing) mix of inputs (deviations from the efficient ray OX_e, in Figure 5.2). This inefficiency can be caused by managerial failures.[4] A reasonable assumption we make here is that the managers are not systematically wrong in choosing an input mix. Thus the average K/L ratio over firms in the industry can be taken as a rough approximation of the optimal mix.

Looking at Figure 5.3, the technical efficiency is represented by the vector OD (measured along the optimal ray) and the optimal input mix is given by angle *g*. The deviation from the optimal ray can be measured as the length of segment *DF*. The vector *DF* has a very easy interpretation: it shows the amount of input per unit of output that should be added or dropped by a firm to achieve the efficient input structure. We consider the linear distance *FD* as a measure of allocative efficiency.

Now imagine that the firm described by point *F* in Figure 5.3 is faced with an adverse technological shock (parameter *A* is decreasing). In order to assess the effect of this technological shock we assume that the firm continues to use the same proportion of inputs (*ceteris paribus* condition). That means that point *F* moves north-east along the same ray to the point *F'*. Therefore point *D* is also moving along the same optimal ray (because of the homotheticity of the isoquants) to point *D'*. Thus the technical efficiency is decreasing (*OD* growing to *OD'*). Because angle β is supposed to remain unchanged, the length of *FD* increases to *F'D'*.

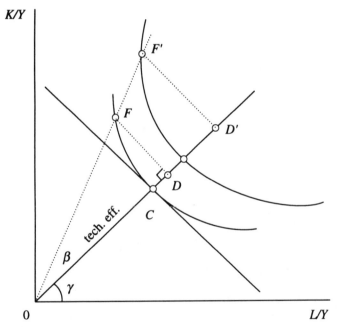

Figure 5.3   An alternative way of presenting cost and technical efficiencies

Finally, the technical efficiency of firm *i* is estimated by (*OD*)$_i$ and the allocative efficiency by (*FD*)$_i$.[5] The algebraic expressions for these efficiencies are as follows:

$$E_T^i = \sqrt{l_i^2 + k_i^2}\ \cos\!\left(arctg\!\left(\frac{k_i}{l_i}\right) - arctg(\gamma)\right) \tag{5.1}$$

$$E_A^i = \sqrt{k_i^2 + l_i^2}\ \sin\!\left(arctg\!\left(\frac{k_i}{l_i}\right) - arctg(\gamma)\right) \tag{5.2}$$

where k_i, l_i are capital–output and labour–output ratios for firm i.

Now we know how to calculate the allocative and technical efficiency for individual firms. Taking the weighted average of the technical and allocative[6] efficiencies, we can assess efficiencies (technical and allocative) for an industry of N firms:

$$E^{industry} = \frac{\sum_{i=1}^{N} OUTPUT_i^* E^i}{\sum_{i=1}^{N} OUTPUT^i} \tag{5.3}$$

EMPIRICAL TESTING OF EFFICIENCY[7]

The main source of data we used for the empirical testing is a unique database of approximately 2000 large Czech firms originally designed for the purpose of the voucher privatization scheme. The second source is the official Czech industrial statistics, either compiled at the Czech Statistical Office (this also included a sample of small firms) or provided by the Czech Association of Industries. It must be admitted that, as the process of the transformation of the Czech economy went on, the problems with the accuracy of statistics grew. This precluded us from using the panel data techniques by individual firms even for 1990–92.[8]

Our enterprise data cover the years 1990–94. It should be noted that the figures for 1990 can be taken as a starting point for transition. With the exception of the first export losses on the CMEA markets and the devaluation of the Czech crown by 18 per cent, there were hardly any fundamental changes in the functioning of the former centralized economy. If 1991 was a year of dramatic breakthrough, with price liberalization, free trade and a tight monetary and fiscal policy, 1992 was a year of relative stability with massive privatization effecting approximately a third of production, while 1993 was marked mainly by the crucial restructuring of the whole fiscal system and, to a lesser extent, by the division of Czechoslovakia.

In this chapter we consider only large-scale firms which have a similar basic production technology. A typical capital–labour scatter pattern and the dependence of the capital–labour ratio on capital are given in Figures 5.4 and 5.5. We discarded all firms which had capital less than the minimal capital among all firms in 1990 (the starting year of transition) because these firms are supposed to be new companies created after the year 1990 with different technology. In the remaining sample, the dependence of the capital–labour ratio on capital is either weak or negligible.

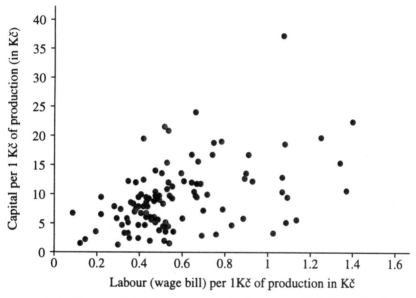

Figure 5.4   Unit capital–labour scatter plot for the textile industry in the Czech Republic, 1992

In order to proceed with the efficiency analysis we first need to estimate the capital–labour ratio pertinent to each particular industry. We consider three sorts of capital–labour ratios: average K/L ratio for the whole industry, $(K/L)_A$; average K/L ratio over the firms with higher profitability than the average profitability of the industry $(K/L)_H$; and average K/L ratio over the firms with lower profitability than the average profitability of the industry $(K/L)_L$.

Table 5.1 presents the K/L ratios estimated for the textile and clothing industries and their percentage changes for 1990, 1991, 1992 and 1994.[9] We used a total wage bill as a measure of labour, implicitly assuming an equal wage rate among firms. Not surprisingly, textile is more capital-intensive than clothing. More interesting is a different evolution of the ratios in time. In both industries the K/L ratio was growing, but the growth of the K/L ratio in

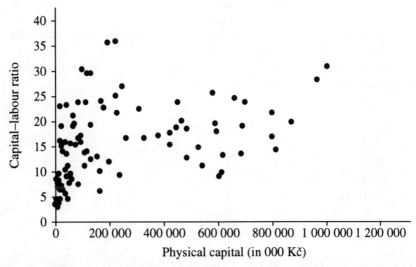

Figure 5.5   Dependence of the capital–labour ratio on the physical capital

the textile industry was more rapid than in clothing before the year 1994. Some minor investment did take place in the industries considered, but it cannot explain such a large increase in the K/L ratio. In both industries some workers may have been fired or real wages may have decreased, and the K/L ratio thereby increased.[10] However, the whole picture changed in 1994. We can observe stabilization in the growth of the K/L ratio in textiles, while in clothing it was still growing.

We also tested for the presence of sunk costs. Our test reveals a clear presence of sunk costs in clothing in the years 1992–4. The test was done by comparing the means of K/L ratios of the firms more and less profitable than the average over the whole industry. In 1992–4 the mean of the K/L ratios of the more profitable firms in the clothing industry was found to be significantly higher than that of the less profitable ones. That firms in the textile industry are quite homogeneous and that there is no clear leader in terms of profits may be an explanation for our failure to find a presence of sunk costs in this industry.

We use the average K/L over the whole industry as an estimate of the optimal input mix for the industry. With the estimates of the optimal input mix known, we can estimate the efficiencies by using the technique designed earlier for the estimation of the allocative and technical inefficiency.[11] These are shown in Tables 5.2 and 5.3.

Since, by our definition, the allocative efficiency is the deviation from the industrial optimal K/L line, its mean should be close to zero. (We assume that

Table 5.1   Capital–labour ratio estimations for the textile and clothing industries in the Czech Republic

	Capital–labour ratios	1990	1991	1992	1994
Textile	Average over the whole industry	0.923 (0.292)	1.715 (0.569)	1.939 (1.079)	1.787 (1.141)
		100%	186%	210%	194%
	Average over the more profitable firms	0.990 (0.307)	1.634 (0.530)	1.959 (1.142)	1.729 (1.161)
		100%	165%	198%	175%
	Average over the less profitable firms	0.862 (0.267)	1.820 (0.607)	1.905 (0.978)	1.949 (1.083)
		100%	211%	221%	226%
Clothing	Average over the whole industry	0.356 (0.110)	0.557 (0.235)	0.561 (0.276)	0.968 (0.645)
		100%	156%	158%	272%
	Average over the more profitable firms	0.352 (0.091)	0.547 (0.247)	0.526 (0.216)	0.838 (0.543)
		100%	155%	149%	238%
	Average over the less profitable firms	0.363 (0.157)	0.566 (0.238)	0.600 (0.332)	1.249 (0.767)
		100%	156%	166%	345%

Note: Variance in parentheses.

Source: Computation results.

the allocative inefficiency is distributed normally around zero mean.) The absolute value of allocative inefficiency which gives us the most important information shows how large the dispersion in the use of resources is. The increase in both technical and allocative inefficiencies may indicate a widening gap in the quality of management or a widening span in the factor prices used in different firms.

A comparison of the efficiencies over time can provide us only with a general assessment of the industrial performance. We can see that there was

Table 5.2   Technical and allocative inefficiency in the clothing industry in the Czech Republic

Year	Technical inefficiency	Allocative inefficiency	N
1990	4.52	0.25	12
1991	6.65	0.65	19
1992	5.63	0.58	38
1994	6.95	1.48	60

Note: N is the number of observations.

Source: Computation results.

Table 5.3   Technical and allocative inefficiency in the textile industry in the Czech Republic

Year	Technical inefficiency	Allocative inefficiency	N
1990	4.52	0.25	11
1991	7.89	0.78	81
1992	10.45	1.14	97
1994	9.56	1.33	132

Note: N is the number of observations.

Source: Computation results.

an increase in technical and allocative inefficiency in both the textile and clothing industries. This is quite natural, given the problems by which these industries were challenged during transition. Our argumentation regarding behaviour of producers in transition (see Figure 5.1) is consistent with these findings. The technical inefficiency increased at first, decreasing parameter A of the production function, but stabilized afterwards. The increase in the allocative inefficiency was almost the same for both industries in the beginning. However, in 1994, the allocative inefficiency in the clothing industry had risen sharply. This increase can be partially explained by the break-up of the large enterprises, which could not change the technical inefficiency. However, if new smaller enterprises have different K/L ratios, the industrial allocative inefficiency may increase over time more than the inefficiency of the original firms would have done.

DOES EFFICIENCY REALLY RELATE TO PROFIT?

The relationship between the firms' profitability and efficiency is of particular interest because this enables us to test the hypothesis that the market environment influences the firms' performances. Since the increase of inefficiencies is supposed to have a negative effect on profit per unit of output as a basic indicator of firms' performance, a significant relationship between inefficiencies and profit would support the idea that the 'invisible hand' was at work. To test this we use the following specification:

$$\pi_i = Const + \alpha \cdot E_{T,i} + \beta \cdot |E_{A,i}| + \gamma \cdot Sign + \varepsilon_i \qquad (5.4)$$

where

p_i = the profit of firm i per unit of output,
$E_{T,i}$ = the technical inefficiency of the firm i,
$E_{A,i}$ = the absolute value of allocative inefficiency of the firm i.
Sign is a dummy variable representing the sign of the allocative inefficiency. (Sign = 1 if the k_i/l_i is greater than or equal to the industrial optimum and sign = 0 otherwise.)

Before running this regression, we normalized unit capital k and unit labour l across the industry, dividing them by their maximal values. After that, we recalculated the optimal input mix and technical and allocative inefficiencies, of course, without losing generality. One can expect negative signs of a and b coefficients, since the technical inefficiency reflects the use of inputs per unit of production and the allocative inefficiency reflects the divergence of the input mixed from the optimum. Table 5.4 shows the results of the regression (equation 5.4).

On the basis of the fact that our estimations for 1990, 1991 and 1992 are clearly weaker than those for 1994, we conclude that during 1990 and 1991 the market economy could not have functioned well. Profits were still dissociated from allocative efficiency and, to less extent, technical efficiency. It is well known that profits at that time did not serve as an objective criterion for the allocation of resources. They could be endogenously manipulated inside the planning system and earned on the grounds of administrative decisions, such as manipulations by prices or subsidies.

The increase in the statistical significance of both coefficients for 1994 can be interpreted as a signal that the market economy had begun to operate. Before 1994, changes in profits may be explained by the changes in the technical, but not in the allocative, efficiency. However, since 1994, the trends in both efficiencies are responsible for the changes in profits. The last test we did here concerns the interdependence between technical and allocative

Table 5.4 *Estimates of coefficients for model*

		Const	E_T	$|E_A|$	Sign	R^2_{adj}	Estimation type	N
Clothing	1990	0.348 (5.82)*	-0.072 (-1.24)	-0.465 (-2.39)*	-0.009 (-0.25)	0.42	OLS	12
	1991	0.873 (8.37)*	-0.916 (-8.41)*	0.30 (1.30)	-0.049 (-1.00)	0.79	OLS	19
	1992	0.786 (9.94)*	-1.10 (-8.47)*	0.044 (0.19)	-0.037 (-0.93)	0.73	RR	38
	1994	1.325 (10.56)*	-1.453 (-7.93)*	-1.766 (-4.40)*	-0.069 (-0.85)	0.71	RR	60
Textile	1990	0.312 (8.93)*	-0.035 (-0.58)	0.170 (0.78)	-0.047 (-1.77)	0.01	RR	58
	1991	0.509 (9.39)*	-0.448 (-3.80)*	0.378 (1.02)	-0.025 (-0.59)	0.15	RR	81
	1992	0.538 (11.19)*	-0.710 (-7.43)*	-0.406 (-1.63)**	-0.033 (-0.92)	0.50	RR	97
	1994	1.112 (14.17)*	-2.460 (-12.51)*	-1.445 (-2.89)*	0.053 (0.88)	0.66	RR	132

Notes:
RR = robust regression estimation.
OLS = ordinary least square estimation.
* = significance at the 5 per cent level.
** = significance at 10 per cent level.

inefficiencies. Correlation between technical inefficiency and absolute value of allocative inefficiency appeared to be weak. To summarize our results:

- Dynamics of the *K/L* ratio show a rising pattern for both the textile and the clothing industries. In the period 1990–94 this ratio increased more in the clothing industry than in the textile industry, reflecting the presence of sunk costs.
- There is a growth in technical inefficiency in the textile and clothing industries. This growth was higher for the textile industry than for the clothing industry before 1992. Since 1992, the growth in the technical inefficiency slowed in the case of the clothing industry, and even reversed in the textile industry. The sharp increase in the allocative inefficiency in the clothing industry in 1994 could be a result of the splitting of enterprises.
- Real profit per unit of output was decreasing with an increase in technical inefficiency. From 1994, it also began to depend on the allocative inefficiency, which may indicate the appearance of the 'invisible hand'.

We have made an attempt here to approach the problems of falling production efficiency by using a standard methodology aimed at quantifying the underlying processes. The survey was made for the Czech textile and clothing industries which were among those most harshly hit by the transition. The adjustment undertaken by the majority of these firms seemed paradoxical and was not marked by strategies widely used in the developed market economies under recession. This behaviour may be justified, at least partially, by the presence of sunk physical capital costs.

A microeconomic model explaining the behaviour of the textile and clothing firms in transition was introduced. A simplified technique of statistical estimation of the technical and allocative inefficiencies has been adopted and applied to data of the former state-owned enterprises in the textile and clothing industries. Empirical tests showed that the efficiency in both industries studied was falling during 1991 and 1992, while the capital–labour ratio was rising. The test of the relationship between efficiency and profits of individual firms in 1990–94 has confirmed that at the end of this period these two indicators were more strongly correlated than in 1991, the beginning of the transformation period. This signals that, after the period of distortion of profit maximization behaviour, the market mechanism had begun to exert its pressure on the decisions about the optimal allocation of resources and thereby set sound conditions for the long-term economic progress of the economy as a whole.

Table 5.1 suggests that the years 1992–4 may become the watershed during which the J-curve of the Czech transformation reached its lowest point. The

Table 5.5   Profits in the Czech textile and clothing industries, 1990–94 (in million crowns, normal price)

Sectors	1990	1991	1992	1993	1994
Textiles	3 960	4 502	1 396	−388	1 779
Knitting	948	1184	446	−34	590
Clothing	615	443	324	473	620

Note: *   Forecast of the Ministry of Industry based on statistics for January–June 1994.

Source: Statistics of the Ministry of Industry, Annual Report of ATOK (1994).

developments after 1993 probably led to a break-even point and stabilization. Given the strong negative correlation between profits and the technical inefficiency that we found, we can suppose from the rising profits in 1994 that the most painful part of the economic transformation in textile and clothing manufacturing is over, and that since 1994 those industries lie on an upward-sloping growth trajectory, approaching the standard patterns of market behaviour and development. We can see from Tables 5.2 and 5.3 that the growth in technical inefficiency was stabilized for the clothing industry, while in the textile industry it even decreased. This is in accordance with the results of our regression (equation 5.4).[12] Table 5.5 shows the fluctuations in profits of textile and clothing industries in the Czech Republic during 1990–95.

NOTES

1. This ambiguous general approach is best summarized in the *Financial Times* (19 December 1994, FT Survey on the Czech Republic, pp. i–viii) where the macro praises go along with cautious micro reserves. For example: '[In the Czech republic] the most painful part of microeconomic adjustment at the enterprise level is probably to begin' (p. i); 'Czechs … have hardly started the painful microeconomic surgery on former state owned enterprises' (p. iii).
2. The years shown in Figure 5.1 are hypothetical and may differ from firm to firm.
3. Farrell (1957) saw the inefficiency as a realized deviation from an idealized isoquant of a production under full capacity and Pareto-optimal use of resources.
4. Nevertheless, it is also likely that a good part of the technical inefficiency is caused not only by bad governance, but also by some exogenous factors (more productive machineries, more skilled labour, and so on).
5. Note that the right measure of technical efficiency should be the segment *OC*. However, for relatively small values of the angle β, the segment *CD* is very small relative to *OD* and can be neglected.
6. Given the way we construct our measure of the allocative efficiency, its average should be close to zero. Therefore we estimate the allocative efficiency of an industry as a weighted average of the absolute values of individual efficiencies.

7. At this stage we are circumventing the problem of comparing the differences in technical efficiency between the east and west (see Bergson, 1987; 1992). Our computations are based on comparing the local efficiencies and their relative ranking inside the given industry. Now are we attempting at this stage to make a comparison with other estimations of East European efficiency (for example, with Danilin *et al.*, 1985), which would otherwise require using the same methodology, for example the stochastic frontier production functions.
8. For a detailed description of the data for textile and clothing, see Benáček and Mejstrik (1995) and Corado *et al.* (1995).
9. We do not have reliable data for 1993.
10. The firms were short of financial capital and credits for purchasing new equipment. Therefore the upgrading of their old technology could not become a quick alternative.
11. For convenience, we use the terms 'inefficiency' and 'efficiency' interchangeably. Larger values of E_T and E_A imply greater inefficiency.
12. Note that we used profits per unit of output in the regression. While Table 5.1. contains data on the total profits. Evidence that the total profits in the clothing industry were increasing when technical efficiency was stabilizing means that total production was increasing as well (probably because of emerging new firms).

REFERENCES

Benáček, V. (1995), 'The Transformation of Small Businesses and Entrepreneurship in the Czech Republic', Occasional Papers (5), University of Essex .

Benáček, V. and M. Mejstrik (1995), 'Czech Textile and Clothing Industury during the period of Transition', Prague: CERGE.

Bergson, A.M. (1987), 'Comparative Productivity: the USSR, Eastern Europe and the West', *American Economic Review,* **77,** 342–57.

Bergson, A.M. (1992), 'Communist Economic Efficiency Revisited', *American Economic Review,* **82,** (2), 27–30.

Corado, C., V. Benáček and W. Caban (1995), 'Competitiveness of the Textile Industry: Comparison of Adjustment and Performance in the Czech Republic, Poland and Portugal', *Working Paper of Universidade Nova de Lisboa,* Lisbon.

Danilin, V.I. *et al.* (1985), 'Measuring Enterprise Efficiency in the Soviet Union: A Stochastic Frontier Approach', *Economica,* **52,** 225–33.

Farrell, M. (1957), 'The Measurement of Productive Efficiency', *Journal of the Royal Statistical Society,* 253–81.

Kopp, R. and W. Diewert (1982), 'The Decomposition of Frontier Cost Function Deviations into Measures of Technical and Allocative Efficiency', *Journal of Econometrics,* **19,** (2/3), 319–32.

6. Public investment expenditure and regional development in transitional economies

Aleksandar Bogunović

Public investment expenditure or public investment is a form of income redistribution by the government, for reasons ranging from legal to political and economic. The social character of public investment expenditure is determined by its use on public goods, thereby generating equality and availability. A relatively high level of investment over a relatively long period of returns, the manner of financing investment, the external economies and diseconomies, overriding the partial and local interests and so on influence the primary motive for public investment, which is increasing the size and volume of public goods (Stiglitz, 1988).

Public investment is channelled into various activities of public good in different parts of the national territory. The basic characteristic constraints of such an investment are the large sums required; long periods of time for expected returns; risk and uncertainty of returns, and no possibility of its exclusion from use. These determine the character of the contents of activities such as infrastructure, education, health and national security. They are thus a matter of vital interest to society and should be available to all sections of the people, irrespective of their financial capacities. This very fact stresses the need for the allocation of natural resources and space. Through public investment the social standard of the people in the country as a whole, as well as in its various parts and sections of the population, is ensured. Public investment in infrastructure and similar activities in the interior of the country activate regional development potentials and, thus, finally development of the regions.

To stress the importance of public investment and its regional allocation does not necessarily imply the role of investment by the private sector. Regional public investment is made in every society and mostly with the objective of developing a particular region. Since the ownership structure of economies differs, it could be vital for the allocation of investment, growth and development. The growth of the public sector, the consequences of nationalization and the growing size of public investment could also become constraints to development.

Restructuring of the former planned economies into market ones requires substantial time and investment. The process of transition is full of contradictions and conflicts, not only from an anachronic content point of view, but also in the manner of creating a market economy. Because of the existing heterogeneity in the old and new economic structure, no single possible approach to transition can be homogeneous. In this sense, public investment expenditure and restructuring and transition are contradictory.

Restructuring and transition mean changes in the economic and political conditions for the development of initiatives and innovations by encouraging private entrepreneurship. Earlier, the transitional economies were basically organized into a small number of large companies. Today, in contrast, the number of newly registered companies has increased by 20 to 30 times (Lavigne, 1995). But the dispersion by economic activities is rather unfavourable. Two-thirds of these companies deal in retail sales, catering, household services, and financial and intellectual services. Very few are left in the sphere of production and infrastructure. This can be explained by the fact that most entrepreneurs are interested in a quick profit and low investment requirements and by a lack of incentives for production activities.

Since private investments are not multidimensionally oriented, growth and development cannot be expected to be all embracing. The need for productive activities and interregional services is an imperative. This will spur the development of the interregional market through growth of the private sector in different parts of the country. On the other hand, the growth of the public sector and public investments calls for an increase in taxes, so wages are thereby reduced, as are the available overall sums for investment. Public investment is a means of correcting disparities and is particularly desirable in three key sectors, regional development, infrastructure and ecological protection.

Public investment expenditure, restructuring and transition, privatization and regional development in a broad sense can be interpreted as complementary. Public investment can be considered from two aspects. First is the creation of a framework for financial investment which is linked to the distribution and redistribution of gross domestic product. Irrespective of whether the resources are ensured by domestic or foreign resources, the taxpayers have ultimately to foot the bill. Contradictions are present in the budget allocation of resources for public investment because, for the same amount, taxes could be reduced and more money could be made available to the private sector for investment. The second perspective is that of solving basic development problems through the efficiency of investment. If the development projects have been well designed and efficiently executed, their returns will indirectly stimulate private initiative, innovations and investment over time. It follows that there is no contradiction here. This argument is frequently used in support of the regional development of those areas which are rich in resources but are underdeveloped because of the lack of financial inflows.

Restructuring and privatization both mean creating favourable conditions for the development of a market, including even those segments in which the private sector is not sufficiently interested. This lack of interest is, at times, due to the large amount of investment required. This problem can be solved by regional public investment, which in turn will invite private investment because, once the costs have been externalized, the returns of the private-sector investment rise. Since the autonomous public sector has a low intensity of investment, public investment expenditure is ensured by the transfer of private funds through the budget. As the public sector provides administrative and other services, which are not available on the market, the resources for such activities are usually assured by levying taxes on the output, sales, profits and wages.

Usually, the private sector is oriented towards the market. By offering products and services and earning profits it has a very high degree of self-financing. It continuously stimulates initiatives, innovations, entrepreneurship, investment in new technology and so on. The growth of the non-market sector implies a speedy and progressive growth of the financing of public expenditure, thereby increasing the pressure on both the household and private sector.

The significance of the public sector is best illustrated by the fact that developing countries alone, in the 1990s, will invest some US$200 billion in infrastructure. This constitutes roughly 4 per cent of their national output, or 20 per cent of their total investment. This has directly resulted in the growth of infrastructural services in transport and communication, energy, water supply and irrigation, improvement in health and education, and so on. Such improvements have raised not only the level of their standard of living but also the rate of growth in their overall productivity.

While the public sector includes activities and services of a collective nature, a large part of the servicing of this sector, including the supply of goods, is provided by the private sector. This constitutes a large part of the national economy. This is very true of the transitional economies of Central and Eastern Europe today. This is particularly so because many large companies and conglomerates in these countries are facing difficulties with the process of privatisation. Accordingly, the companies are increasingly passing into the ownership of the public sector.

Evidently, it follows that the allocation of national resources through the public expenditure policy remains the most significant instrument of the public policy for influencing growth rates, productivity and the standard of living in different parts of the country. The fundamental motives for preserving the regional character of the allocation of resources could be related to the following.

- Regional imbalances cause a retardation of growth and development, and weaken the functioning of the market in establishing a value system in and among countries.
- The national economy is an aggregate of regional economies. Regional disproportion and the absence of a consistent policy towards the regions reduce the efficiency of the overall national economic policy (Higgins and Savoie, 1988, p. 2). Naturally, the acceleration of the growth rate of the total national economy demands a solution to the developmental problems of economically backward regions.
- For a variety of reasons, a much better management and allocation of resources (natural, demographic and productive) is possible at a regional rather than national level.
- Respecting the regional economic policy and its symbiosis with the sectoral and national development policy, it acts as a factor of the democratization process in the country.

The guiding principles of the regional allocation of resources are the dispersion of productive capacities and putting the available potential in the country into a proper use; respecting the strategic (economic, military and political) goals of the country; and solving the problem of regional imbalance and disproportion among the underdeveloped regions within the country.

Over and above these factors, each and every government, irrespective of the degree of democracy in the society, needs the popular support of the entire country (Mckee *et al.*, 1970, p. 111). This, at times, reduces the significance of economic criteria and motives in resource allocation. Accordingly, underutilized, uneconomic and inefficient production units, infrastructural objects, power plants and cheap housing schemes have often been located in remote areas.

The decision on public investment is made by the government and thus falls under the joint jurisdiction of economics and politics. Obviously, contrary to the wisdom of theory and policy, particularly in developing and transitional economies, the government's decisions on public expenditure and investment policy are not motivated by the idea of maximum dispersion of the projects over the entire country.

The regional allocation of public investment expenditure and project dispersion over the regions have positive externalizing effects through the growth of local initiatives, the emergence of a number of small firms, innovations and entrepreneurship, and ultimately result in a significant increase in the regional growth rate (Maillat, 1995, pp. 161–5), thereby imparting dynamism to total economic growth. The allocation of resources for the public sector investment is of utmost importance in all phases of development (Friedman, 1966). In the underdevelopment phase, characterized by regional disparities, public-funded projects could have a great impact on regional growth rates. The government's decision on public investment expenditure may involve an alternative use of resources on a variety of projects.

The transition process that has begun in Central and East European countries, right from the beginning, has been burdened with cumulative negative characteristic factors: the centrally planned allocation of factors of development and growth generated a number of failures, partial and global inefficiencies and resulting disparities in the sectoral and regional structure. The inherent structural weaknesses further slowed down the pace of transition. Thus additional fresh resources need to be employed.

While the existing economic, political and social framework on a national level were suitable under the centrally monopolized system of economic and social management, the transition from such a system has opened up avenues for the development of individual, group, local and regional initiatives and innovations. There is an expressed desire in these countries to create the basic preconditions of growth and development, such as infrastructure.

During 1990–94, all the transitional economies, except Poland which had a positive GNP growth rate of 1.6 per cent, recorded a decline in growth rates by almost one-fifth, so that countries like Hungary, which has gone far in creating a market-oriented system, has experienced a decline of 2 per cent (The World Bank, 1996, pp. 208–9). This decline is surely much greater in the countries of former Yugoslavia, particularly in view of the war and social upheavals that have taken place in the region, but the statistics are not available. Such a trend could be attributed to the victimization by quantity at the expense of the quality of growth and development. However, future growth in these economies, at least to a certain degree and for some time to come, will depend upon the intensity and size of the public sector's investment in development of the backward regions. Moreover, it is very logical to expect that the emerging private sector will follow suit.

In the context of the future growth process in transitional economies, there is an emerging dilemma that needs some thought. A threat to growth is posed by a limited supply of resources within the countries and a constraining availability of foreign capital. While domestic resources are, in most cases, insufficient to meet the growth demands, direct foreign investment, multilateral aid and soft loans are not coming up to expectations. Accordingly, one of the dilemmas, among many others, is whether to finance regional and overall development through budgetary resources and risk inflation or, alternatively, at the expense of growth and development, to ensure the stability of prices and exchange rates, as is usually recommended by the IMF.

Except in the case of transport and communication, energy, water supply and primary health care, particularly because of the delocalization effects, special attention needs to be paid to preserving the ecology. The state of natural resources, of space, of the biosphere and so on is rather distressing. Examples such as the 'black triangle of Central Europe', the Albhasan Valley in Albania and so on, are not only the by-products of the former system and of negligence in the use of resources (Ascher and Healy, 1990, p. 11), but are also due to the lack of public investment in environment protection. As a result, today, the future costs of ecological revitalization of these areas in transitional economies are estimated in billions of US dollars. The autarchy, fragmentation and polarization of interests have not contributed to the ecological development, so far.

Another dilemma concerns the future direction of regional growth – the concentration of or dispersion growth factors. The degree of urbanization and its correlation with the growth process is of primary concern to growth planners, because the attained growth and development in many of these transitional economies, so far, is concentrated in a few areas only. In transitional economies the concentration of population in urban areas is in excess of 60 per cent, the only exceptions being Albania, with 37 per cent, Macedonia FYR (59 per cent), Romania (51 per cent) and Slovakia (58 per cent) (The World Bank, 1996, pp. 204–5). The result of such a trend in the postwar years is that vast territories of land within national boundaries are empty. The question now arises: growth and development for whom? The numerous examples of depopulated areas include the Albhasan valley in Albania, hilly and rocky areas in Bosnia and Herzegovina and the Adriatic islands and Lika region in Croatia. Along with the creation of an infrastructural base, as a precondition of future growth in these economies, development of tertiary activities for gainfully employing people and retaining them in the underdeveloped regions could become a source of dispersion of population over each entire country.

The measures and instruments of the government's policy for encouraging growth are heavily dependent on regional support. The frequently used measure of direct transfer of resources through specialized funds has proved to be successful to a great extent for many development projects such as roads, irrigation, energy, telecommunication, health and educational facilities, but has failed miserably to attract the growth of entrepreneurship following the regional interests.

During 1994, the transitional economies recorded a growth rate 10 per cent lower than that of the west. Within the group there are notable differences in performance. Albania, which is the least developed European country, had only 1.6 per cent of the GNP of the high-income economies, and 5.4 per cent of that of Slovenia. Slovenia has the highest per capita income, US$7040, which is almost 30.6 per of the average per capita GNP of the high-income economies (see Table 6.1).

Table 6.1   Structure of the (1994) economy: production and demand

			Distribution of gross domestic product (%)		
Economies	GNP per capita (dollars)	Average growth rate 1990–94	General government consumption	Private consumption	Gross investment
Albania	380	–4.2	15.0	100.0	13.5
Bulgaria	1 250	–5.9	15.0	64.0	20.8
Croatia	2 560	—	28.0	60.0	13.8
Czech Republic	3 200	–4.7	13.0	58.0	20.4
Hungary	3 840	–2.0	13.0	72.0	21.5
Macedonia FYR	820	—	7.0	89.0	18.0
Poland	2 410	1.6	19.0	64.0	15.9
Romania	1 270	–3.7	13.0	62.0	26.9
Slovak Republic	2 250	–5.4	24.0	53.0	17.1
Slovenia	7 040	—	21.0	55.0	20.8

Source: *World Development Report 1996*, pp. 188–9, 208–13.

From the beginning of the transition process until 1994, all except Poland experienced a real decline in gross domestic product. The growth rates are characteristically low in the newly independent states, which can be attributed to the accumulated developmental problems and half-hearted reforms. Such a trend had determined the distribution of growth of GDP during 1994. It deeply affected personal consumption, which in Albania, Macedonia FYR and Moldavia is just sufficient to meet requirements. Thus it follows that public investment needs to be covered by external sources.

The government expenditure in these least developed countries is hardly sufficient to meet the current account expenditure of the state. A major part of the budget is being used irrationally, not only on services, such as health and education, but also to cover the losses of state sector enterprises which have not been privatized for one reason or another.

Evidently, the scope for public expenditure is fairly narrow. In the transition phase it is, so far, disproportionately in favour of the infrastructural projects which still remain in state ownership. As we know, the infrastructural problems were dominant in the earlier system of centralized management, so that, in the transition process, sizeable sums are required for creating new output, improving quality of output and stimulating new business entries in the private sector. Since the needs for public investment are greater than the capacity, when allocating resources, a rigorous and selective choice of projects having explicit advantage in externalities must be adhered to. This does not mean forgoing regional development. Well selected sectors and rational investment will have an indirect effect on regional development: regional potentials can be hooked up to a major growth activity, such as the development of energy, roads, water supply, health and environment protection.

It must be emphasized that, as far as public investment is concerned, it creates preconditions of growth and development. These are badly lacking in the transitional economies. After an initial investment has been made, the preconditions of growth are created; the need for public investment will evidently be reduced in the years following. This will help release pressure on the government budget and eventually taxes can be reduced. Further investment can be made out of the net returns of previously completed projects. Also greater attention can be paid to the regional dispersion of investment. Since transitional economies have suffered from structural disparities for so long, at least in the case of the global distribution of funds, it is rather difficult to determine the priorities. The choice is limited because of economic and political constraints.

Private investment is generally a residual category in poor countries and is subject to limitations due to a low level of output and increased pressure on wages, taxes on profits, and so on. The case is similar in transitional economies where gross domestic investment, excluding Albania and Croatia, with 13.5 and 13.8 per cent respectively, range between 15 and 27 per cent of GDP. However, Albania, Croatia, Macedonia FYR and Romania have investments in excess of domestic savings (for example, in Albania savings are minus 15 per cent, and in Macedonia FYR 4 per cent of GDP). The distribution of GDP by expenditure (see Table 6.1) shows that it is all used up and a negative difference appears in cases like Albania, Macedonia FYR, Hungary and Romania.

In today's transitional economies, maximum attention was previously paid to global projects such as oil and energy, black metallurgy, chemical plants and so on, at the expense of the consumer products of mass consumption. But the basic problems were of a technical nature, of the quality of production and that of the deficient demand for these products in the west. Since all these heavy industrial projects were financed by public money, they were basically irrational and disfunctional.

If we consider the energy consumption structure in transitional economies, we find it not in line with the level of production. The per capita energy consumption is far above the per capita output (see Table 6.2), and there is a

Table 6.2   Commercial energy use

Country	(1)	(2)	(3)	(4)	(5)
Albania	422	28	4.0	1.24	1.2
Bulgaria	2 786	63	54.4	6.37	3.3
Croatia	1 057	28	16.2	3.39	6.8
Czech Republic	3 902	13	135.6	13.15	13.5
Hungary	2 455	44	59.9	5.80	6.2
Macedonia FYR	—	—	4.1	1.99	8.4
Poland	2 563	5	341.9	8.91	9.8
Romania	1 750	27	122.1	5.36	4.6
Slovakia	—	—	37.0	6.97	20.7
Slovenia	1 506	19	5.5	2.76	5.3
HIE	5 168	—	10 087.4	12.03	13.6

Notes:
Col. 1: energy use (oil equivalent) 1994 per capita kg.
Col. 2: net energy imports as percentage of energy consumption in 1994.
Col. 3: CO_2 emission (1992) total metric tons.
Col. 4: CO_2 emission (1992) per capita metric tons.
Col. 5: nationally protected areas (percentage of total surface area) in 1994.
HIE: High Income Economies.

Source: *World Development Report 1996*, pp. 202–3, 207.

further demand for investment in the energy sector, which is highly irrational. Analysis of the energy production, transmission, consumption and import in the transitional economies shows the inefficiency of the energy sector. So, to rationalize this sector and intensify environment protection, in the absence of any substantial involvement of the private sector in the near future, large public investments will be required.

As compared to the energy sector, transport and communications (road, rail, air, telecommunications), water supply and control systems are in much worse shape in many of these countries. The situation is not any better in the field of health and education, which suffer from excess capacity, lack of equipment and so on. Again, all these sectors require further public investment.

Lack of capital is characteristic of transitional economies. It would therefore be natural to invest in advanced technologies which would be cheaper in the long run because the ultimate costs of ecology protection will be much higher. Because the environment is a public good, and because of the degree of devastation and of desired regional dispersion, public investment expenditure for its protection, in all transition countries, requires special attention. It is worth observing that, if we compare the per capita output and the degree of pollution in transitional economies with that of the developed market economies, particularly the degree of emissions of carbon dioxide and sulphur dioxide and other pollutants, we find that it is extremely high. The situation is much better in Macedonia FRY, Slovenia and Croatia than in the newly independent states and Central European countries. Just to illustrate the point, Slovenia, with its 30 per cent share of the output of the developed countries, emits 22.9 per cent more cabon dioxide than Russia, which has a 20 per cent higher emission and only a 10 per cent share of the output.

If we consider nationally protected spaces (national parks, forests, natural beauty spots and so on), some 14 per cent of developed countries is under protection. With the exception of Slovakia, all the transitional countries have less. With respect to the use of space, in most countries in the past there was a general misconception that there is an unlimited and inexhaustible supply of the resource. Such a view had a negative effect on the rate of economic growth. In order to reduce the costs of future growth, an intensive effort of spatial and environmental protection is desired. The protection measures need not only to minimize the existing degree of pollution, but also to put a check on future pollution. In order to achieve this, attention must be paid to adequate legislation, a penalty system, standardization of the norms of pollution, an early detection information system, education, economic incentives and so on.

REFERENCES

Ascher, W and R. Healy (1990), *Natural Resource Policy Making in Developing Countries: Environment, Economic Growth and Income Distribution*, Durham and London: Duke University Press.

Friedman, J. (1996), *Regional Development Policy: A Case Study of Venezuela*, Cambridge, Mass.: MIT Press.

Higgins, B. and D.J. Savoie (1988), *Regional Economic Development*, Boston, Mass.: Unwin-Hyman.

Lavigne, M. (1995), *The Economics of Transition*, New York: St Martin's Press.

Maillat, D. (1995), 'Territorial Dynamic Innovative Milieus and Regional Policy', *Entrepreneurship and Regional Development*, **7**, (2).

Mckee, D.L., R.D. Dean and W.H. Leahy (1970), *Regional Economics*, New York: The Free Press.

Stiglitz, J. (1988), *Economics of the Public Sector*, New York: W.W. Norton.

World Bank (1996), *The World Development Report 1996*, Washington, DC.

7. Policies for control of air pollution in Central and Eastern Europe

Jennifer Steedman

Several parts of Central and Eastern Europe (CEE) suffer from high levels of air pollution, particularly from sulphur dioxide (SO_2) and particulate matter (PM). This poses serious threats to human health, damages and destroys physical capital, and threatens coasts, lakes, forests and mountain habitats. The precise magnitude of the total cost of environmental damage in CEE countries remains controversial. However, with most estimates ranging from 2 to 10 per cent of GDP, the costs are clearly significant.

Air pollution in CEE is the unfortunate consequence of a number of interrelated factors. First and foremost, it is a legacy of the central planning approach to resource allocation, which, with its extensive reliance on physical planning targets and soft budget constraints, produced energy-intensive economies. This is demonstrated in Table 7.1.

These figures show that CEE countries consume significantly higher amounts of energy per unit of GNP than their OECD counterparts. A second and related factor is the dominant use of low-quality coal in CEE economies; this exacerbates the environmental impact of the high energy figures. Third, the

Table 7.1   Energy intensity for OECD and selected CEE countries, 1988

Countries	Energy use / GNP
OECD	1.0
USSR	2.7
Romania	2.5
Bulgaria	2.2
Poland	1.9
Czechoslovakia	1.9
Hungary	1.3
All CEE	2.5

Source: Bates *et al.* (1994a).

failure of environmental policy and the lax enforcement of regulatory measures in CEE countries have also made an important contribution to the current air pollution problems.

Air pollution has been recognized as a serious problem and governments
are naturally keen to devise policies to improve the situation. The problem is
that most of these economies are still in the throes of transition and the
resources available for environmental improvement are severely constrained.
In this context, it is essential that governments design and implement pollution control policies which are cost-effective. They have three tools at their
disposal: economic, energy and environmental policies. Although environmental policy is the most direct means of reducing pollution, economic and
energy policies can also have a significant, positive impact on air pollution.
For example, economic reforms have affected and will continue to affect the
structure of industry; this restructuring will change the pattern of energy use
and resulting environmental damage. Similarly, energy policy decisions, from
increasing fuel prices to restructuring the sector, can reduce the extensive
environmental effects of energy production, distribution and use. Most OECD
countries have formulated their energy, economic and environmental policies
separately, which has resulted in sometimes conflicting objectives, higher
economic costs and less effective policies in all areas. CEE economies cannot
afford to do the same.

This chapter defines the precise role which should be played by economic,
energy and environmental policies to reduce air pollution in CEE, in the most
cost-effective manner. The specific characteristics of the principal air pollutants – SO_2, NOx (nitrogen oxide) and dust – are analysed. Air pollution in
CEE differs in some important respects from that in OECD countries and this
has important implications for the applicability of economic instruments,
such as pollution charges and tradable permits. Our analysis shows that the
transition process leading to economic reform, already has led, and can be
expected to lead, to a reduction in the production and consumption of energy,
with attendant consequences for air pollution. The key factors which will
bring about this reduction include enterprise restructuring, increases in energy prices and hard budget constraints on public and private enterprises. It is
concluded that, although price and enterprise reform will make a significant
contribution to the reduction of pollution, these by themselves will not be
sufficient to achieve the environmental objectives of CEE countries and will
have to be coupled with selective environmental policies.

It is also shown that most changes in energy policy, in most CEE countries,
have been limited to supply-side measures, particularly organizational and
ownership changes, increases in energy prices and the removal of some subsidies. It is argued that, while these are important and should continue, there are
also a number of demand-side policies which should be introduced to help

overcome a number of barriers, which are currently preventing the full effects of economic reform from being realized. We also turn to assess the potential role that can be played by environmental policies and explain how economic instruments such as charges and permits have the potential to achieve set standards of air quality at lower cost than traditional regulatory mechanisms alone. We set out the changes that would be required in existing environmental policy to take advantage of the benefits offered by such instruments.

The main lesson provided by this chapter is that improvements in air pollution in CEE depend on continued economic reform, better energy policies and selective environmental policies, based on economic instruments.

CHARACTERISTICS OF AIR POLLUTION IN CENTRAL AND EASTERN EUROPE

As in most western countries, air pollution in CEE is largely confined to cities and regional hotspots where there are concentrations of industries, power plants, homes and vehicles. Prague, for example, records the highest average daily concentrations of air pollution in any European capital and regions such as Northern Bohemia and Northern Moravia (Czech Republic), Upper and Lower Silesia (Poland) and Southern Saxony (Germany) are also severely affected.

Air pollution in CEE originates not only from high-stack sources, such as the large power stations, heat plants and heavy industry, but also from numerous low-stack sources, including small boiler houses, small businesses and domestic open hearth coal fires. When discussing the relative importance of each source, one must distinguish between contributions to emissions and to ambient concentrations (or, alternatively, emissions and immissions). High-stack sources typically account for the vast majority of PM, SO_2 and NOx emissions. For example, in 1990, energy production and use in most CEE countries by high-stack sources typically accounted for 70–80 per cent of the emissions of PM and SO_2, and nearly 50 per cent of the emissions of NOx. However, because most of this pollution is dispersed from high stacks, this does not constitute the most serious air pollution in CEE countries. Rather, it is the local ambient concentrations of pollutants which pose the most serious threats to human health. It is the low-stack sources which make the greatest contribution to concentrations both because they are so numerous and because they release pollutants close to ground level. The emissions from burning coal from low-stack sources therefore are not dispersed and, given the number of sources, cannot easily be controlled.

These characteristics contrast strongly with the situation in the west, where the great majority of air pollution (emissions and concentrations) is produced by power stations and a small number of industrial sectors. In the west, therefore, pollution control policy is simpler to devise as it can focus on a handful of stationary sources rather than the numerous small and medium energy sources that exist in CEE countries.

TRANSITION AND AIR POLLUTION

The process of transition and associated changes in energy policy are expected to lead to large reductions in energy-related air pollution. There are two aspects of economic reform that are especially important in this context. First, economic reform will make a significant contribution to a reduction in air pollution by changing the structural features of economies. Under central planning, the CEE economies were dominated by industrial production, especially metallurgy and other heavy industry. These industries were energy-intensive and thus contributed significantly to the air pollution problem. Industrial restructuring will change the composition of the CEE economies away from heavy industry to other less energy-intensive and, hence, less polluting sectors.

The second aspect of economic reform that is expected to generate substantial reductions in air pollution is price reform. One essential reason for the inefficiency of energy use in CEE economies was that energy prices, until recently, were decoupled from the world market; they were artificially low and did not reflect production costs. In the west, it was increases in relative energy prices (caused by the oil shocks of 1973 and 1979) which induced industries and consumers to use energy more efficiently. The reduction in fuel use was, in turn, a major factor contributing to a significant reduction in the level of air pollution in the west.

Similar forces can be expected to operate in CEE. Higher energy prices are expected to promote energy efficiency, thus reducing energy intensity, and to encourage a shift in the composition of fuel use. Industry, for example, will substitute oil products and gas for coal and electricity, and households will substitute coal for other, cleaner fuels, such as gas.

One important area of work that has been undertaken in some CEE countries is to develop models to estimate the effects of economic reform on energy demand and pollution levels in the future (Bates *et al.*, 1994b; Hughes, 1994; Bollen *et al.*, 1994). Most of these projections have been undertaken by the World Bank and the OECD, in preparation for the Environmental Action Programme for CEE.

The models vary in numerous respects, for example in terms of the countries studied, the method used, scenarios that are tested and the assumptions that are adopted. Despite this, a number of common results emerge. For example, the results of all models suggest that, even if no particular measures are taken to control pollution, emissions of PM and SO_2 are likely to fall and remain below 1990 levels until after the year 2000. This is mainly the result of the fall in large-scale industrial output (due to industrial restructuring) and a reduction in industrial and residential coal use (the impact of higher energy prices). Emissions of NOx are the exception to this pattern because growth in the number and use of vehicles, in a number of countries, is expected to outstrip the decline in emissions from stationary sources.

At various points after 2000, emissions are expected to increase owing to the recovery in large-scale industrial output that is expected to take place, which more than outweighs factors such as increasing fuel efficiency and changes in the structure of production. However, in most cases, aggregate emissions of SO_2, NOx and PM are expected to be lower in 2010 than their pre-1990 levels. For example, a model of the Polish economy, developed by the World Bank (Bates, Cofala and Toman, 1994) estimates that SO_2, NOx and PM emissions will decline by 7, 3 and 44 per cent, respectively, compared with 1988. Simulation analysis also suggests that, despite significant decreases in air pollution emissions from economic restructuring and energy price reforms, the resulting levels of pollution will remain well outside EU ambient air quality standards.

The Impact of Transition

The replacement of central planning by market-oriented economies has already resulted in large reductions in air pollution in CEE. For example, in Poland, there was a 34 per cent reduction in SO_2 emissions and a 22 per cent reduction in NOx emissions, between 1988 and 1993. Similarly, there was a 15–45 per cent nationwide reduction in emissions in Bulgaria between 1990 and 1994. It is difficult to say how much of this observed decline in emissions reflects economic restructuring and how much the cause is the temporary decline in economic activity. Economic decline in CEE countries provides nothing more than a temporary abatement of the pressure on the environment. The critical question is whether emissions can be stabilized or reduced further as economic activity begins to recover from the deep recessions that have accompanied the early stages of economic transformation.

There is no doubt, however, that a significant amount of the observed reduction is due to increases in energy prices. In many countries in the region, energy prices have risen drastically. In Poland, for example, the prices of coal, oil and natural gas increased significantly in 1990 and 1991, reaching levels near those of the world market in early 1992. In dollar terms, the price of coal for industry increased by 3.8 times and district heat and hot water for households rose by 20.5 times; natural gas prices increased by 18.8 times for households and 2.3 times for industry. Electricity price rises were also severe: 12.6 times for households and 3.4 times for industry. Clearly, the increases have been greatest for the residential and commercial sector, which paid much lower prices than industry before the transition. Heating prices, however, continue to be subsidized and still only cover about 40 per cent of real current costs.

In the Czech Republic, prices have also increased significantly for industry's purchase of coal, electricity and natural gas, to close to market levels. However, fuel, electricity and heating prices for households are still well below market levels and do not cover economic costs.

Despite increases in energy prices, energy intensities in CEE countries, although decreasing, remain high. Price changes, therefore, are not translating into energy efficiency improvements as rapidly as was expected. This however, is due to the lack of complementary demand-side policies. Energy efficiency involves real costs of adaption and investment for those enterprises, institutions and households which have to adjust and, while it is realistic to presume that supply-side measures, such as increases in energy prices, will induce such efficiency, it is not realistic to think that such inducement would take place automatically. There are a number of barriers which face agents in transitional economies and which will have to be dealt with before enterprises and households can respond fully to the new set of incentives in the manner expected.

The barriers to energy efficiency improvements vary for residential and industrial sectors, as do the policy measures required to overcome these barriers. In what follows, therefore, we analyse both under their respective sector headings.

Barriers to Energy Efficiency in the Residential Sector

At present, energy use in the residential sector is influenced only by prices and, in some countries, by the standardization of household appliances. There are three key barriers to improved energy efficiency in this sector. First, although there have been significant increases in the price of energy in recent years, most CEE governments continue to subsidize residential energy use. In the Czech Republic, for example, the owners of buildings are currently reimbursed for the difference between the amount paid to the energy supplier for the real cost of energy and the amount received from the renters, that is the state-regulated price of the energy. Thus, as apartment renters do not bear (or even know) the full heating costs, they have no incentive to economize on their use of heat and a significant amount of heat is wasted. This waste of energy will only be reduced by the elimination of subsidies. The reason, of course, for subsidies not having been eliminated is that the price of energy for households would increase to an often unacceptably high level, but this argument is not sufficient, as a number of measures could be taken in tandem with the elimination of subsidies, to reduce adverse social impacts. The Ministry of Industry and Trade of the Czech Republic, for example, is trying to transfer the funds for subsidies into a social fund for housing support. In this way, households will be made aware of the full costs of their energy use and will make a greater effort to save energy.

Second, even though governments have increased residential energy prices and reduced subsidies, residents are limited, both in incentive and in their ability to respond. This is due to the free-rider effect in household energy consumption, caused by the lack of meters to measure individual use of hot water or gas, in many apartments and houses. Payments for energy use are made collectively, by apartment building or housing complex, and thus individual heating bills are based, not on the amount of heat actually consumed, but on the size of the dwelling. This weak link between payment and consumption means that current and future pricing incentives can, at best, only have a limited impact on energy use. This problem is aggravated by the fact that, in many countries, the valves on radiators do not work, leaving residents with no means of regulating heating levels, except by opening the windows.

The measurement of heat consumption is critical to promoting energy savings and hence emissions. One short- and medium-term priority, therefore, should be the provision of individual meters and controls that provide the means and the incentive for individual, household control over levels of energy consumption. Some countries have already introduced measures. For example, a regulation issued by the Czech Ministry of Economic Policy and Development in 1991 required meters for heat consumption in all buildings connected to district heating by the end of 1993 and in every apartment by the end of 1996. Further, in January of this year (1996), a new decree on billing for heat in residential buildings went into effect in the Czech Republic. The billing system will consist of a so-called 'two-layer price structure', for the heat consumed and for hot domestic water. Some 30 per cent of bills will be a fixed cost, with the remaining 70 per cent based on consumption.

Third, a lack of finance is also regarded as an important barrier to the implementation of energy efficiency projects in CEE countries. In most of these countries, financial institutions do not provide consumer loans and, even if they do, long-term loans are difficult to obtain. This, together with the impact of high rates of inflation on savings, both past and present, means that private energy users often lack funds to undertake energy efficiency improvements. Such imperfections in the capital market cannot be easily or quickly remedied. The Czech Republic government has attempted to overcome this problem by issuing grants, constituting up to 70 per cent of the cost of approved expenditures.

Energy Efficiency Barriers in Industry

In industry, the low level of energy efficiency is caused by the unsatisfactory technical condition of equipment. The main barrier does not appear to be a lack of knowledge, since progressive technologies are sufficiently well known. A more likely reason lies in the attitude of top management of industrial enterprises, where the practice of devoting only minimal attention to energy efficiency issues still prevails in most countries. It seems that many do not believe that energy savings would be significant enough to have much effect on their businesses. While it is true that, in many sectors of industry, energy costs make up only a small part of the enterprise's total expenses, experience shows that energy savings can reach values of 20 per cent or higher in practically every industrial enterprise once current technologies are applied.

Two ways in which governments could intervene, at low cost, to bring about the desired change would be to run information campaigns and to fund demonstration projects. These would be aimed at top management, informing them of the cost savings that can be generated by energy-efficient technologies. Both methods would reinforce the economic incentives for energy users to switch to more energy-efficient technologies or ways of working.

It is clear from the discussion above that, while current energy reforms have contributed to a reduction in energy use and, consequently, a reduction in air pollution, these alone will not capture the energy savings that are available in different sectors of the economy. The extent to which energy savings are captured depends not only on the continued liberalization of prices paid for energy, by both industries and households, but also on the introduction of appropriate government initiatives, to address barriers to energy efficiency.

ENVIRONMENTAL POLICIES

Transition, has already made, and will continue to make, a large contribution to the reduction of air pollution in CEE countries. However, this process needs to be reinforced by specific environmental policies aimed at reducing air pollution.

Most countries in the CEE have environmental legislation which sets out binding limits on the emissions and concentrations of air pollution, for different sources. For example, in Poland, the Ordinance of the Ministry of Environmental Protection (1990) sets emission standards for SO_2 and PM which apply only to power stations, industry and combustion plants with capacity exceeding 200 Kw. The second type of standards relate to all sources and are set in terms of air quality, that is, maximum allowable concentrations of pollutants in the air.

Ambient standards for air quality in most CEE countries are considerably more strict than EU ambient standards but are routinely exceeded in many industrial urban areas. Given the goal of joining the EU, several CEE countries have proposed or adopted emission/concentration standards that are based on EU precedents. A number have also signed and ratified various pan-European treaties on air pollution. Poland, Hungary and the Czech and Slovak republics, for example, have signed and ratified the UN Convention on Long Range Transboundary Air pollution and the subsequent 1985 (Helsinki) and 1988 (Sofia) protocols to reduce SO_2 and NOx emissions, respectively. The costs involved in meeting the obligations set out in such agreements will inevitably be high, for countries in the west and in the east. It is essential, therefore, that governments design and implement cost-effective environmental policies to control air pollution.

Until recently, environmental policies in most countries, whether OECD or CEE, relied exclusively on direct regulatory instruments as the main mechanism for implementing environmental goals. Direct regulatory instruments, or command and control (CAC) measures, are mandatory controls on activities that specify the environmental performance of polluters directly. Direct controls can operate in a variety of ways; for example, they can take the form of bans on specific substances, technology-based standards which specify the use of best available techniques, or national or local emission standards. In most countries, polluters either comply with the regulations or face penalties through administrative or judicial procedures.

The popularity of direct regulation indicates that it has advantages: it can remove the worst excesses of unregulated activity quickly and with certainty. Thus, when the environmental impact of a particular pollutant is very severe, regulation can be the most effective instrument. Regulation, however, is a poor means of minimizing resource costs because it imposes the same requirements on all polluters, irrespective of their abatement costs. Thus, with the introduction of tighter pollution control standards and hence a significant increase in the costs, regulation has been found wanting as a means of controlling pollution.

In recent years, therefore, attention in the west has turned to the use of economic instruments – such as pollution charges or tradable permits – to control air pollution. These two instruments are rather different: pollution charges involve putting a price on each unit of pollutant that is emitted (for example, per tonne of sulphur dioxide emissions), while a tradable permit scheme allocates permits to polluters for particular shares of emissions, and then allows these to be bought and sold. Although both instruments internalize externalities by imposing an implicit price on emissions, there is an important difference with respect to the establishment of this price. In a charge system, the price is set politically and total emissions result endogenously, mainly as a function of abatement costs. With a tradable permit scheme, the level of emissions is set directly and the price is a result of that level.

Economic instruments have a number of advantages over direct regulation. First, there is overwhelming evidence (both theoretical and empirical) that, under the right conditions, they can obtain set standards of air quality at significantly lower costs than a regulatory regime. The reason is that the cost of cleaning up emissions is not the same for all sources. Therefore the cheapest method of meeting the reduction target is to encourage those with the lowest costs of cleaning up to reduce their emissions by more than those facing higher abatement costs. In essence, polluters should clean up more when they have a comparative advantage in terms of the costs of abatement.

Second, they provide a continuing incentive to invest in lower-cost pollution abatement technologies rather than simply encouraging minimum compliance. With permits, for example, such investment enables polluters to reduce permit purchases or increase permit supplies (for later use or to sell). Emission charges also induce innovation in pollution reduction, since even sources in compliance have an incentive to reduce their tax liability. In contrast, rigid approaches provide little incentive for technical innovation, particularly when the controls specify the means for abatement.

The choice of policy instruments is sometimes posed as one between CAC approaches which use regulatory instruments and market-based approaches which rely on economic incentives. However, those countries which have adopted economic instruments as part of their air pollution control policies (notably the USA), have used them as an adjunct to, rather than a replacement of, the existing regulatory systems. Thus, in reality, the choice is not between one or the other but the most appropriate combination of economic instruments and regulation.

Economic Instruments in Central and Eastern Europe

Prior to transition, it was not feasible to consider the application of economic instruments to the economies in transition, since these instruments rely on the existence of an effective system of property rights and a high degree of cost consciousness. Because of the central planning approach to resource allocation, firms had weak incentives to minimize costs because of direct subsidies, soft finance windows or direct government intervention in enterprises. Zylicz (1993), for example, has argued: 'financial instruments were doomed to failure in an economy where all essential inputs were allocated administratively, and plant managers had little incentive to pay attention to price stimuli'. However, recent reforms in the enterprise and banking sectors are resulting in a hardening of budget constraints and an improvement in resource utilization.

Furthermore, privatization is introducing more effective property rights and there is encouraging evidence that firms are becoming more cost-conscious. It is now feasible, therefore, to consider the application of economic instruments to countries in CEE.

There are two factors which suggest that there is a particularly important role for the application of economic instruments to air pollution control in the economies in transition. First, the magnitude of the costs required to meet environmental objectives, and the substantial competing claims for limited resources, suggest that CEE governments might have to give more serious consideration to economic instruments than has been usual in Western Europe. Second, several countries, including Bulgaria, the Czech Republic, Hungary, Poland, Russia, the Slovak Republic and Ukraine, already impose, or have the legislation to impose, emission fees and fines on polluters. In many other countries, such as Belarus and Croatia, such legislation has recently been introduced or is being actively considered.

It is important to stress, however, that fees in CEE countries, as in many West European countries, are used to contribute to government revenue. This purpose is fundamentally different from the use of emission fees to internalize the external costs generated by pollution. The general level of fees therefore, is too low and does not reflect the damage caused by emissions of air pollutants. The differentiation of fees is also, in general, poorly matched to regional variations in pollution levels. Nevertheless, existing systems of emission fees and fines can form the basis for efficient systems of pollution charges. If pollution charges are deemed the most suitable economic instrument to control the principal air pollutants, it will be necessary to raise the level of the charges dramatically and then to enforce payment of the charges levied. This will provide a powerful incentive for enterprise to find low-cost methods of abating their emissions even if they cannot afford to make large investments in new plant and technology.

In some countries this process is already well under way. For example, in Poland, the level of pollution charges has been raised more than tenfold, in real terms, since 1990. The revenue collected in this manner goes to national and provincial funds and is used to finance various environmental investments. In the Czech Republic, pollution charges are levied on PM, SO_2 and NOx (US\$103, 34 and 28 per tonne, respectively). If emission charges are exceeded, pollution charges are increased by 50 per cent. They are reduced by up to 40 per cent when companies modify processes or install pollution control equipment. If these measures fail to achieve compliance, the company is subsequently liable to pay the avoided charges. These charges are not high enough to reflect external pollution costs and do not, therefore, provide sufficient incentive for polluters to take abatement action.

Estimated Saving from Economic Instruments

Some studies have been conducted to assess the savings in abatement costs that might be achieved if a particular set of standards is implemented using policies that rely on economic instruments rather than regulatory measures. While most of these have focused on western countries, a group of studies has recently been undertaken for Poland as part of a World Bank research project (Bates, Cofala and Toman, 1994a; Bates, Gupta and Fiedor, 1994b). Other simulation studies in other parts of Eastern Europe are also currently under way, one in a heavily polluted region of Eastern Europe, dubbed the 'Black Triangle', which consists of neighbouring districts in Poland, Germany and the Czech Republic.

One of the studies (Bates, Cofala and Ioman, 1994) involved developing a dynamic model of least cost energy supply in Poland. This model allows examination at a national level of the effects of different pollution standards and policies. A number of different incentive-based policy scenarios were then analysed and compared with the more traditional command and control approach. The cost of controlling PM, SO_2 and NOx emissions over 1991–2015, under CAC, is estimated at US$12.56 billion (discounted to 1990, 12 per cent real discount rate). When economic incentives are applied to all pollutants, the cost falls to US$5.73 billion. The cost saving therefore is significant: control costs are more than halved.

Which Economic Instrument?

Although charges and permits are theoretically equivalent in their effects, they are not equivalent policy instruments. Each possesses characteristics which makes one more effective than the other in different circumstances. The choice between them depends on the nature of the pollutant and of its source, its geographical setting and various political and administrative considerations. Detailed assessments are needed of the suitability of different economic instruments and combinations of instruments and direct controls, for dealing with the principal air pollutants for each country in CEE. These must focus on practical issues of implementation as well as on economic assessment of the relative costs of the alternative approaches. However, even at this point, it is possible to reach some general conclusions.

First, economic instruments, whether charges or tradable permits, are most appropriate for reducing pollutants from large, stationary sources, such as power stations and heavy industry. They are less appropriate for the numerous, low-stack sources such as households, where the problems of monitoring to ensure the right level of tax is paid are much more intractable. For these low-stack sources, specific regulations or indirect market incentives via the cost of inputs may be more effective alternatives.

Second, for regional pollutants, such as PM and SO_2, a tradable permit system is likely to be most suited to controlling emissions from large high-stack sources, rather than pollution charges. This is because, with regional pollutants, the relationship between the quantity of emissions and air quality is not monotonic. Rather, it is strictly dependent on the characteristics of the emitting source and the meteorological and geographical conditions in which these emissions take place. This contrasts with uniformly mixed pollutants such as carbon dioxide (CO_2), for which location does not matter and damage depends solely on the aggregate volumes of residuals emitted. It is inefficient to control a regional pollutant in a way which disregards location; such a policy either expends more resources than is necessary to deal with the damage or fails to deal with as much damage as an efficient policy would do for the same resource cost. While, in theory, either economic instrument could be designed to take the spatial dimension fully into account – with differentiated emission charging structures and deposition permit schemes – both have been judged to be too complex and administratively impractical to implement. This explains why there is no real-life example of either system anywhere in the world.

However, an equivalent effect can be achieved with tradable permits if exchange rates are introduced between permits from different sources. That is, permits would be issued on the basis that the most damaging sources pay two or three times as many permits for each tonne of emissions. This avoids the administrative penalties while allowing a useful degree of locational differentiation.

If one considers the characteristics of the principal air pollutants in CEE, it is clear that a single instrument, whether economic instruments or command and control, will not provide an adequate solution to the air pollution problems. It is likely that a mix of economic instruments and direct regulation will be required. Although no definite conclusions can be made without detailed modelling, on the basis of available evidence it seems that tradable permits will be more appropriate than emission charges for controlling emissions from the large static emitters and, further, that traditional direct controls are likely to be more efficient at controlling emissions from the area pollution sources, where emissions trading would be costly and complex to arrange and taxes are technically and politically difficult to apply.

Disadvantages of Economic Instruments

Economic instruments are not without problems. The principal problems in introducing economic instruments arise from the heavy fiscal burden which an efficient system of pollution charges or permits would impose on enterprises. This is particularly important for transitional economies since the financial position of many enterprises is already weak. However, there are certain transitional arrangements to mitigate the worst impacts of the new control system. For example, it may be feasible to impose a relatively low charge on emissions up to the level specified in each plant's emission permit but require that the full charge should be payable on emissions above that level. This is equivalent to the system of fees (low charges) and fines (full charges) which currently operates in certain countries. It provides an incentive to reduce emissions to the permitted level, but sacrifices a significant amount of the efficiency gains which would be generated by encouraging plants with low abatement costs to reduce their emissions below the level specified in their permit. However, this would only be a short-term measure with the quantity of emissions subject to the lower charge being gradually reduced to zero, in two to four years.

In conclusion, although economic and energy reform will go a long way in reversing the perverse incentives introduced by central planning and hence alleviate the accompanying air pollution, these by themselves will not be sufficient to ensure that CEE countries fulfil the obligations they have set out for themselves. Economic reform, however, is a prerequisite for the success of environmental policy and it is essential that this process continues. However, additional measures, specifically adapted to the transition process, are required. First, government initiatives are required to address barriers to energy efficiency. Second, governments need to assess whether, and to what extent, tradable permits or pollution charges would reduce the costs of controlling air pollution. If as expected, the estimated savings are significant, these should be built into the existing system of pollution control as a matter of some urgency.

BIBLIOGRAPHY

Bates, R., J. Cofala and M. Toman (1994a), 'Alternative Policies for the Control of Air Pollution in Poland', *World Bank Environment Paper,* No. 7, Washington, DC: World Bank.

Bates R., S. Gupta and B. Fiedor (1994b), 'Economy-wide Policies and the Environment – A Case Study of Poland', *World Bank Environment Paper,* No. 63, Washington, DC: World Bank.

Bollen, J., J. Hettelingh and R. Maas (1994), *Scenarios for the Economy and the Environment in Central and Eastern Europe*, The Netherlands, Environmental Action Programme for Central and Eastern Europe, Conference Proceedings, Lucerne, 28–30 April 1993.

Hughes G. (1994), 'Economic Reform, Industrial Restructuring and the Environment', Washington, DC: World Bank.

London Economics (1992), 'Study of Economic Policy Instruments for the Control of Air Pollution in Poland' (unpublished).

OECD/IEA (1992), *Priorities and Opportunities for Co-operation and Integration*, Proceedings of Conference on Energy and Environment in Central and East European Economies in Transition, Prague, 17–19 June, Paris: OECD.

Zylicz, T. (1993), 'Environmental Taxes in Poland', paper presented at the Workshop on Taxation and Environment in European Economies in Transition, OECD Environment Directorate, CCEET/ENV/DAFFE (92)243.

8. Regional dispersion of foreign direct investment in Eastern Europe

Ivo Družić

A number of studies, research projects and projections of the economic development in the transitional economies of Eastern Europe begin with a hypothesis that domestic saving is insufficient but that there is enough foreign capital to nurture intensive investment activities, which will result in high growth rates. Nevertheless, studies point to the fact that, on a global level, there is significant investment capital which is considered to be the basic developmental factor both for the developing (LDC) and for transitional economies (Kozul-Wright, 1996, pp. 11–12). Therefore, if LDC and transitional economies are grouped together on the basis of similar features of certain economic indicators, a relatively favourable picture of capital transactions emerges.

However, if transitional economies are grouped separately it becomes apparent that international financial investors have shown a relatively modest and decreasing interest in investing in former planned economies of Eastern Europe. In the 1990–95 period, the global gross total of investment capital amounted to US$1650 billion. Eastern Europe and the former Soviet Union had only a 15 per cent share in that amount (World Bank, 1996, p. 136). If we take into consideration the gross capital transactions that are being considered here, the net result is even more unfavourable: numerous transitional economies have achieved a negative financial inflow owing to the fact that the capital outflow of servicing external debts and investments abroad was higher than the inflow. Thus the capital flight in the former Soviet Union alone was US$50 billion between 1992 and 1995.

Within Eastern Europe, excluding the NIS (New Independent States – the former Soviet Union), there is also a great lack of uniformity since the majority of western investments were poured into two or three countries, while all others, including Croatia, saw no significant inflow of foreign investment.

SUB-REGIONAL INVESTMENT FLOWS

The study of interdependence between the efficiency of transition and the inflow of foreign capital into transitional economies leads to the conclusion that heterogeneity in both categories (transitional economies and capital transactions) hinders any analytical judgements being reached. Therefore it is necessary to examine both categories with the aim of reaching a more consistent insight into the level of correlation between the inflows of foreign capital and the transition efficiency by finding more homogeneous categories.

When dealing with regional features, the analysis shows the specific position of Eastern Europe as a whole and points to the notion that the dispersion of intraregional flows of financial capital within Eastern Europe corresponds to a narrower division into subregions within Eastern Europe.

When dealing with capital transactions, an effective analysis points to the need for isolating the foreign direct investment (FDI) category from the total capital transactions. The other financial transaction categories, such as official financing and bilateral financing, have a tendency to stagnate or decline in their relative significance in the total capital transactions, while FDI records exponential growth along with changing the structure of the global investment capital. The isolation of FDI discloses the tendency of intensive investment growth in the 1990–93 period when the average investments in Eastern Europe rose more than sixfold, from approximately US$600 million to almost US$4 billion. However, in 1994, a falling trend in foreign investors' interest in Eastern Europe was noted and FDI was cut by almost one-third. A more precise analysis would show that foreign investors' interest declined as early as 1993, which was 'hidden' by a US$900 investment in the purchase of the Hungarian telecommunications company MATAV, that is by the fact that only Hungary kept a stable FDI inflow (UNECE, 1996, p. 158).

A similar downward trend in investment inflows was also noted in 1995. A certain amount of time is still needed to judge realistically whether significant changes in the direction of financial inflow have occurred, or whether we are dealing with only short-term oscillations. Future FDI trends are bound to be under the influence of various factors. Since the highest weight is attributed to the privatization dynamics, it is believed that the second privatization wave, or the so-called 'mass privatization' which affected the majority of transitional economies at the end of 1995 and the beginning of 1996, will have a positive effect on FDI trends.

This falling tendency in the flows of direct investments into Eastern Europe is of special concern since joint ventures are the principal means of bridging the technological gap. It is widely known that technological lag is one of the shortcomings inherent to the system of planned economies which make them inferior in competition with the west. Thus intensification

Table 8.1 Private foreign investment (FDI) in transitional economies, 1990–94, US$ millions

	Net inflows					Cumulative inflows					FDI per capita
	1990	1991	1992	1993	1994	1990	1991	1992	1993	1994	1994
Albania	—	—	20	48	48	—	—	20	68	116	36
Bulgaria	4	56	42	55	48	4	60	102	157	205	23
Croatia	—	—	16	40	48	—	—	16	56	104	22
Czech Republic	180	511	983	517	779	436	947	1 951	2 519	3 319	319
Hungary	311	1 459	1 471	2 328	1 097	526	1 985	3 456	5 795	6 941	670
Poland	88	117	284	580	527	94	211	495	1 075	1 602	42
Poland[1]	89	298	665	1 697	—	218	509	1 187	2 884	—	—
Romania	—	37	73	95	294	—	40	120	207	501	22
Slovak Republic	18	82	100	144	79	28	110	210	354	434	102
Slovenia	—	41	113	112	88	7	72	183	294	374	185
Macedonia FRY	—	—	—	—	5	—	—	—	—	5	126

Note: 1. Balance of payment statistics.

Source: UNECE (1995), *Economic Survey of Europe*, Geneva.

of this trend in the transitional period slows down the market transformation.

An unfavourable regional trend also covers a vast subregional disproportion. Homogenization of smaller units within the vast concept of Eastern Europe is becoming more and more apparent. Comparative analyses that seek and find similarities and differences between individual transition models are not mere researchers' extravagances but reflect concrete interests of individual subregions within Eastern Europe. At the very beginning of the period of intensive all-encompassing transformation, countries like Poland, Hungary and what was Czechoslovakia defined the need for coordination of efforts aimed at joining the European Union by creating the Vishygrad group. Thus it has become frequent to group the 12 countries of Eastern Europe into two blocks: the countries commonly known as Central European Transitional Economies, or CETE-4 (Poland, the Czech Republic, Hungary and the Slovak Republic), and SETE-8, or South European Transitional Economies (Albania, Bosnia and Herzegovina, Bulgaria, Croatia, Macedonia FRY, Romania, Slovenia and the remains of Yugoslavia).

In the five years (between 1990 and 1994) of the process of economic transition in East European countries, the cumulative amount of FDI was US$13.6 billion, of which 95 per cent or US$12.9 billion was invested in CETE-4. It is obvious that the principal recipient was Hungary, having received a half of the total amount, or US$6.9 billion, followed by the Czech Republic and Poland. SETE-8 countries, which include Croatia, are evidently treated as a European subregion, that is countries with a relative high investment risk, which, combined with the general instability in the region, currently results in minimal interest on the part of international entrepreneurial capital in this area. Minimal participation of SETE-8 becomes even more unfavourable if we take into consideration the balance of FDI in the developing countries, which amounted to US$489 billion in 1993. In that case the cumulative amount of FDI in SETE-8 was only 2 per cent of the FDI flows in the developing countries (see Table 8.1). A more complete picture of investment flows can be obtained only by comparing the level of FDI with the external debt of transition economies, which contributes to a more realistic evaluation of the net effect of foreign investments on the level of the national economy's economic activity.

EXTERNAL DEBT AS A LIMITING FACTOR FOR FDI

Economic theory holds a somewhat contradictory attitude to the external debt of the national economy and its effect on FDI inflows. According to some theories, a high external debt has a negative impact on the stability of the economic activity within the national economy, thus discouraging foreign investors. At the same time, long-term high foreign indebtedness can be detrimental to the economic and general sovereignty of a country. Others quote a saying, which is often ascribed to Keynes, according to which a small debt is the debtor's problem, but a large debt is primarily the creditor's problem and only subsequently the debtor's. Along with that, a high debt regularly indicates a high FDI level. Thus investors will be more inclined to grant additional investments in an attempt to secure return from the investment rather than to reduce possible losses by disinvestment.

The current issues concerning Mexican and Polish debts confirm this notion to some extent. These are the two most indebted countries in the world in absolute and, especially, in relative terms. The most developed countries have been involved in consolidating the debts of these economies by facilitating favourable rescheduling, partial interest rate fixation, partial write-offs, or freezing of both the principal and the interest repayment. Also, judging by financial flows, these economies have high FDI inflows, that is, their access to the international capital market is far easier than that of less indebted economies, such as Croatia.

Nevertheless, a sensible national economic policy will avoid all extreme situations. It is a commonly known fact that Poland's high debt at the end of the 1980s was the key factor of instability and, in part, a cause of the transition process. It is also a fact that low or zero external indebtedness can be a factor of internal instability. This is the case with Romania, whose economy almost totally eliminated external debt at the cost of falling into recession and a drastic decline in living standards during the 1980s. All this increased the internal tensions to the point that Romania was the only Eastern European country where democracy was brought in by violent dismantling of the old regime and not through elections, as was the case in other transitional economies. Bearing in mind these historical and practical experiences, it is realistic to observe foreign debt in its developmental function.

Eastern Europe met democratic changes and economic transition with a foreign debt of approximately US$100 billion. During the 1990s, a slower but still continuous growth of foreign debt in the region as a whole is noticeable, so that in 1994 it reached approximately US$106.5 billion, which is close to a US$1000 debt per capita (see Table 8.2).

Insight into the intraregional structure of foreign debt mirrors both the intensive preparations for the transition in the mid-1980s and a gradual differentiation of CETE-4 and SETE-8. At the beginning of an intensive debt growth in the second half of the 1970s, the two groups could be identified according to loan-taking dynamics. It is clearly perceptible that CETE-4 debt grew faster than the average, as it increased 20 times, while SETE-8 debt increased only seven to nine times. In the 1980–85 period of stagnation in

Table 8.2   Gross debt of the transitional economies,   US$ billions

	1990	1991	1992	1993	1994
Albania	0.3	0.5	0.6	0.8	0.8
Bulgaria	10.4	11.9	13.0	13.2	11.0
Croatia	2.5	2.5	2.5	2.5	2.7
Czech Republic	4.4	7.5	7.5	8.5	9.3
Hungary	21.3	22.7	21.4	24.6	28.5
Poland	48.5	48.4	47.1	47.2	41.9
Romania	1.2	2.2	3.5	4.2	5.0
Slovak Republic	2.0	2.6	2.8	3.6	4.2
Slovenia	1.9	1.9	1.7	1.9	2.2
Macedonia FRY	0.5	0.4	0.7	0.9	0.9
Eastern Europe	93.0	100.6	100.8	107.4	106.5

Source: UNECE (1995), *Economic Bulletin for Europe*, Geneva.

debt growth, there is no recognizable difference between these two groups. Although Hungary and Poland continued recording a steady debt growth, we cannot speak about a uniform upward trend since what was Czechoslovakia saw a fall in loan taking during the same period. However, in the 1985–90 period, significant differences in the position of these two groups of countries can be noted. CETE-4 countries doubled their already high external debts, while SETE-8 countries, with the exception of Bulgaria, kept decreasing their external indebtedness. For example, Romania entered the transition with almost no foreign debts.

If we take into consideration the said tendency of stagnating or falling GDP in Eastern Europe during the 1980–90 period, it is evident that SETE-8 countries, including Croatia, entered the transition under additional increased economic pressure of debt repayment at the expense of domestic spending, a falling standard of living, and stagnation and regression in the development.

After 1990, the general transition to democracy in Eastern Europe did not bring any significant changes to intraregional relations. CETE-4 continue to occupy the attention of western investors by increasing external debts, while SETE-8 are experiencing no prosperity in relation to the position they have been in during the last 25 years. There are exceptions on both sides, where Poland succeeded in reducing and Romania in increasing their external debts. To explain this we have to be aware that in Poland's case what happened is due to the old debt relief rather than the boost in internal efforts towards reducing the debt. Romania, on the other hand, entered the transition without external debt and reached significant indebtedness in transition, although it is still not so high as to seriously burden the national economy.

The level of indebtedness per capita has similar trends. If we compare the years 1985 and 1995, a relatively high indebtedness of CETA-4 countries is manifest. In 1985, the debt per capita was US$800 in Poland and US$1400 in Hungary, and this increased in 1995, to over US$1000 and US$2700, respectively. On the other hand, SETE-8 countries, with the exception of Bulgaria, recorded a per capita foreign debt between US$300 and 800 in 1985, which fell to US$200–500 in 1995.

The level of the debt is also measurable by relating the GDP to it. Still, because of the different methodologies used in calculating the GDP, especially international comparisons based on purchasing power indicators (PPI) on the one hand, and on the official exchange rate on the other, this indicator seems to be rather ambiguous. In such a situation, a more appropriate indicator of the level of indebtedness would be the level of debt per employed person. However, the first step in the process of restructuring transitional economies regularly has the greatest impact on the employment rate, which means that not even this indicator can give a realistic picture. Therefore, at this stage of transition, indebtedness per capita seems to be the most stable indicator of the strength of the economy and its capacity to comply with international commitments.

CONFLICTING INVESTMENT AIMS

Analytical indicators undoubtedly point to the conclusion that there is a basic difference in the expectations of Eastern Europe and the intentions of Western Europe with regard to investments in transitional economies. It seems that, following a long economic stagnation in the 1980s and the upsurge of democracy in the 1990s, Eastern Europe expected foreign investments to give a boost to their exhausted economies and lead them to the road to prosperity. Contrary to this, western countries probably expected eastern countries to undergo market and all-embracing changes in order to create a favourable economic environment, including legal regulations and market pricing of factors in order to make this area globally competitive.

A deeply disappointing or lacking external investment support to the transition is partly caused by the differences between the economic philosophy which has prevailed in the east for a long time and economic standards of the west. In the east we could see that the economic philosophy has gradually been reduced to ensuring high growth rates. Such a reduced model had a starting point in the relative scarcity of factors, or in a relative abundance of the available labour force and a shortage of capital. The increase of saving, that is investment in fixed capital, produced the growth rate as a relation between the investment rate and the marginal capital–output ratio. The maximum saving rate, and the high capital investments rate based on it, was the basic instrument of economic policy. The sources of saving were based on the low standard of living of the country's population at the beginning, and later on foreign capital. With such a growth model the primary aim is achievement of the desired growth rate, and efficiency or investment profitability is the secondary aim. In a nutshell, the model relied on investing in the factor which was scarce (the capital) in order to employ the factor which was abundant (the labour force). Thus maximum growth was achieved via full employment. Eventually, this led to artificial shortage and hidden unemployment, and so to an unrealistic cost of this factor.

Contrary to this, western economic philosophy is based on the principle of economic efficiency. By way of market evaluation of factors, that is market prices, this principle imposes the use of abundant factors, and that is the labour force in the case of transitional economies. Thus the real cost of labour results in optimal economic structure and a corresponding savings and investment rate. We can see that here the real cost of the abundant factor (the labour force) is used to attract the scarce factor (the capital) in the form of foreign investments. Studies show that only a few transitional economies have managed to embark on this preferred route towards market transformation. Those are economies, like the Czech Republic, where foreign investment inflows were transformed primarily into the restructuring of industrial corporations (Zemplinerova, 1996, p. 18). Thus over 50 per cent of FDI is concentrated in large foreign investments: Volkswagen, Philip Morris, Nestlé, Linde and TelSource. These five major projects have had a key impact on the successful restructuring of the Czech economy.

OPTIMIZATION OF CROATIAN EXPECTATIONS

Foreign investment inflows are the basis of the official Croatian development policy. All official documents of the Croatian government are directed towards Croatia joining the world market and attracting foreign investments. However, foreign investment inflows are hindered by the regulation of investment policy execution for at least two reasons. Primarily, the legal procedure lacks transparency: the realization of foreign investments in Croatia is regulated by about 20 legal acts, which in principle discourage potential investors (Jurković, 1994, p. 9). The second reason is the policy of limited foreign investments in the real estate sector and forcing reciprocity in the financial sector, for example, which facilitates direct or indirect preference for Croatian investors. Even in Hungary, where most foreign investments were attracted, the preference for domestic investors is considered to be one of the key reasons for the slowing down of foreign investment inflows (Hunya, 1996, p. 9).

Since the key condition for investment inflow was the stabilization of economic trends and privatization, Croatia has successfully implemented an anti-inflation programme despite great war losses and damages. The macro-economic aggregates have been stabilized with the country's own efforts, and the stabilization policy in particular gave exceptionally good results in the general price level by transforming the hyperinflation into a stable currency situation with full internal and partially external convertibility in a very short period. The inflationary financing of public spending, as the prime source of inflation, was interrupted and the balance of payments was stabilized (Škreb, 1995).

Having fulfilled the basic goals of macroeconomic stabilization as the principal condition for joining the international capital market, the war-ridden and high-stabilization cost-weary Croatia expected foreign investment inflows as its chief incentive for boosting economic activity. Let us for the moment set aside the need to discuss the realism of the possible contribution of foreign investments to privatization and through that to the optimal alloca-tion of resources of the former planned economies. Even in highly developed market economies, the privatization process has not yet fulfilled its key task, which is to facilitate the competition of bidders by deregulation, that is market fixing of real prices, as was intended with the CEGB (Central Elec-tricity Generating Board) in Great Britain.

The fundamental need for foreign capital as the economic activity booster is probably partially the cause of the drastic differences in the statistical records of the private investment inflows into Croatia. Great expectations have prompted various official institutions to record foreign investments dif-ferently, that is to present foreign investors' intentions as the real capital inflow. In addition, owing to different roles of various governmental institu-tions, the record and data collecting forms differ. Thus, for example, the Croatian Ministry of Economics approved (up to 1995) and recorded all contracts on joint ventures or foreign investments, which means that statistics show all contracted deals, regardless of whether the joint ventures were really effectuated. In contrast to this, BOP statistics record the real financial flows, that is only the real financial transactions. Still the BOP statistics do not record the part of foreign investments in kind, which are given in the external trade balance statistics. Therefore it is evident that certain differences in presenting the total FDI referring to the source of reporting dates may appear with almost all countries in transition. In the case of Croatia, what cannot be completely accounted for is the excessive discrepancy in the data coming from various sources. In the 1992–4 period, the Croatian Ministry of

Economics recorded a total of US$ 1 billion worth of private foreign invest-
ments (FDI) in Croatia. The FDI cumulative according to BOP statistics in
the same period amounts to approximately US$200 million (see Table 8.3).

Table 8.3   Inflows of FDI in Croatia 1992–5 US$ millions

Institution	1992	1993	1994	1995
Ministry of economics	412	317	273	—
Croatian privatization fund	103	93	123	82
Croatian central bank	17	56	72	63

Source: Calculated by the author based on the official statistics.

Another reason for this discrepancy of FDI recorded in the different official
institutions is that the Croatian Privatization Fund, for example, treats investments from the other republics of former Yugoslavia inappropriately. A typical example is the INGRA (an international construction company from
Croatia) which was turned into a joint stock company with 357 stockholders,
some of whom are from Bosnia and Herzegovina or from Macedonia FRY.
Some stockholders have sold their shares and some have kept them. The
Croatian Privatization Fund treats the latter stockholders as foreign investors
in spite of the fact that there has been no actual inflow of investments (Marin,
1996, p. 12).

We believe that a much more serious reason for these discrepancies could
be the sophisticated fiscal evasion of domestic entrepreneurs. This notion is
supported by the fact that a large share of FDI is channelled towards smaller
mixed joint stock companies, and that the greatest share of investments is
those in kind. This makes it possible to achieve two aims: investment in kind
may mean imports of cars, office equipment and so on as a means of fiscal
evasion for smaller companies. Profit gains which can be repatriated are
treated according to more favourable fiscal regulations, especially when reinvested. The domestic entrepreneur who starts an off-shore company can
also become his/her own 'partner' in the country by achieving duty and fiscal
evasions and by exporting instead of importing capital. Such a rent-seeking
business strategy is achieved more effortlessly in smaller companies because
of lower costs. Empirical studies in Croatia indicate that such practices of
joint ventures are quite widespread, which is reflected in FDI statistics as the
intention recorded by the Ministry of Economics, but not as a real inflow of
capital which should be registered in BOP statistics. The imperfection of the
privatization model in large companies can also turn a foreign investor into a
rent seeker. Thus, for example, one of the largest foreign investments in

Croatia is the purchase of a 49 per cent share of the Nikola Tesla national electronic company by the Swedish multinational corporation Ericsson for approximately US$40 million. This sum will be registered by the Croatian Privatisation Fund as foreign investment. But in reality the Swedes will invest US$25–30 million in equipment and know-how, that is, in kind. The remaining sume will be paid through Ericsson's procurement of the tele-communication equipment for the state-owned HPT (Croatian Postal and Telecommunication Company). Thus BOP statistics will register zero foreign investment inflow referring to the largest foreign investment in Croatia in 1995. Only the current transactions will show an outflow based on HPT payments for the imports as well as outflow of repatriated profits if they are not reinvested.

Nevertheless, the difficulties and problems with efficient regulation that would stimulate foreign investors, and not discourage them, only increase the need for a more accelerated and more relevant approach that Croatia should adopt on the international investment market. Croatian expectations from FDI are influenced by exogenous and endogenous forces whose balance influences the stability of economic trends. The former refers to the inad-equate subregional position of the Croatian economy on the international investment market, while the latter refers to the suboptimal post-transitional changes in Croatian economic structure.

The exogenous placing of the Croatian economy into the SETE-8 subregion does not comply with real development level indicators and structure of the Croatian economy, neither does it suit Croatian economic and other interests. The key indicators locate Croatian economy far closer to the Vishygrad group (CETE-4). Croatia even entered the market transformation process with an advantage concerning the progress of the ingredients of the free market economy over almost all Eastern European economies. Undoubtedly, the Greater Serbian aggression in Croatia, numerous human losses and vast property and infrastructure destruction have reduced the efficiency of the market transformation of the Croatian economy, but regardless of the war losses and destruction according to economic criteria, the Croatian econ-omy's performance places the country much closer to the Central European than to the Southern European group of countries. Therefore it is clear that the positioning of Croatia in the SETE-8 group of countries is based on non-economic reasons.

It will therefore be necessary to deal with the position which is contrary to the nation's desires, which does not make it less realistic. The level of FDI in CETE-4 varies between US$100 per capita in the Slovak Republic and US$700 per capita in Hungary. In contrast to this, and excluding Slovenia, the level of FDI in 1994 fluctuated between US$3 per capita in Macedonia FRY and US$36 per capita in Albania. With an FDI of US$22 per capita, Croatia falls in the middle of the described subregional dispersion of foreign investments. The strategy for attracting foreign investments into Croatia ought to be built up around these relatively unfavourable facts, instead of ignoring them.

As for the endogenous factors, it is worth mentioning that the foreign investments inflow has a dimension that is often overlooked, and that is the national economy's capacity to absorb efficiently the swollen inflow of foreign investments and turn them into profitable ones. Although there are no reliable instruments to measure absorption capacity, it can be evaluated indirectly by average maturity period, tendencies in the rate of return and so on. Another indicator of the absorption capacity is the degree of market transformation of the individual economic sectors. Market transformation can be measured by the level of privatization in each sector. Taking structural differences within the economy into consideration, the higher level of privatization is a strong indicator of greater market efficiency of individual industries, that is of their greater investment absorption capacity.

According to this criterion, the greatest prospects lie in investing in housing and utility industries, finance, and tourist and catering industries (see Table 8.4). Agriculture is not mentioned here, even though its level of privatization is over 50 per cent, because this is not a result of the transition but of earlier land reforms. Only by completing the privatization of the former state-owned so-called 'agricultural combines' will it be possible to evaluate realistically the market transformation in agriculture. The degree of privatization as an indicator of FDI absorption capacity is (also) restricted by limitations in

Table 8.4   Sectoral dispersion of private ownership in Croatia

Sectors	Ownership			
	State	Private	Cooperative	Mixed
Mining and industry	82.7	7.8	0.0	5.0
Agriculture and fisheries	37.9	52.5	4.1	5.5
Forestry	99.6	0.4	—	—
Water management	100.0	—	—	—
Construction	47.0	27.8	3.4	21.8
Transport and communication	88.9	7.7	0.4	3.0
Trade	49.0	43.9	1.5	5.6
Hotels, restaurants and tourism	71.0	24.3	0.1	4.6
Craft and trades	24.4	69.2	4.8	1.6
Housing, utilities and public services	94.5	47.0	—	0.8
Financial and other services	52.1	41.3	0.3	6.3
Education, culture and the arts	86.4	—	—	13.6
Health care and social services	100.0	—	—	—

Source: *Statistical Year Book*, Zagreb: CROSTAT (1994).

the market efficiency in individual industries, especially in the large infrastructure. Therefore dominant state ownership in traffic and telecommunication infrastructures is not a limiting factor for FDI, since the liberal concessions policy and state guarantees stimulate foreign investors. Consequently, most negotiations with foreign investors in Croatia revolve around the modernization of the old and construction of new roads, where mainly Italian, French and German investors would invest over US$2 billion in the principal road network.

The global financial flow structure, as a framework of every strategy including that of Croatia, suggests that private investment or joint ventures are the most dynamic category of international capital. As opposed to official investment, whose role is becoming less and less significant, private capital is what Croatian investment efforts should be aimed at. Primarily, this means that the international market does not accept mere preliminary projects for industrial or infrastructural investments. The potential private investors, as a first indicator of feasibility of a project, seek detailed concrete projects, clear ownership relations and land and structures that are fully prepared. Croatian entrepreneurs should enter the international financial market offering projects with detailed analyses of economic purpose and sound rates of return.

Secondly, for the Croatian economy to be competitive with the global economy, liberalization of property laws and of real estate sector is imminent. Since the real estate industry along with the finance industry is the second most dynamic factor in FDI, liberalization is all the more important.

Thirdly, by careful examination, Croatia should identify the specific interest and preparation of individual international market factors which will be offered large projects. Thus, for example, German and British investors will probably show most readiness to invest in tourism, the French will be prepared to invest in telecommunications and the electronic industry, and the Italians will be most likely to invest in road construction. Market evaluation of the geographic and road communications position is bound to identify the interest of the Pacific Basin economies in Croatia as the entry point of their efforts to penetrate the European market. Communication and market openness of the Croatian economy and the cosmopolitization of the economic activity is the key prerequisite for both fast development and preservation of national independence. For a small economy such as Croatia, openness to all is essential in order to harmonize the different interests of various international capital sources through careful sectoral and spatial location of investments, preventing the domination of any of them over the national economy in the process. Therefore a sensible national strategy should optimize foreign interests and national requirements.

REFERENCES

Hunya, G. (1996), 'Foreign Direct Investment in Hungary: A Key Element of Macro-economic Modernization', *Vienna Institute Monthly Report*, (226).

Jurković, P. (ed.) (1994), *Investment in Croatia*, Zagreb: Masmedia.

Kozul-Wright, Z. (1996), 'Enterprise Development and Catalytic Industrial Policy in Transitional Economies: The Case of Croatia', *Most*, **6**, (2), 11–12.

Marin, N. (1996), *BOP Statistics of FDI in Republic of Croatia*, Zagreb: National Bank of Croatia.

Škreb, M. (1995), *Recent Macroeconomic Developments and Financial Sector Changes in Croatia*, Zagreb: National Bank of Croatia.

UNECE (1995), *Economic Survey of Europe 1994–1995*, Geneva. p. 136.

UNECE (1995), *Economic Bulletin for Europe*, Geneva, (47), p. 158.

World Bank (1996), *World Development Report 1996*, Washington, DC. p. 136.

Zemplinerova, A. (1996), 'The Role of Foreign Enterprises in Czech Economy', *Vienna Institute Monthly Report*, (226).

9. Technological integration and global marginalization of Central and East European economies: the role of FDI and alliances

Slavo Radošević and David Dyker

It is still too early to attempt to give any kind of overall assessment of the impact of foreign direct investment (FDI) on the transition economies of Central and Eastern Europe (CEE) and the former Soviet Union (FSU). General levels of FDI into the region have been modest (see Tables 9.1. and 9.2). Perhaps partly for that reason, no clear pattern of correlation between levels of FDI into particular countries and levels of economic performance by country has emerged. Hungary, in particular, stands out as a country with a relatively very high level of FDI and a rather moderate level of economic

Table 9.1   Total and per capita FDI in selected countries in US$ (estimated inflows for 1995 and stocks, end 1995)

Countries	Inflows		Stocks	
	Total (millions)	Per capita	Total (millions)	Per capita
Czech Rep.	2 500	242	5 900	571
Hungary	4 000	392	12 700	1 245
Poland	2 500	65	600	176
Slovak Republic	140	26	700	131
Slovenia	150	75	100	754
Bulgaria	130	15	600	71
Romania	310	14	1 600	70
Russia	1 600	11	5 000	34
China	35 500	30	131 500	110

Source: Hunya (1996a, p. 4).

Table 9.2   Number of FDI projects (flow)

Countries	1989	1990	1991	1992	1993	1994
Hungary	—	—	5 642	4 101	4 286	4 331
Poland	—	1 216	3 151	5 335	5 157	4 570
Slovak Republic	—	—	—	—	2 318	2 064
Slovenia	174	616	491	1 490	485	—
Bulgaria	—	—	—	817	1 097	1 021
Romania	—	—	6 368	12 780	8 457	13 986
Russia	—	1 529	2 022	3 552	7 989	—
Ukraine	—	—	400	2 000	2 800	—

Source: Hunya (1996a, p. 11); for Russia and Ukraine, Jermakowicz (1994, p.7).

performance, while in Poland, one of the top-performing transition countries, levels of FDI have only recently started to pick up from relatively low levels.

But there is a clear upward trend in FDI in the region as a whole, and it is striking that, in Russia, where in the 1990s the perception of medium-term political risk has changed considerably, FDI doubled between 1994 and 1995. All of this is at least consistent with the *a priori* case that FDI will tend to improve economic performance in the host country, which can be argued on the following grounds:

1. It will increase the aggregate rate of investment.
2. It will generate transfers of 'hard' technology.
3. It will generate transfers of 'soft' managerial technology.
4. It will tend to induce patterns of networking and subcontracting with other firms in the host country which are conducive to a general increase in levels of technology and productivity.
5. It will generally help the host economy to integrate into the global economy.

In this chapter we take a sceptical view of these *a priori* propositions and argue that the effects of FDI, and of the opening up to trade, on CEE and the FSU are more complex than is usually assumed. In particular, we question the implicit assumption that post-socialist economies, emerging from an extended period of isolation, will be able, more or less automatically, to engage in technological integration at the global level. By technological integration we understand a process whereby the given economies are assimilated into the dynamic learning patterns of international companies. Technological integration means that the host economies and their constituent firms are not just passive recipients, but rather active adapters and sources of technological knowledge. In the opposite case, where countries are technologically marginalized, their constituent firms are not in any significant degree involved in processes of technological accumulation at international level.

What are the conditions for effective technological integration through FDI? First, FDI effects technology transfer to the extent that countries have developed indigenous technological capabilities (ITC). The critical factor in the success of particular major pieces of FDI, or the subcontracting ramifications thereof, is always the domestic environment in the host economy (Bell, 1996). Chain-reaction technological upgrading consequent on FDI will only occur if domestic firms are prepared to make the effort to raise their game. Effective assimilation of major elements of foreign technology is crucially dependent on the existence of congenial market structures in host countries. It is for that reason that FDI-led growth is very rare, and that FDI pulled along by indigenously generated growth is much more common.[1]

Second, the structure and pattern of FDI inflows are the result of a complex interaction between the corporate strategies of domestic and foreign companies, as moulded through government policies. It is for that reason that it is difficult to explain the huge variations in FDI inflow between the FSU and CEE countries, and indeed between individual CEE countries, purely on the basis of factor endowment differences. Put another way, international firms will undertake far-reaching investments in developing or transition countries only where they believe they can impose their 'soft' management technology comprehensively, so that they can keep control of productivity, and where they believe the local environment will support them in that task. If these conditions are not met, there will simply be no basis for the kind of FDI that can produce technological integration.

Third, technological integration can only take place if the general pattern of globalization reaches beyond a certain critical level. Standard liberalization packages tend to integrate transition economies very strongly at the level of shallow integration (trade and finance), but do not necessarily integrate them at the level of production networks, let alone at that of technological networks (deep integration). In practice there can be no technological integration without deep integration at the level of production networks.

There is every reason, therefore, to be sceptical of any assertion that FDI is a sufficient condition of technological integration. There is, furthermore, plenty of evidence to suggest that FDI is not even a necessary condition of such integration. There is, for instance, plenty of evidence of effective technological integration of software firms in transition countries through forms of cooperation with international firms that do not involve FDI as such (Dyker, 1996). There is, indeed, a whole gamut of (sometimes overlapping) forms of international business cooperation, running from classic FDI through subcontracting to strategic alliances, all of which may – or may not – provide the necessary conditions for technological integration. In this chapter we concentrate on two of these, FDI, as such, and alliances. Specifically, we pose three questions:

1. Are alliances in CEE countries only a step forward towards FDI, or are they essentially different from FDI?
2. What technological capabilities are transferred through FDI and alliances?
3. In what ways can FDI and alliances integrate – or marginalize – CEE economies *vis-à-vis* the global economy? More specifically, how can intra-firm productivity improvements be transformed into intrasectoral productivity improvements?

Before proceeding, it is necessary to clarify the notions of FDI and strategic alliances as used in the chapter. FDI is defined in terms of those investments which are made with a view to acquiring a lasting interest in a foreign enterprise, and of having an effective voice in its management.[2] In the case of the CEE and FSU countries, it is important to distinguish between greenfield FDI, on the one hand, and indirect acquisitions (joint ventures) and direct acquisitions (majority stakes through privatization) on the other. Alliances or collaborative agreements are defined in terms of the establishment of common interests between independent industrial partners (that is, partners not connected through majority share holding) (Hagedoorn, 1990).

ALLIANCES: TRANSITIONAL OR DISTINCTIVE FORMS IN THE CEE AND FSU COUNTRIES?

While international production (in the sense of intra-firm trade) is currently stagnating in relative terms (not, of course, in absolute terms), there is a growing trend towards sourcing through subcontracting, joint ventures and alliances, as organizational forms for coordinating production internationally (see Radošević, 1996a). As FDI expands, so too does a whole range of different types of purchasing agreements. This tendency forms part of a shift in the direction of externalization of markets for intermediate products, and towards new organizational modes of international sourcing. One indicator of the process is the increasing importance of subcontracting (which will not be discussed here) and strategic alliances. Both developments reflect a trend towards non-equity-based trade and linking, going beyond the purely arm's length level, in east–west trade. Are minority ownership and non-equity forms of cooperation only transitory phase towards the acquisition of full control, or are they distinct forms where considerations other than outright control are predominant? In the case of the developed countries, both empirical research (see Hagedoorn and Sadowski, 1996) and theoretical inquiry (Chesnais, 1996) suggest that strategic technology alliances are not transitional phase towards mergers and acquisitions, but rather represent a distinct category.[3] Alliances as distinctive organizational forms may be based on what Chesnais calls relational economies – economies that cannot be achieved within a single company, but only within semi-integrated or network relationships.

In the case of the CEE and FSU countries, however, no testing has yet been done on any such hypothesis on the true nature of alliances. Lack of a systematic database, subcritical numbers of observations and still relatively short-time series, are obvious problems for econometric testing. Our provisional hypothesis is that both aspects – alliances as transitional phase towards mergers and acquisitions and alliances as a distinctive form – may be present in this particular case. In order further to clarify that proposition, it is necessary first to look back at the different forms of technology transfer that may be operational in CEE and FSU countries, and the factors which have conditioned them.

Diversification of Technology Transfer Forms

The opening up of previously closed economies clearly changes the patterns and modes whereby these economies are integrated into the global economy. In the past, the CMEA countries were linked into the world economy predominantly through trade, with the import of equipment and licences serving as the main vehicle of technology transfer. Now the whole gamut of mechanisms available to the open economy is at their disposal. Simple trade, FDI and the various forms of minority equity or non-equity type of relationship are all now possible as vehicles for technology transfer (see Table 9.3). Three

Table 9.3   Technology transfer channels before and after 1989

Before 1989	After 1989
Import of equipment	FDI
Licences	Alliances (including joint ventures)
Joint ventures (only from 1988)	Import of equipment
	Subcontracting
	Licences

Source: Radošević (1996b).

phases can be discerned regarding the relationship between FDI and alliances within this general context.

In the first phase, before, and at the early stage of, transition, foreign investors concentrated on joint ventures (JVs). It is estimated that over the period 1988–90 the number of JVs in CMEA countries rose from 383 to over 10 000 (see Table 9.4). In practice, this was very much a transitional phase, and many of these JVs were transformed into direct investments after 1989.

In the current, second, phase, FDI is the preferred mode of entry. From 1990, the importance of FDI has grown sharply in all post-socialist countries. But while minority shareholdings (joint ventures, minority acquisitions) have diminished in importance, they still make up a significant proportion of total foreign business involvement in the CEE countries, and indeed still dominate in Russia.

Table 9.4   Joint ventures in Central and Eastern Europe and the FSU

	No. of Jvs in 1987	1 Jan 1988	1 Jan 1989	1 Jan 1990	1 March 1990	1 July 1990	31 Dec 1990
Hungary	11	102	270	1 000	1 000	1 600	5 000
Poland	38	13	55	918	1 000	1 550	2 400
Czechoslovakia	16	7	16	60	60	60	n/a
Bulgaria	9	15	25	30	30	30	n/a
Romania	23	5	5	5	5	5	n/a
USSR	286	23	291	1 261	1 480	1 734	2 800
Total	383	165	662	3 274	3 575	4 979	Over 10 000

Source: Dunning, J. (1991), *The Prospects for Foreign Direct Investment in Eastern Europe*, Discussion Papers in International Investment and Business Studies, No 155, University of Reading.

The Hungarian pattern is, perhaps, typical. In that country, in 1990, 62 per cent of FDI capital was placed in minority-owned foreign investment enterprises (FIEs). By 1991, however, only 34 per cent of cumulative total foreign capital was placed in minority companies, and by 1993 only 25.5 per cent (Hunya, 1996b). In Russia the share of joint ventures in the total number of FIEs decreased from 95.7 per cent in 1992 to 55.4 per cent in 1995 (Astapovich, 1995). It is only in the telecommunications sector that foreign minority shares are still the rule, as a function of the enormous volumes of investment involved and, in some cases, the political complications surrounding a basic infrastructural element. Even here, however, the situation may change significantly, indeed is already changing in some countries. In Hungary, for example, foreign partners which initially controlled just 27 per cent of Matav, the national telecommunications company, obtained majority control in 1995.

In general, the data indicate a decrease in the importance of joint ventures as a form of foreign involvement, on account of general liberalization which allows for direct acquisitions, greenfield investment with 100 per cent foreign ownership and other, more advanced, forms of intercorporate cooperation.

In the coming, third phase, further increases in the weight of non-equity forms and minority shareholdings are to be expected, as the transition economies recover and start to grow steadily, and as domestic firms start to 'go global'.[4] An exclusively FDI-based scenario is, therefore, unlikely.[5] Worldwide experience indicates that, when the process of 'catching up' is accompanied by FDI, direct investments are usually complemented by strategic alliances, including technological alliances. Certainly, technological alliances are less in evidence among developing countries (see Hagedoorn and Freeman, 1994). Even here, however, there is evidence of an upward trend in the most recent period (see Vonortas and Safioleas, 1996). Among the developing countries, it is the group of highly dynamic Asian economies such as Hong Kong, Taiwan, South Korea and Malaysia that show the biggest concentrations of alliances. This suggests that technological alliances as a distinctive form of inter-company cooperation will become a specific feature of the CEE and FSU economies only as recovery speeds up and technological catching up begins.

Data from the Strategic Alliances in Information Technologies database (ITSA) (see Table 9.5) do, in fact, indicate that the number of strategic technology alliances in the IT sector in FSU countries is the highest among the groups of developing countries (including the economies in transition), at least up to 1994. The number of alliances (294) formed by FSU countries (in practice mainly by Russia) in the period 1989–94, is higher than for China, Hong Kong or South Korea. While the comparison with countries like Hong Kong and Korea may be misleading, in view of the small size of those economies, that with fast-growing China is really quite startling. There is obviously a need for further investigation into the true nature of strategic alliances in the Russian case. Two plausible *a priori* explanations suggest themselves. First, alliances in Russia could be very much transitional phenomena, ploys to circumvent restrictions on mergers and acquisitions imposed in an attempt to control insider privatization. Alternately, the high number of IT alliances could simply reflect unexploited opportunities for science and technology cooperation, in an area where the human capital resources of Russia – and indeed of a number of other transition economies – are substantial. Case study material from the software sector would tend to corroborate this latter thesis, with licensing and franchising agreements with international companies furnishing software firms in transition countries with

Table 9.5   Strategic alliances in information technology, 1984–94*

FSU	294	China	270
Hungary	80	Hong Kong	247
Poland	77	South Korea	239
Czechoslovakia	47	Taiwan	179
Bulgaria	20	Mexico	165
Romania	13	Singapore	158
Albania	1	India	105
		Israel	105
		Brazil	80
		Thailand	74
		Malaysia	60
		L. America	45

Note: *   Based on the IT Strategic Alliance (ITSA) database, which records publicly announced inter-firm strategic alliances in IT worldwide. All alliances that include at least one firm from the developed OECD countries are covered.

Source: Vonortas and Safioleas (1996).

a springboard for technological dynamism, which the latter are then able to exploit as a basis for integrating back into the global system which provided the licences and franchises in the first place, ultimately generating a process of two-way technology transfer (see Dyker, 1996). All of this lends support to the argument that alliances can be considered as a distinctive form.

TECHNOLOGY TRANSFER THROUGH FDI AND ALLIANCES

FDI and alliances involving CEE and FSU countries aim to exploit the existing factor endowments and cumulated capabilities of these economies, as well as to compensate for their weaknesses by bringing in competencies which are otherwise lacking. FDI usually involves complete packages of skills, finance and organization, while technology alliances are normally based on complementarities between partners. In order to understand the real content of technology transfer within FDI and alliances, it is necessary to take into account the specific competence profile that firms have inherited from the centrally planned system. Table 9.6 indicates how that competence profile changes in the post-socialist period.

Table 9.6   The changing competence profile of enterprises in post-socialist economies

Centrally planned system	Post-socialist economy
Production know-how, technical complexity, cost- and user-insensitive	Marketing, finance, organization, system integration at product level, network building at firm level, cost-driven

Source: Radošević (1996b).

Swaan's empirical research on the Hungarian economy (1995) produced similar conclusions. Swaan found that the group of capabilities in which the Hungarian economy can be considered (very) strong involve either a high level of definable, transferable knowledge (high level of education) or types of tacit knowledge which are not related to commercial application and marketing (abundance of qualified engineers and skilled labour). The aspects in which the Hungarian economy is weak are all related to complex organizational capabilities involving a high degree of market-related tacit knowledge and complex (inter)organizational cooperation, capabilities without which it is not possible to control the effectiveness of strategies, the time required for product development and marketing, the implementation of total quality management and the general level of technology and R&D.

In a system where the top-down, linear innovation model was totally dominant, we would expect that research and design capabilities would be relatively better developed than capabilities relating to process improvements, networks and the organization of distribution. In market conditions, learning from the marketing side becomes all-important, while technical complexity per se is no longer an issue. This is especially important for FSU and CEE economies, which at present mainly export products for which demand is saturated, and where collective brands and dislocated distribution are the norm. Significantly, empirical research shows that downstream activities are precisely the area where restructuring is most intensive. In 96.4 per cent of cases of post-acquisition activities in Poland, for example, the reorganization of marketing activities has taken first priority, followed by the introduction of new production programmes (see Jermakowicz, 1994).

Taking into account the high degree of imbalance in the distribution of R&D, production and marketing competencies, alliances in post-socialist economies can be classified, following our earlier analysis, into three distinctive types: R&D alliances, production alliances and marketing alliances[6] (see Table 9.7).

Table 9.7   A taxonomy of alliances

	R&D alliances	Production alliances	Marketing alliances
Areas of technology cooperation	Research Software development Design	Process improvements Quality control Packaging	Distribution and marketing of partners' products Franchising

Source: Radošević (1996).

In the case of R&D alliances, we would expect to find strong complementarities between partners founded on the developed research base inherited from the old system. In the case of production and marketing alliances this may not necessarily be the case. This suggests that R&D alliances are a distinctive form, while production and especially marketing alliances are transitional forms towards mergers and acquisitions. In countries where privatization into foreign ownership is already at an advanced level, much of FDI is motivated by the quest for access to distribution channels. That again suggests that alliances in such cases are temporary solutions, pending full takeover. In countries with mass privatization schemes (the Czech Republic, Russia and Lithuania) marketing alliances are, after all, the only way to acquire (at least a degree of) control over distribution channels.

Production alliances seem to be the rarest form of alliance, presumably on account of a general lack of complementarities here and the problems involved in radical 'turnaround' of domestic enterprises. (The exception is production-sharing agreements, which are, however, confined to the Russian oil and gas sectors. Technological complementarities are an important consideration in these agreements, but are nevertheless secondary to the negotiation of specific legal constraints in relation to privatization.[7]) In the case of large investments in the production and services spheres, joint ventures as transitional forms and wholly foreign-owned subsidiaries (these are as a rule new enterprises) have proved much more attractive to foreign investors, particularly in the motor vehicle and paper industries, construction and tourist/travel and financial services (UNECE, 1995, p.13).

It is our guess that mutual technological exchange is present in the case of R&D alliances, and is much less frequent in the case of production alliances. In the case of marketing alliances, technology transfer does take place, but is unidirectional and generally motivated by the prospect of full takeover.

TECHNOLOGICAL INTEGRATION OR MARGINALIZATION?

'Deep Integration' Issues

The CEE and FSU economies are now within reach of global or regional companies whose business strategies are governed by considerations of global competitiveness.[8] How the CEE and FSU economies will integrate into the global economy will depend, not only on the extent of trade and financial liberalization (shallow integration), but also on the degree to which they integrate at the level of international production and technology networks (deep integration) (UNCE, 1995). The positions that domestic subsidiaries occupy within international production networks will to a significant extent determine the extent of technology inflows. The higher the technological position of the affiliate, the greater are technology inflows likely to be. Technological integration into the world economy will depend crucially on whether FDI is integrated into the respective national economies, and whether alliances, as distinctive vehicles of technology transfer, will spread. Specifically with regard to FDI, the critical question is whether individual direct investments will remain isolated enclaves, with technology inflows and modernization confined to the level of intra-firm productivity improvements, or spread into the larger environment through the development of local supplier linkages and through movement towards higher value-added activities.

Initial Patterns of 'Deep Integration'

In Radošević (1996c) we analysed the initial patterns of 'deep integration' in FSU and CEE countries through typical examples of FDI and sourcing factory types. Scattered evidence at the micro level shows that almost every type of factory exists in the post-socialist economies, with the exception of outposts, world product mandate factories and miniature replicas (see Table 9.8).

The Interface between FDI, Trade and Technology

FDI, trade, finance and technology transfer are increasingly interlinked in the world economy (Hatzichronoglou, 1996). FDI accounts for disproportionately high shares of exports and imports in the transition countries, notably in the case of Hungary, where FIEs are responsible for 50 per cent of export sales (see Table 9.9). In a very real sense, then, FIEs are the main agents of deepening and extension of the trade of the CEE and FSU economies. Of course, the effects of this on the balance of payments are not always positive, and in the early phases of transition foreign direct investments were a net

Table 9.8 Typology of FDI and sourcing factory types, with typical examples from transitional economies*

Enterprises	The direction of technological deepening		
Resource-based	*Extractors* Oil and gas industry in Russia, Kazakhstan and Azerbaijan Gold and diamond ventures in Kazakhstan Wood industry in Estonia	*Processors* Food-processing industry in Central Europe	*Focused factories* Car industry in CEE *World product mandate* ?
Cost-reducing	*Offshore* Clothing industry in Poland Furniture industry in Poland	*Source factories* Car industry in CEE	
R&D-driven	*Outpost companies* ?	*R&D subcontracting* A few Russian institutes	*High-tech joint ventures* Russian ventures in aerospace and aviation
Domestic market-driven	*Importers* Trading companies	*Local servers* Telecom investments in EIT; Ford investment in Poland	*Miniature replica* ?

Notes: *   Resource-based, cost-based and R&D-driven = predominantly foreign market-oriented.

Source: Radošević (1996b).

Table 9.9   Share of foreign investment enterprises in the total economy, in 1993/94 (per cent)*

	Czech Rep. 1994	Hungary 1993	Slovak Rep. 1994
Nominal capital	7.4	26.6	5
Employed persons	6	20.1	3.8
Output	9.4	30.9	7.7**
Export sales	n.a.	50	n.a.
Investment	16.5	34	11.8

Notes:
* Czech companies with at least 25 employees; Hungarian companies filing tax returns; Slovak Republic non-financial corporations with at least 25 employees.
** Value added.

Source: Hunya (1996b).

burden on the Hungarian trade balance. Thus the trade extension and trade deepening aspect of FDI raises serious issues in terms of the value-added content of FDI, and the degree of integration of FDI into the domestic economy. From our perspective, the critical point is that in deepening trade FDI does not necessarily deepen technological value-added.

Intra-firm Productivity Improvements

The primary effects of (successful) FDI are in terms of increasing productivity and efficiency in the acquired companies (intra-firm productivity improvements) – not surprisingly, given the relatively higher share of investment and R&D in the typical foreign direct investment, as compared to domestic enterprises (see Table 9.9). This is the conclusion that emerges from studies on developing countries as well as from the research that is going on in the case of post-socialist economies (see Hunya, 1996b, for the case of Hungary). But big intra-firm productivity improvements have not so far been accompanied by employment creation in the CEE and FSU countries. As Hunya (1996b) shows, the net employment effect of FDI in Hungary is only 33 000 jobs. In other CEE and FSU countries, employment in multinational corporations' (MNCs') subsidiaries is still quite nugatory. This strongly suggests that much of FDI bears an enclave-type character, with rather limited employment-generation effects and technological spillovers.

Intra-sectoral Productivity Improvements Through FDI?

This is an important but under-researched topic for developing countries in general, and for transition countries in particular. Where (potential) improvements are represented simply as spillovers, the real content of the technology and capabilities transferred from foreign to domestic enterprises remains unclear. The majority of the studies that have been tried to pin down the notion of spillover emphasize the importance of competition, which is strengthened by foreign presence and which induces intensive processes of intra-firm learning and learning through demonstration effects. A second mechanism for spreading productivity improvements works through labour mobility from affiliates to entirely local companies. The experiences of developing countries in this respect have been rather divergent.[9] What is clear is that spillovers are weaker in the case of green fields than in that of acquisitions, because green fields are erected *ab novo* while acquisitions bring with them their inherited network of suppliers and customers. In the case of Central and Eastern Europe, the share of greenfield FDI has risen from 2.6 per cent in 1988 to 36.1 per cent in 1993 (Jermakowicz, 1994. p. 14), which is strongly indicative of an enclave pattern of development, with only weak ramifications beyond the initial investment. The enclave syndrome is, indeed, already acute in the Hungarian economy, and this pattern will probably be followed in other countries as the volume of foreign investments mounts. Closer integration into domestic economies is bound to emerge as a key concern for CEE and FSU governments.

In that context, the rise of alliances in the CEE and FSU countries, as distinctive rather than transitory forms, may be of some importance, to the extent that it indicates the existence of mutual technological complementarities and firm spillovers between the partners involved. While FDI may sometimes be an antidote to the disadvantages of the given domestic economic environment, alliances assume the existence of virtuous circles within that domestic environment, which makes positive effects on intrasectoral productivity more likely. The fact that domestic companies have the capability to become involved in alliance indicates the existence of a potential for higher productivity potential, right up to the intrasectoral level. That is as far as *a priori* analysis can take us, and we must wait for the results of systematic empirical investigation before making a final judgement. Still, the question must be posed: given that alliances may involve genuine technological integration, and given that the more general effects of FDI are, to say the least, problematic, is it not time to shift the balance of policy attention from FDI to alliances? Would it be better still to forget about the traditional system of classification of international business cooperation by type and focus on the essence, that is, the question of whether a given deal will, or will not, help the given economy to raise its economic game in the most general sense?

The main points to emerge from the foregoing are as follows.

- International business cooperation involving transition economies can take a wide range of forms. While the importance of some specific forms, in particular periods, such as joint ventures in the late communist/early transition period, can be explained in terms of the need to negotiate specific institutional and legal peculiarities, other specific developments, such as that of some types of strategic alliance, may be of a much more 'organic' nature.

- In concentrating on two key forms of international business cooperation – FDI and alliances – we have demonstrated how much easier it is to provide necessary than to provide sufficient conditions for 'deep integration'. Both FDI and alliances may generate such integration, but there is nothing in their organizational forms as such that guarantees that.

- The ever-present danger of marginalization is not a function of any specific organizational form. Thus both FDI and alliances are, in essence, 'organizationally neutral'. What matters, in both cases, is the content of the particular cooperation and the extent of its generalized ramifications, and it is on that that governments should concentrate in seeking to maximize the beneficial impact of foreign economic involvement on their own economies.

- This is a vast, and vastly under-researched area. Much of the relevant basic data series without which serious analysis – and serious policy making – are impossible remains to be collected.

NOTES

1. FDI moves into branches that have domestic or regional markets with relative stability or growth potential. They do not move into collapsing branches with shrinking markets. As Hunya (1996b, p. 24) puts it: 'Once market access is consolidated there remains little interest to make further investments if the targeted market is not growing.'
2. IMF, *Balance of Payments Manual*, 1993.
3. This proposition has not yet been tested in the case of production and marketing alliances. The probability is that these do not have distinctive features, and do, in fact, represent an essentially transitory form on the road to full control.
4. For a rare presentation of globalization of a central European firm (the Czech company Škoda at Plzen) see *Business Central Europe*, April 1996.
5. Vigorous growth in FDI is, nevertheless, expected. Projections by the Economist Intelligence Unit for the period up to the year 2000 indicate that the total stock of FDI by that year will be as follows: in Russia, US$ 27 billion; in Poland, US$ 22 billion; in the Czech

Republic, US$ 15.5 billion; and in Hungary, US$ 11 billion (*Business Central Europe*, April, 1996).
6. In practice it is, of course, unusual to find any of these in its pure form. In most cases we find mixtures of the three types.
7. Among large foreign investment projects in European transition economies, production-sharing agreements made up US$ 2.4 billion or 14 per cent of total initial investment commitments and 39 per cent of total pledged investment at year end 1994 (see UNECE, 1995).
8. Global competitiveness can be defined in terms of the need for firms to be able to mobilize a range of skills simultaneously in different regions or even continents (Hatzichronoglou, 1996).
9. The literature gives a number of examples of failure to spill over (the Mexican *maquilla* industries, the Dominican Republic Processing Zone), but also describes very successful spillovers from FDI in Singapore and Taiwan.

REFERENCES

Astapovich, Z.A. (ed.) (1995), *Foreign Investment in Russia: Salient Features and Trends, Second Report*, Moscow: Infomart.

Bell, M. (1996), 'Technology Transfer to Transition Countries: Are There Lessons from the Experience of the Post-war Industrialising Countries?', in D.A. Dyker (ed.), *The Technology of Transition: Science and Technology Policy for Transition Countries*, Budapest: Central European University Press.

Chesnais, F. (1996), 'Technological Agreements, Networks and Selected Issues in Economic Theory', in R. Coombs *et al.* (eds), *Technological Collaboration: The Dynamics of Co-operation in Industrial Innovation*, Cheltenham: Edward Elgar.

Dyker, D.A. (1996), The Computer and Software Industries in the East European Economies – A Bridgehead to the Global Economy?, *STEEP Discussion Paper No. 27*, SPRU, University of Sussex, February.

Eden, L. (1991), 'Multinational Response to Trade and Technology Changes: Implications for Canada', in D.G. McFetridge (ed.), *Foreign Investment, Technology and Economic Growth*, Calgary: The University Press.

Hagedoorn, J. (1990), 'Organizational Modes of Inter-firm Co-operation and Technology Transfer', *Technovation*, **10**, (1), 17–30.

Hagedoorn, J. and C. Freeman (1994), 'Catching Up or Falling Behind: Patterns in International Inter-firm Technology Partnering', *World Development*, **5**, 771–80.

Hagedoorn, J. and B. Sadowski (1996), 'Exploring the Potential Transition from Strategic Technology Partnering to Mergers and Acquisition', mimeo, Maastricht: MERIT.

Hatzichronoglou, T. (1996), 'Globalisation and Competitiveness: Relevant Indicators', *STI Working Papers, No. 5*, Paris: DSTI, OECD.

Hunya, G. (1996a), 'Foreign Direct Investment in Transition Countries in 1995', *Vienna Institute Monthly Report*, (1), 2–8.

Hunya, G. (1996b), *Foreign Direct Investment in Hungary: A Key Element of Economic Modernization*, Research Report, No. 226, The Vienna Institute for Comparative Economic Systems, February.

Jermakowicz, W. (ed.) (1994), 'Foreign Privatization in Poland', *Studies & Analyses No. 30*, Warsaw: Center for Social and Economic Research.

Radošević, S. (1996a), *International Technology Transfer Policy: From 'Contract*

Bargaining to Sourcing', Maastricht: UN University Institute for New Technologies.

Radošević, S. (1996b), 'The Baltic Post-socialist Enterprises and the Development of Organisational Capabilities', in Neil Hood (ed.), *Transition in the Baltic States: Microlevel Studies*, London: Macmillan.

Radošević, S. (1996c), 'Technology Transfer in Global Competition: the Case of the Economies in Transition', in D.A. Dyker (ed.), *The Technology of Transition: Science and Technology Policy for Transition Countries*, Budapest: Central European University Press.

Swaan, Wim (1995), 'Capabilities and Competitiveness of the Hungarian Economy', mimeo, Budapest: Institute of Economics, Hungarian Academy of Sciences.

UNECE (1995), *East–West Information News*, (2), Summer.

Vonortas, N.S. and S.P. Safioleas (1996), 'Strategic Alliances in Information Technology and Developing Country Firms: Recent Evidence', mimeo, Washington, DC: Private Sector Development Department, World Bank, 26 March.

10. Financial fragility in the banking system of transitional economies in Eastern Europe

Jan Toporowski

The banking system plays a crucial financial role in the capitalist economy, facilitating economic activity but also generating problems of indebtedness and instability. This is contrasted with its more passive accommodating role in the former socialist economies of Eastern Europe. It is argued that an essential feature of the market relations, introduced as part of the transition to a capitalist market economy, has been the enforcement of financial claims and liabilities. This has introduced greater fragility to the financial systems of the transitional economies. This fragility is enhanced by the overcapitalization of banks that is a feature of institution building aimed at replicating in the specific circumstances of contemporary Eastern Europe the institutions of advanced capitalist economies.

In his only published comment on the worker-managed socialist market system of former Yugoslavia, made during a UN-sponsored visit to Belgrade in May–June 1958, the famous Polish economist Michal Kalecki criticized price liberalization as undermining the dynamic stability of the socialist economy. He argued that, with market forces determining demand and supply, there would be a tendency for excess capacity to appear in the consumption goods sector because of monopolistic practices in that sector. Such excess capacity would depress investment below the level needed to secure full capacity utilization in the investment goods sector. This, he thought, would tend to hold down economic activity, leading to the economic stagnation which he felt characterized the mature capitalist economies that did not have the benefits of Keynesian demand management. He concluded:

> This is certainly a fundamental issue. There is no doubt that when prices are wholly determined by the enterprise... the level of investment may be lower than the optimum level... An indispensable condition for ensuring the full use of economic potential is central control of price formation...Finally, a further problem arising out of autonomous price-fixing by enterprises should be pointed out. This is the possibility that unwarranted differences in income between workers in

different enterprises may arise, which may cause dissatisfaction. This in particular cannot be a matter of indifference from the point of view of socialist relations in society. (Kalecki, 1958, pp. 52–3)

In almost every respect, Kalecki appears to have been wrong. The 'socialist relations in society' were undermined, not by differences in income between workers in different enterprises, but by income differentials between different professional strata frequently within the same enterprise (cf. Sachs, 1993, pp. 20–22). In federally organized socialist countries, such as former Yugoslavia, such income differentials gave rise to invidious comparisons which narrowed the scope for central fiscal redistribution between federal states, discrediting federalism among the wealthier states making net payments into the central budget and among the poorer states as their net subsidy from the central budget was reduced over time. As for Kalecki's prediction of slow economic growth in former Yugoslavia, following the adoption of free prices and market relations, this was not borne out partly because, in practice, prices and market relations were never as free as envisaged in Kalecki's model and in the models of most economists writing about worker-managed economies. Indeed, partly through control of prices, but mainly through a centrally planned investment policy, former Yugoslavia managed to maintain high growth rates until the 1980s. Moreover, its worker-managed firms proved to have fairly high rates of surplus reinvestment (cf. Ward, 1958; Horvat, 1982, pp. 339–44; Horvat, 1986). Kalecki appears to have thought that income-maximizing worker-managers would follow the same underinvestment strategies as profit-seeking capitalists, even though, in a discussion of Chinese rural cooperatives, he recognized that cooperatives were a way of ensuring that enterprise surplus was reinvested (Kalecki, 1955).

This propensity for the reinvestment of cooperative enterprise surplus may be contrasted with a fundamental microeconomic principle underlying Keynes' and Kalecki's macroeconomics of capitalism. In their macroeconomics, all private-sector expenditure categories (which in turn determine output, inflation and so on) are dependent upon and largely determined by income. The sole exception among these categories is investment. However, investment can only be independent of firms' current income if there exists an accommodating financial system to facilitate the financing of investment in excess of current income (Minsky, 1976, pp. 134–5; Keynes, 1936, ch. 7). Once capitalist firms build up liquid reserves, due to successive incomplete reinvestment of their surplus, these savings may then be used to finance investment in excess of current surplus. Furthermore, the existence of these savings implies a capital or credit market, allowing other firms without accumulated surpluses to finance investment in excess of their current surpluses, by borrowing other firms' surpluses through financial intermediaries (banks). Moreover, while successive phases of underinvestment and overinvestment form the basis of business cycles in the capitalist economy, the illiquid nature of fixed capital undertakings means that capitalist firms are therefore prone to financial crises emanating from the liabilities to the financial system which those firms may have incurred to finance their investment (Toporowski, 1994; See also Keynes, 1971, ch. 18). These financial cycles exacerbate the business cycle.

This active, but also periodically pathological, character of the financial system in a capitalist economy may be contrasted with the contribution of the state-owned banks to the relative financial stability of the socialist economy. Notwithstanding crises in consumer goods markets, slow growth and economic inefficiency, one of the strengths of the communist system of central economic administration was its financial stability. Essentially, industrial companies which spent more than they obtained in sales revenue obtained automatic credit from the banking system, provided that their expenditure was undertaken to fulfil the economic plan. In this way, any financial deficit was automatically covered by bank credit and, because the banking system was state-owned, became thereby a claim on the central government. The central government balanced these liabilities with its own claims on the profits or surplus of state companies. Financial stability was obtained because the corporate, financial and government sectors effectively operated as one sector in which each economic unit's financial liabilities were automatically met by claims on the central government, which could meet those liabilities by its own claims on state companies. This financial stability was subverted, not by developments within the banking or financial system, but by the failure of governments to balance their liabilities to industry with their claims on the surplus of industrial enterprises. Underlying this fiscal imbalance was a political failure to maintain that ratio of wages to prices which balanced the demand for consumer goods with the supply of these goods from the domestic consumption goods sector and from imports. The rise in that ratio of wages to prices not only imposed inflationary pressure on consumer markets, but also reduced the surplus of state enterprises from which government claims could be met.

This system of accommodating finance inspired Kornai's famous criticism that the resulting operations of state companies were inefficient and led inevitably to shortages because of this 'soft budget constraint' (Kornai, 1986). However, it has to be pointed out that this criticism rests on a misinterpretation of the role of the budget constraint in capitalist enterprises. With the exception of marginal, small businesses, capitalist companies are not constrained by their cash flow because (as we have noted above) they usually have internal savings or reserves, and have access to credit. A much more fundamental characteristic of capitalist companies is their obligation (to the capital market) to secure a return on their capital. It is this obligation or liability, rather than any need to keep total expenditure within the limits of sales revenue, which makes capitalist enterprises seek out profitable business, but also leads to financial crisis if the profits on their business fall (cf. Minsky, 1976, pp. 133–5).

The most obvious consequence of the introduction of market disciplines into the formerly centrally planned economies has been to force companies to seek out profitable business. A less obvious, but possibly even more fundamental, consequence of such disciplines is the enforcement of financial claims and liabilities rather than their automatic accommodation by claims against the state. The enforcement of claims and liabilities on companies in transitional economies has been a major factor in some of the controversial changes that have been apparent in those economies. For example, the collapse of the system of automatic financial credits against corporate financial deficits left companies with liabilities to their workers and to their suppliers which greatly exceeded companies' cash inflow from sales. Measures to eliminate the resulting financial deficit led to reductions in employment, rapid price inflation as a means of securing increased sales revenue and the growth of inter-company debt as companies postponed payments to their suppliers. Rising unemployment then led to increasing government liabilities for financial assistance to the unemployed. This, combined with a drastic fall in the profits of state enterprises, has led to rapidly expanding fiscal deficits. The reduction in workers' financial security and their real household incomes resulted in a fall in demand for wage goods, reducing sales revenue in the consumption goods sector. This was not compensated for by the rise in demand for luxury goods, following the rise in private sector profits, because of the high import content of such goods. Rising profits in the private sector and foreign direct investment in Eastern Europe, rather than the recovery of the state sector, have been the basis of the slow economic recovery in those countries in the former communist bloc that have avoided civil war.

BANK INFLATION AND THE RISING FINANCIAL RISK

A key factor in economic crises generated within the financial system is the layering, or pyramiding, of financial claims. Financial crisis occurs for an economic unit if its inability to pay its liabilities causes it to cease functioning and creates major losses for those holding claims against that unit. Minsky's Financial Instability Hypothesis is essentially the view that, during economic booms, companies' liabilities rise faster, because of increasing debt and rising interest rates, than their capacity to meet those liabilities. Eventually, a company or a group of them are unable to service their liabilities, and the defaulters collapse, often taking with them creditors and other companies, whose claims have been made worthless by the initial collapse (Minsky, 1978; Toporowski, 1994). Excess liabilities can be avoided by matching claims against liabilities very exactly, but this usually entails forgoing profits which are the reason for speculative undertaking of liabilities balanced by claims of uncertain value that may yield a profit over the cost of the liabilities, but may instead yield a loss. Moreover, financial markets complicate the picture because the more sophisticated are those markets, the greater is the layering of claims and liabilities, so that a default by an economic unit affects many more units. This can lead to financial market paralysis and collapse. Typically, an economic unit defaults on a liability, causing creditors to default on their liabilities due at the same time. The inability of the market to enforce these layered claims undermines the operations of the market. When the market loses its ability to settle transactions, it cannot operate effectively and ceases to function. To avoid this possibility, certain markets, such as the London International Financial Futures Exchange, operate a central clearing house which acts as the counter-party to all transactions. However, this is only a partial solution: a default brings action by the clearing house to secure payment, which causes claims against other agents (or the clearing house) to be brought forward or to be liquidated. The liquidation of claims causes further defaults which may then accumulate and cause another market collapse. An advantage of a state-owned banking or financial system is that, in an age of fiat money, their liabilities can always be met with claims against their owner, except obviously in the case of foreign liabilities.

Minsky's Financial Instability Hypothesis is a theory of financial cycles in a mature capitalist economy. It is relatively easy to show that it applies *a fortiori* and catastrophically in an economy through an over-rapid expansion of bank balance sheets. While the example of Polish banking is used in this part of the analysis, the conclusions are broadly applicable to transitional economies in Eastern Europe. Since the mid-1980s, the regional and national bank networks have been built up in Poland, initially with the aim of reducing the dependence of state industry on government finance. This policy has been extended since 1990, under the auspices of the International Monetary Fund (IMF), the World Bank and the European Bank for Reconstruction and Development (EBRD), with the aim of creating efficient capital markets. However, retail banking is weakly developed and with low levels of liquidity in the household and company sectors it operates with a high risk that financial firms will collapse. This fragility of the financial system is due to a number of factors arising out of the combination of bank capital inflation, with monetarist anti-inflationary measures (principally high real interest rates) in labour and product markets. Among these factors is a high incidence of fraud: the monetarist anti-inflationary strategy pursued since 1990 is intended to confront households and companies with the dilemma that, if they raise their wages/prices to obtain liquidity through higher income, this will result in a proportionate or more than proportionate loss of work or sales. With liquid savings in the household and company sectors devalued by hyperinflation, there are correspondingly higher incentives to acquire liquidity illegally or semi-legally. Certain desperate customers obtain liquidity by getting a bank loan secured on an illiquid asset. The customer then disappears with the loan, leaving the bank with an illiquid asset (waste land or old factories, for example) which neither brings in revenue, nor can be realized quickly, except at a loss. Thus the liquidity profile of bank assets is altered in ways and directions over which the bank has no control. This kind of semi-legal fraud was facilitated by the proliferation of banks, designed to create a competitive banking system in Poland, before the Kolodko policy shift at the end of 1995 renewed the emphasis on consolidating banks into viable units.

A second factor increasing financial risk is the large amount of speculation on asset values, from land to the stock market. This speculation is a means of acquiring liquidity that is at least legitimate compared to the legal and semi-legal fraud described above. Many asset markets are highly unstable, and the measures taken to stabilize the Warsaw stock exchange, the matching of orders and trading halts if the price of a stock moves more than 10 per cent away from its previous notation, have made this market less effective and unpredictably illiquid.

A third factor increasing risk is the large amount of capital devoted to money centre activities. Such activities are more speculative than normal retail banking, where lending margins are much wider. Moreover, the size of the interbank market increases the systemic risk among institutions that do not have stable retail sources of deposits as a source of liquidity. The inter-bank market ensures that problems in one bank rapidly become problems for the banking system as a whole, unless the central bank takes an accommodating role. It is difficult for a central bank to take such a role without breaching limits on lending to state enterprises. The high share of money centre activities in transitional banking is well illustrated in Table 10.1, showing the balance sheet of the Polish banking system at the end of 1993. In contrast to the banking systems of the advanced capitalist countries, Polish banking does only a small proportion of its business with industrial and commercial companies and households. Most of its business consists of taking positions in wholesale financial markets and in government paper. This makes the banking system correspondingly more vulnerable to the sudden changes in prices and financial flows, to which central financial markets are more prone than retail markets. Moreover, a recent study showed that, with the decreasing exception of the old state savings banks, the larger the bank, the higher is the proportion of its assets and liabilities in money centre activities (Chick and Toporowski, 1995).

Table 10.1   Balance sheet of the Polish banking system at end of 1993

	Billion zloty	Per cent of total	Per cent of GDP
ASSETS			
Total assets	1 302 017.0	100.0	83.7
Foreign assets	261 349.4	20.1	16.8
Claims on financial institutions*	180 266.4	13.8	11.6
Claims on:			
Central government	37 278.5	2.9	2.4
Local government	784.9	—	—
Public corporations	0	0	0
Claims on enterprises	309 362.6	3.8	19.9
in domestic currency	245 868.2	8.9	15.8
in foreign currency	29 396.7	2.3	1.9
Claims on households	22 594.4	1.7	1.5
Financial assets	320 947.2	24.7	20.6
of which			
government obligations	14 356.1	11.0	9.2
government bonds	16 844.5	12.9	10.8
Other assets	169 433.8	12.5	10.9
LIABILITIES			
Total liabilities	1 302 017.0	100.0	83.7
Foreign liabilities	88 209.1	6.8	5.7
Liabilities to financial institutions	157 911.8	12.1	10.2
Deposits of:			
Central government	22 923.8	1.8	1.5
Local government	11 488.8	0.9	0.7
Public corporations	15 367.7	1.2	1.0
Cash (money in circulation and in bank tills)	12 183.0	9.4	7.8
Zloty deposits of enterprises	135 858.6	10.4	8.7
of which			
demand deposits	82 588.5	6.3	5.3
term deposits	53 270.1	4.1	3.4
Zloty deposits of households	162 655.0	12.5	10.5
of which			
demand deposits	14 061.7	1.1	0.9
current deposits	1 487.8	0.9	0.7
term deposits	137 105.5	10.5	8.8
Foreign currency deposits of enterprises	6 597.4	0.5	0.4
Foreign currency deposits of households	154 309.6	11.8	9.9
Financial assets in circulation	10 281.5	0.8	0.7
Interest payments on loans	274.2	—	—
Own funds and reserves	52 712.2	4.0	3.4
Other liabilities	361 597.5	27.8	23.2

Note: *   including Polish-owned banks, foreign exchange businesses, post offices.

Source: *Rocznik Statystyczny*, in Chick and Toporowski (1995).

A fourth factor increasing bank risk is the policy of positive real interest rates, and high nominal interest rates because of high inflation, followed by successive governments since 1990. In this situation businessmen prefer to finance their activities out of their own cash flow (Kornai would perhaps have approved). In an emergency, it is common for businessmen in Poland and elsewhere in Eastern Europe, as in other countries with undeveloped banking systems, to obtain short-term loans from business associates, usually on a non-interest-paying basis. The value of the loan may be maintained by denominating it in foreign currency, and the price of the loan is the moral obligation to reciprocate should the lender need such a loan in the future. With the option of such terms, businessmen have a strong incentive to take out only such bank loans as they do not intend to repay. These arrangements strengthen the community of business activists, as well as being an important factor in the coherence of market systems (Weber, 1930, chs 1 and 2). Whereas in a fully banked system a firm's survival in unstable markets depends on its liquidity and the lines of credit available to it from one or more banks, in a market system with undeveloped retail banking, a firm's survival depends on its liquidity and the lines of credit available to it from other businesses.

BANK CAPITAL INFLATION

Current policy in the transitional countries of Eastern Europe is to emulate advanced capitalist economies by establishing and expanding financial markets and financial intermediation. Such a policy is supposed eventually to create a financial system rooted in strong retail banking activity. The means of creating such a system are the establishment of new financial markets and the strengthening of existing markets by increasing the capital of intermediary firms operating in them. Since the development of retail markets requires the confidence and active participation of households and firms, both of which are now beyond the direct influence of the state, policy has concentrated on facilitating new money centre activities and increasing the capitalization of financial firms. This is in line with the conventional wisdom underlying financial deregulation in advanced capitalist countries and the Basle Accord approach to financial risk, namely that more capital supporting a given portfolio of assets means less risk. In other words, asset risk can be avoided by liabilities management. In Eastern Europe, the lower risk of more highly capitalized banks is supposed to give confidence to households and firms to use more financial intermediary services.

However, in a capitalist market economy, retail bank business can only develop autonomously. Not having any intrinsic use value, the demand for bank services can only rise with the demand for those goods and services with which bank services are associated (Toporowski,1993, pp. 46–7). Moreover, the development of normal loan services is positively discouraged by a monetarist anti-inflation policy based on positive real interest rates. While in the more advanced capitalist countries banking has developed historically to service growing retail demand, and only in the last two decades to service growing money centre demand, in the transitional economies, the banking system is being expanded in advance of retail demand.

New deposits and additional capital are therefore more likely to be directed towards the inflation of wholesale money and capital markets. Indeed, a prominent adviser to the Polish Finance Ministry has recently argued that increasing the capital of Polish banks, while increasing the government bond issue, would enable Polish banks to improve the overall quality of their portfolios by diluting their bad commercial debts with low-risk government paper (Gomulka, 1994). However, this would require modifications in the Polish government's agreements with the International Monetary Fund, under which the government is supposed to reduce its fiscal deficit. Under such a constraint, a government only has discretion to move along the maturity spectrum, rather than increase borrowing, as this proposal suggests. If the government does increase borrowing, in order to place a large amount of debt among bank assets, then such a wholesale issue of new paper is likely to cause bond prices to fall, undermining the speculative positions of banks and institutions already holding bonds.

If, however, the intention is that existing banks increase their capital and invest the capital so raised in already issued government paper, it is easy to show that this will actually increase banks' engagement in risky business, rather than diminishing it. Privately capitalized banks, like any other capitalist undertaking, need to obtain a return on their capital that is on average greater than the cost of that capital, the excess return being necessary to set against the risks of loan default. Banks with the worst quality loan books prior to recapitalization have the worst credit ratings or reputation, and hence can only attract new capital by offering a correspondingly higher yield on that new capital. The new capital therefore has to be turned over, or invested in securities, to obtain an even higher yield. This is unlikely to come from government bonds, the more so if banks in general are buying in government stock and the price of that stock rises. The higher yield is therefore more likely to come from engaging in even more risky business than that which got banks into difficulty in the first place. Moreover, the issue of a large amount of new bank stock would have important portfolio implications. The stock market in Warsaw, for example, is already overbanked and, without a major and potentially destabilizing inflow of foreign funds from abroad, it would be practically impossible to issue large amounts of new stock without setting off a fall in stock prices. This in turn would undermine the speculative positions of bank stockholders.

Recapitalization therefore tends to exacerbate existing difficulties rather than resolving them. In this way, the inflation of capital markets that has been a policy of successive post-communist governments is increasing financial instability and risk, rather than facilitating the emergence of normal capitalist finance and banking.

A successful banking system is based on relatively liquid corporate and household sectors; its job is to enhance growth potential without damaging either its own liquidity or that of its clients. Eastern European banking systems entered the transition from centrally directed socialism to market capitalism burdened not only by a stock of bad debts, that were the outcome of the collapse of the previous system of mutually accommodating finance between the government, the banks and state enterprises. These banks also face special risks because of the illiquidity of corporate customers, which is also inhibiting the development of normal business. Increased liquidity in Polish companies could come from more active government and overseas purchasing from Polish companies. Such increased sales would put liquidity without liabilities into the corporate sector, providing earnings on investment undertaken in that sector. Such liquidity would be available for redeposit within the banking system, but redepositing liquidity requires confidence in the systems of company regulation and taxation of households and firms. In the long term, the soundness of a domestic banking system depends on the encouragement of banking use by households and businesses. The greatest danger of the inflation of banking systems that is taking place in transitional economies is not that it will give rise to banks failures, but that these in turn will discredit the development of healthy retail banking.

ACKNOWLEDGEMENT

The contributor is grateful to Grazia Ietto-Gillies for financial assistance from the Centre for International Business Studies towards the research on which this chapter is based (see Chick and Toporowski, 1995). The research was conducted in collaboration with Victoria Chick, with assistance from Aleksander Janiszewski and using data supplied by Halina Sopniewska.

REFERENCES

Chick, V. and J. Toporowski (1995), 'Evolution and Sudden Transition in Banking: The Polish Case Considered', *Research Papers in International Business,* No. 29, London: South Bank University.
Gomulka, S. (1994), 'The Financial Situation of Enterprises and Its Impact on

Monetary and Fiscal Policies, Poland 1992–1993', *Economics of Transition*, **2**, (2), 189–208.

Horvat, B. (1982), *The Political Economy of Socialism*, London: Martin Robertson.

Horvat, B. (1986), 'The Theory of the Worker-Managed Firm Revisited', *Journal of Comparative Economics*.

Kalecki, M. (1955), 'Uwagi o referacie Mao Ze-duna' (Comments on the Report by Mao Zedong) in *Dziela: Tom 6 Analizy gospodarcze Miscellanea*, Warsaw: Panstwowe Wydawnictwo Ekonomiczne, (published in Polish, 1988).

Kalecki, M. (1958), 'Central Price Determination as an Essential Feature of the Socialist Economy', in *Selected Essays on Economic Planning*, Cambridge: Cambridge University Press.

Keynes, J.M. (1936), *The General Theory of Employment, Interest and Money*, London: Macmillan.

Keynes, J.M. (1971), *The Collected Writings of John Maynard Keynes: Volume V, A Treatise on Money, Volume 1 The Pure Theory of Money*, London: Macmillan for the Royal Economic Society.

Kornai, J. (1986) 'The Soft Budget Constraint', *Kyklos*, **39**, (1).

Minsky, H.P. (1976), *John Maynard Keynes*, London: Macmillan.

Minsky, H.P. (1978), 'The Financial Instability Hypothesis: A Restatement', *Thames Papers in Political Economy*, London: Thames Polytechnic.

Sachs, J. (1993), *Poland's Jump to the Market Economy*, Cambridge, Mass.: MIT Press.

Toporowski, J. (1993), *The Economics of Financial Markets and the 1987 Crash*, Aldershot: Edward Elgar.

Toporowski, J. (1994) 'Corporate Liquidity, Capital Markets and their Valuation', *Économie Appliquée*, **XLVI**, (3).

Ward, B. (1958), 'The Firm in Illyria: Market Syndicalism', *American Economic Review*, **48**, (4), September.

Weber, M. (1930), *The Protestant Ethic and the Spirit of Capitalism*, London: George Allen & Unwin.

11. The transformation and demise of self-managed firms in Croatia, Macedonia FRY and Slovenia

Will Bartlett

The transition process in the successor states of former Yugoslavia has brought about the almost complete elimination of the 'self-management' form of enterprise governance which had been a characteristic feature of the former Yugoslavia. Social property has been transferred largely to employees, managers or state funds (although some lingering examples of the labour managed firms (LMF) persist in areas most affected by the war and outside the main jurisdiction of new state powers). Workers' councils have simultaneously been largely abolished, partly as a result of property transformation, in other cases by direct liquidation. Nevertheless, as has been the case in some other East European economies, the potential conditions for new and transformed forms of employee participation have been created in cases where enterprise shares have been sold to employees, often at large discounts. Employee ownership is emerging as the most prevalent form of enterprise governance in the former social ownership sector, although it should be noted also that in many cases managers rather than employees hold a controlling interest.

The economic transition process, however, is not completely described by the fate of the self-managed enterprises. In parallel with the top-down process of privatization, another equally important process of bottom-up transformation is taking place through the large-scale entry of new, small firms under a more traditional form of private ownership. In most of the successor states, the new small-scale sector is emerging as a substantial and dynamic element of the emerging market economies (Bartlett and Prasnikar, 1995; Bartlett, 1996). In these small firms, employing an increasingly large proportion of the labour force, the mechanisms of employee participation and employee ownership are almost entirely absent.

In order to understand the emerging industrial structure in the successor states, therefore, there is a need to analyse the role and interaction of the newly transformed employee ownership sector and the new small-scale sector under private ownership. Two possible modes of interaction are theoretically possible. In one model, the large transformed employee-owned firms compete with the new small-scale firms for market share. Models of Cournot and Stackleberg competition would be appropriate to this type of competitive dynamic. In the second model, large employee-owned firms interact with the new small private firms on a network basis, either as contractors and subcontractors in a supply chain relationship or through ownership linkages in the form of holding companies and spin-offs in which the large transformed enterprise has an ownership stake in the newly established small firms. The consequences and influence of employee participation and employee ownership in the successor states need to be understood within such newly emerging industrial structures as a whole. In sectors in which the competitive model is appropriate, the interesting questions concern the outcome of the evolutionary process of competition between employee-owned firms and private firms. Potential competitive advantages or disadvantages of employee ownership may eventually result in the dominance or demise of employee ownership within such a sector as a result of the competitive struggle with the new private sector. In sectors in which the networking model is more appropriate, the interesting question concerns the extent to which the economic behaviour of the sector as a whole would be determined by the strategies and policies adopted by the employee-owned firms as dominant players in the networks.

SELF-MANAGEMENT AND WORKER PARTICIPATION IN FORMER YUGOSLAVIA

Yugoslavia had been distinguished from other East European economies by its unique system of workers' self-management as a system of enterprise governance. Standing astride the east–west division of the continent, it had abandoned central planning in the early 1950s and introduced a limited market economy, heavily circumscribed by political management by the ruling Communist League, especially at local and regional level. Extensive decentralization of powers had led to the emergence of distinctive regional economies, which eventually developed their own political elite, creating the basis for the disintegration of the country into rival successor states in 1991.

For most of the postwar period, enterprise governance in former Yugoslavia was based upon the concept of social ownership of the means of production and the management of enterprises by their employees. Capital assets were formally owned by the collectivity of citizens (a system known as 'social ownership') and managed on their behalf by the employees of the enterprises. This principal–agent arrangement was subject to most of the defects for which such arrangements are notorious. In particular, there was a heavy moral hazard problem: the principal (the citizens) could not effectively monitor the use to which the agents (the employees) put the assets under management, or impose any penalties for self-interested and opportunistic behaviour. Employees therefore had an incentive to exploit their position and 'consume' the enterprise capital through excessive wage payments and underinvestment (Furubotn and Pejovich, 1970; Madar, 1992). This problem was intensified by the lack of definition of who exactly held the role of the principal. While formally it was society at large, in practice enterprise management was in a position to exert a powerful influence over corporate strategy. At the same time, however, the interests of society were also claimed by representatives of local and regional government authorities, leading to a persistent trend towards political intervention in enterprise decision making. Moreover, the circulation of the political and economic elite meant that enterprise directors were often closely connected to local political personalities and so there was a conflict of interest between political and economic objectives of company directors. This lack of well-specified ownership rights led to an inefficient industrial economy in which levels of output and productivity were falling throughout the 1980s and in which chronic inflation and continuous currency depreciation were persistent features (Lydall, 1989).

Moreover, in so far as the citizens were interested in exerting control over the enterprise management, this was usually expressed as a desire for employment creation and employment stability, rather than for the promotion of the efficiency of the enterprises. Political interference with management was formalized into rules concerning job entitlements which made lay-off of redundant workers well-nigh impossible. 'Self-management agreements' were used by local authorities to compel enterprises to increase employment levels above the levels which they would have chosen in the absence of intervention. The result was a large surplus labour force employed within enterprises. The *de facto* permanent job rights enjoyed by insiders within the self-management system froze the labour market and institutionalized a queue for jobs. This led to persistently high levels of youth unemployment. In order to free tenured positions inside the enterprises, increasing use was made of early retirement of older workers. This caused further difficulties, since pensions were linked to current average wages with a high average replacement rate, which was in turn indexed to inflation. In order to finance this system, the combined pension contributions of existing employers and employees had reached almost 50 per cent of the net wage by the end of the 1980s (Stanovnik and Kukar, 1995).

Central planning had been abandoned in the 1950s and self-managed enterprises operated in a market-based environment. However, the market was highly regulated. There were extensive price controls, and regional and local authorities had considerable powers to intervene in the decisions of enterprises through the system of self-management agreements which were in effect local plans. The local political authorities also controlled the entry of new firms and they had close connections with the local banks, so that they could influence the distribution of loans and credits to support particular industrial sectors or particular enterprises. In this way the authorities were able to influence the pattern of industrial development at a local level. However, this did not always lead to sensible investment decisions and the integration of economic and political decision making led to the existence of so-called 'political factories'. Moreover, ways could always be found to provide financial support to loss-making enterprises. The lack of hard budget constraints on enterprise behaviour led to inefficiency and weakened the influence of the market as an economic institution (Uvalić, 1992).

These dysfunctional features of the system were already well recognized at the end of the 1980s, when a reform process was started under the Marković regime (Bartlett, 1991; Uvalić, 1992). The reform involved a privatization law and a company law to open up the economy to the development of more effective forms of enterprise governance. This was to be brought about both through the conversion of the socially owned enterprises into enterprises in which ownership was more clearly identified and through the removal of restrictions on the development of small firms. The identification of ownership rights was to be formalized through the creation of share titles. The primary objective was to overcome the lack of definition of property rights and the reduction of political interference in enterprise decision making and activity. The legislation therefore permitted the enterprises to choose their own form of privatization. Shares could be issued for sale to inside employee owners, outside owners or the state. The reform was implemented in Slovenia more vigorously than in other republics. Owing to the regionalization of the economy, and to hidden barriers to labour mobility brought about by language differences and trends towards regional autarky, unemployment levels in Slovenia had been lower than in other republics in the pre-independence period. However, the labour force shake-out which occurred after the Marković reforms pushed unemployment levels up to historically high levels, reaching 14 per cent of the labour force by 1991 (Bartlett and Uvalić, 1992). However, the reform process was too little and too late to reverse the long period of economic decline which had persisted in Yugoslavia throughout the 1980s (though affecting Slovenia to a lesser extent) and dissatisfaction with economic performance and disagreements over economic policy between the different republics led to regional tensions which culminated in the destruction of Yugoslavia as a federal state. Thereafter, the successor states followed independent policies of ownership transformation.

OWNERSHIP TRANSFORMATION IN CROATIA

The first independent privatization law to be passed in any of the successor states of former Yugoslavia was in Croatia in April 1991. Enterprises were to submit privatization plans within one year of implementation of the law, by which time all social capital was transferred to government ownership, mainly to the Croatian Privatization Fund (CPF), but also partly to state managed pension funds. The main method of privatization was the sale of shares to employees and managers at favourable discounts (a basic 20 per cent plus 1 per cent for each year of service) up to a maximum of DM20 000 per employee. Shares could also be sold to outsiders without a discount. By 1994, the majority of the 3000 labour-managed firms in Croatia had completed the process of property transformation, although it can hardly be said that this represented a process of privatization. Although nearly half of all enterprises (47 per cent) were fully privatized, these accounted for only 8.6 per cent of total assets of the enterprise sector (Uvalić, 1996). Most larger enterprises, accounting for 40 per cent of total assets, were effectively transferred to state ownership under the CPF. The remainder of firms (comprising 38 per cent of firms accounting for 52 per cent of asset values) had minority state ownership. Thus, in Croatia, almost half of the social capital of the enterprise sector subject to ownership transformation had become state-owned capital by the end of 1994, and the CPF was the manager of DM6.5 million of capital assets.

Among those enterprises which were sold to employees and managers, in many cases subsequent trading of shares resulted in management control of a large number of firms. Often managers favoured by the ruling party, or outsiders with political connections, were able to obtain privilege loans to buy out enterprises, so that political influence of the state was effectively ensured even in supposedly privatized enterprises. In other cases where enterprises were under the ownership of the Privatization Fund, management teams were replaced by new managers more sympathetic to the ruling party (Bićanić, 1993). Moreover, the public utilities were outside the privatization law and were transferred directly to state ownership. Uvalić (1996) concludes that 'the Croatian economy, rather than being privatized, has been renationalized', a conclusion echoed by other observers (Čučković, 1993).

More recently, a new voucher privatization programme has been introduced which is intended to cover these enterprises and the remaining assets held by the CPF under state ownership which amounted to around DM3.5 million in June 1996. It will therefore result in a complete recapitalization of the stock market. Under the programme, vouchers will be received by 350 000 war-affected citizens, including returning refugees and other categories listed in the draft law. Each eligible person will receive vouchers worth 7000 points or more, depending on their circumstances (having an initial nominal value of DM7000). These vouchers will be swapped for shares in the official list of enterprises to be privatized (the 'supply-side list') or in a Privatization Investment Fund (PIF). The PIFs are yet to be established and will be licensed by the Ministry of Finance. So far only one bank has put itself forward as a potential PIF.

The programme will begin in mid-August 1996 with individuals registering their entitlement to vouchers. The voucher privatization programme will entail three bidding rounds, starting in February or March 1997. Each round will last six weeks, so the process should be completed before August 1997. After each bidding round the prices of shares which attracted bids outside a 33 per cent price band will be reset and the shares involved will be re-auctioned. In the third round all remaining shares will be disposed of in exchange for the remaining vouchers at whatever price the bidding determines.

The Croatian privatization programme has not as yet been extended to cover the labour-managed firms in the UN-protected areas which had seceded from the Croatian state until their reincorporation following the *Oluja* offensive in August 1995. The self-managed enterprises in these war-affected areas are still formally in social ownership, although most are operating at much reduced capacity and many have suffered extensive war damage. They are currently being registered with the Privatization Fund and are to be privatized under a new voucher privatization programme. The shares in the 200 so-called 'special enterprises' (that is, self-managed enterprises) in the war-affected regions will be sold off in a 'zero round' in January 1997. Half will be transferred to former employees and their families, and the rest exchanged for vouchers. The position of ex-employees who have fled to Bosnia and Serbia is not clear. Although they will apparently have an entitlement to vouchers, it seems unlikely that they will be able to register a claim, which has to be done in registration offices in Croatia. Moreover, records or data about the previous and current number of employees hardly exist.

Case Study: SAPONIA

SAPONIA is a large firm based in Osijek which produces washing powders, soaps, other industrial cleaning products and bio-insecticides. The firm was first established in 1894 as a small soap-making workshop owned by Samuel Reinitz. In 1919, it was taken over by Schicht, which integrated with Lever Brothers of Rotterdam in the 1930s. During World War II, it was badly damaged and was recreated as 'The First Soap Works of Osijek', eventually regaining its old name of SAPONIA. In 1969, SAPONIA integrated with Dalmacijabilje as a 'complex firm'. It remained a socially owned firm until

1994, when it became a joint stock company. The privatization resulted in a 51 per cent shareholding by employees, managers and retired workers (small shareholders). Since then the employees have bought more shares from the Privatization Fund and their ownership share stands at 65 per cent. The firm has therefore become an employee-owned enterprise.

Before the war of independence 1991–95, the company was the biggest soap producer in Europe and produced 120,000 tons output. It had a turnover of DM250 million, and operated from two sites in Osijek, one in east Slavonia which has been completely destroyed, and one in Dubrovnik. Now production stands at 30 000 tons, and turnover at DM85 million. Average wages are DM400–500 per month and dividends are zero. Employment has fallen from 2700 to 1370, although no employees have been laid off. The firm's policy has been to retain the labour force and provide jobs as far as possible. They are proud that they retained 500 workers in Dalmatia during the war even though production was impossible. However, this means that they have substantial surplus labour and would welcome a programme of managed redundancies for those who wish to establish their own small businesses. This would reduce surplus labour and increase profits.

Most of their suppliers are based in Osijek, Zagreb, Zadar and Pula and there are two other important suppliers in Slovenia. Before the war, the most important suppliers were based in Serbia (Galenika in Zemun) and in Bosnia (Lukovac in Tuzla). Their biggest overseas suppliers are in Britain. In production packaging there are good opportunities for the development of new suppliers in the locality.

During the 1991 war, the factories were badly damaged. The newest and most modern plant in Nemetin in eastern Slavonia (now the only area remaining under UN protection) was almost completely destroyed. Production continued throughout the war even though 14 workers were killed, several as a result of bombardment of the factories. The Serbian side also destroyed a giant chemical storage plant, putting the health of the inhabitants of Osijek at risk. Total war damage amounts to DM65 million, although the latest data suggest that a figure of DM100 million would be more exact. It is valued by the privatization fund at DM65 million, although the management argued that a figure of DM35 million would be more exact. Their strategic aim now is to rebuild the main facilities destroyed in the war, and to diversify into new activities appropriate to the reconstruction market. For example, they are creating new facilities to produce construction materials. They have a loan of DM5.6 million for this purpose from CBRD.

One of the most interesting possibilities from the perspective of this project is the redevelopment of the site in Nemetin. This covers 36 hectares of land in East Slavonia towards Vukovar. The firm took 12 years to build up the site and now it is destroyed. The idea was to gradually shift their production to that site and it is well supplied with infrastructure. It had been a distribution centre for the whole of the former Yugoslavia, with roads, 10000 sq.m. of parking, a railway track, a heating system and its own resources of gas and electricity. In 1994, the site was destroyed. It is now occupied by the Croatian army but still there is no access to it. The management see this site as one with tremendous potential for redevelopment. Their current ideas for redevelopment include building a hypermarket or creating a free trade zone.

The Nemetin site could be used as a small business development centre or as a business incubator, providing premises to new small businesses. SAPONIA could establish a separate shareholding company. First, there is a need for credits to finance the cleaning of the site. Then they would be willing to offer space in a cooperative way to any new entrepreneurial activity, charging a rent, or receiving dividends from the profits earned by the new shareholding company. They envisage that their own employees would be able to start new companies there. However, they need technical know-how training on how to do this, and training in how to enter new markets.

It would be possible to release workers to set up their own SMEs and SAPONIA has already begun to diversify into construction materials in this way. Discussions have been held with an Italian investor from Veneto to discuss investing in the creation of a ceramics business. These new firms would be a method of diversification by the company in order to facilitate redeployment of surplus workers into independent companies.

The management team are not very impressed by the results of the privatization process and consider that the dispersion of ownership has had an adverse effect upon their efforts to manage the company. They hope that in the future it will be possible to concentrate ownership into a smaller group, so that the managers themselves will hold a controlling interest. The state still has a 35 per cent share, but this will be sold off under the voucher privatization programme. The voucher shareholders will probably sell their holdings off very quickly, which will in itself lead to the development of a new market for shares and a new concentration of ownership.

OWNERSHIP TRANSFORMATION IN MACEDONIA FRY

Although insulated from the direct effects of the war, the Macedonian economy suffered indirectly from the UN sanctions imposed on Yugoslavia which not only disrupted existing trade linkages but also the close inter-enterprise linkages between the two economies. In addition, Macedonian trade was severally disrupted by the unilateral embargo imposed by Greece on the southern border (Bateman, 1996). Social product in Macedonia FRY fell by 14 per cent in 1992 and by a similar amount in 1993. In 1994, it fell by 8 per cent and in 1995 by 3 per cent. It is only after the lifting of these dual sets of sanctions that output began to rise in 1996. Unemployment amounts to over 200 000 or some 24 per cent of the labour force. Macedonia FRY has therefore had to contend with a difficult economic climate which has delayed the process of ownership transformation.

The Macedonian Law on Transformation of Enterprises with Social Capital was introduced in 1993. However, little progress was made until early 1995. Until that time enterprises could opt for voluntary privatization. Enterprises which did not begin this process by a deadline date were then subject to compulsory privatization by the Privatization Agency. For small and medium-sized enterprises the deadline date was the end of 1994, whilst for large enterprises it was June 1995. Enterprises could select from a variety of methods of privatization, including employee buy-out (provided at least 51 per cent of assets are bought), leveraged buy-out (for a minimum of 20 per cent of assets), commercial sale of the enterprise, issue of shares to outsiders (of at least 30 per cent of the shares), debt equity swaps, leasing or liquidation and sale of assets.

In the case of employee buy-outs, employees were offered discounts of 30 per cent plus a further 1 per cent for each year of employment in the enterprise. The maximum amount which could be bought by any employee was restricted to DM25 000. For ancillary units such as enterprise hotels and restaurants, discounts of 50 per cent were made available. In addition, in every case 15 per cent of the shares are to be transferred to the Pension Fund, which therefore receives a large amount of capital. Remaining unsold shares are transferred to the Privatization Agency, which is supposed to offer these shares to the public after a three month period.

The privatization process proceeded rapidly between 1995 and 1996. By the beginning of 1996, 536 enterprises (44 per cent of the total) had been completely privatized. These enterprises employed 55 000 workers (24 per cent of all employees). A further 342 enterprises (28 per cent) employing 103 000 workers (45 per cent) were undergoing privatization. By the end of July 1996, most of these had been fully privatized, so that some 800 firms had been completely privatized out of 1200 enterprises in the privatization programme. A further 200 were in the process of privatization. The remainder are either still to be privatized or are in such difficulties that they will probably be liquidated. Thus the privatization process is approaching the end of its first phase.

The most pressing problem is the existence of 25 very large loss-making enterprises which are being dealt with under a special Law for Restructuring Enterprises. These enterprises account for 13 per cent of GDP and employ 55 000 workers. Their debts account for 60 per cent of the non-performing loans held by the banks. In these enterprises Workers' Councils have been abolished and government nominees have been placed in control of the boards of directors. Over 15 000 workers have been declared 'surplus' and have accepted redundancy payments which have been paid by the state budget. A World Bank credit has been used to establish a Labour Redeployment Fund to assist the workers made unemployed under this programme to set up new businesses of their own. The restructuring programme for these firms also includes measures to liquidate non-viable enterprises, to transfer social assets to local governments, to carve out and privatize non-core commercial assets and to privatize separately the viable components of the enterprises as separate businesses. The restructured enterprises have been placed under a strict hard budget constraint and have been insulated from further credits from the banking system.

In practice, most privatization has been carried out either as management buy-outs (MBOs) or as management and employee buy-outs (MEBOs). Of 750 enterprises privatized by early 1996, 257 (employing 10 000 workers) were privatized through employee buy-outs, and 86 (employing 33 000 workers) were privatized by management buy-outs. A further 158 small enterprises employing 2000 workers were sold to foreign investors. In terms of employment, therefore, management buy-outs were the most significant form of privatization. In terms of the value of equity involved, management buy-outs were also the most important form of privatization, accounting for DM700 000 in value out of a total value of DM1.5 million.

Case Study: TETEKS

TETEKS, the largest textile company in Macedonia FRY, was established in 1951 in Tetovo, the main town in the region of Polog west of Skopje, with a high proportion of ethnic Albanian residents. At the end of the 1980s, TETEKS employed 7800 workers. It is a highly vertically integrated company, with its own independent electricity supply and its own bank (now a private bank with foreign shareholders: Teteks Banka) and produces machinery for textile production and spare parts for the machines. It has a substantial network of retail outlets throughout Macedonia FRY and foreign representative offices in New York, Moscow, Frankfurt and in the other successor states.

The firm was initially privatized in 1990, under the Marković privatization programme, and subsequently re-evaluated under the Macedonian privatization law. The shares are mainly held by employees, with only a residual 7 per cent remaining under social ownership. Since privatization, the workforce has fallen to 5200, and is continuing to fall. Over the next three years the management team intend to further reduce employment to 3500 which they consider the optimum number of employees for their core production activities. Labour force reductions are achieved through a voluntary redundancy programme the main elements of which include the pensioning of older workers and voluntary redundancy with a substantial redundancy pay-off amounting to 24 months' pay. In addition, there is a retraining programme which is a key part of the restructuring process. This involves mainly the large surplus of administrative workers which were employed in the self-management period, and now need to be retrained for production tasks.

Another key component of the restructuring programme is the creation of a number of independently registered small private firms, in which, however, TETEKS has a controlling ownership interest and plays a supervisory role through the company board. As a parent company, TETEKS provides the initial market research and equipment. It sets up the new small firm with its own management team and redeploys labour into it from TETEKS. These new firms have been established in a bewildering variety of sectors, including Teplastic, to produce plastic bags for packaging for clothes and carton box packaging, Teteks petrol, for the distribution of crude petrol and oil, Tegas to distribute technical gases (oxygen and so on) and Tegot to process recycled waste materials. In another case a new bakery firm has been established which supplies bread to TETEKS' employees. This was established with the help of a regional development loan from the government in Skopje and a loan from the local Tetovska Banka. In some cases one can see the logic of these diversifications; in others the motive appears to be the maximization of short-term financial returns with little regard for the long-term strategic position of the company. This strategy appears to be paying off in the short term. The new small firms now account for 27 per cent of group profits, while employing only 5 per cent of the overall workforce. As the strategy continues, output in core activities is planned to fall to only 40 per cent of total group output by the year 2000, the rest being produced by the new diversified small firms.

The restructuring process therefore relies very much on voluntary lay-off and retirement, and redeployment to new activities. The labour force are still conceived of as a work community. The decision makers within the firm consider it to be their social responsibility to seek out new employment and new areas of activity for the employees where voluntary retirement is not desired. There is a minimal element of compulsion involved. The management are clearly very sensitive to the social and economic welfare of workers even though they are now managing a formally private firm. In interview, this perspective came over as a very genuine concern of management. When asked why they did not want to speed up the redundancy programme, they replied that their objective is not only to improve profits and productivity, but also to accept a criterion of protection of the social interests of the workers.

As in the case of SAPONIA, however, the management team are unhappy with the results of privatization in so far as it has led to a dispersal of ownership amongst the employees. Ostensibly, they argue that this will eventually lead to the takeover of the firm by outsiders, as employees retire and sell off their shares. There is also the issue of control within the firm in the short term which may also be an important point of dissatisfaction for the management team, despite their adherence to a paternalistic concern for employee welfare. For either or both these reasons, the management team are in the process of buying up shares from employees, and hope to have established a controlling share ownership within the next five years.

OWNERSHIP TRANSFORMATION IN SLOVENIA

Before Slovenia became independent in 1991, the process of ownership transformation had been governed by the laws introduced under the Marković government, and had created a framework in which enterprises which wished to undergo privatization could develop their own plans. Under this system, a number 'wild privatizations' occurred which attracted critical comment and thereby brought the process into disrepute. In response to this, the Slovenian government, which was already beginning to pursue an independent line in economic and political affairs (Hafner, 1992; Ramet, 1993), established a Privatization Agency and a Development Fund in 1990. The role of the Privatization Agency was essentially that of monitoring and control, whilst that of the Development Fund was to assist the implementation of the process.

The federal law on privatization remained in use in Slovenia until the end of 1992. The introduction of a new law was delayed by an intense struggle at the political level over the form of privatization. As elsewhere in Eastern Europe, the privatization issue has strong political overtones and cannot be understood as a mere technical economic exercise. In Slovenia the approach eventually adopted was a compromise between, on the one hand, those who advocated a decentralized multi-track approach, based heavily on commercial sale and the voluntary choice of privatization methods by the companies themselves and, on the other hand, those who advocated mass privatization based on the issue of vouchers to the population to create a 'people's capitalism' (Korze and Simoneti, 1992).

In November 1992, a privatization Law on the Ownership Transformation of Enterprises was passed. The main objective of the law was to transform all companies with social capital (the self-managed enterprises) into 'companies with known owners'. In addition, employee ownership was encouraged by free internal distribution of up to 20 per cent of shares to employees, former employees and relatives of employees in exchange for ownership certificates (vouchers) and by sale of shares through internal buy-out of up to 40 per cent of the shares by employees at a 50 per cent discount. Enterprises could also select to undergo ownership transformation through a commercial sale of the shares by public offering, public tender or public auction to financial institutions, by the sale of all the assets of the company in combination with its liquidation or by raising additional outside equity, but only if new shares were issued for more than 10 per cent of the existing equity. In all cases, 10 per cent of shares were to be transferred to a Compensation Fund, 10 per cent to the Old Age Pension and Disablement Insurance Fund. A further 20 per cent were transferred to the Development Fund for further allocation to authorized investment companies, which would collect the vouchers .

The privatization law was therefore a very flexible instrument. It allowed for a combination of commercial sales and free distribution through a voucher system, as well as providing mechanisms for both insiders and outsiders to obtain shares. The main emphasis of the law, however, was on employee and management buy-outs through the discounted sales of shares to insiders, that is to employees, former employees and retired employees, and their families (who have preference in exchanging ownership certificates for shares).

The concession to the proponents of mass privatization through free distribution of shares is embodied in the part of the privatization arrangements which is based upon the distribution of vouchers to the general population. These vouchers are known as ownership certificates and were issued to the population in the first half of 1993. Their value depended on the age of the recipient and ranged from 100 000 tolars (equivalent to about US$1000) for young people up to the age of 18, to 400 000 tolars for people aged over 48. These non-transferable certificates could be used to buy shares of the company where a person worked, to purchase shares of companies offered for sale, or to buy shares of a new set of financial institutions known as Privatization Investment Funds (PIFs).

These new financial institutions provide an intermediation between the population who receive vouchers and the privatized companies. The investment funds can use the ownership certificates they collect to buy shares of privatizing companies either directly or from the Development Fund. Since there are several PIFs competing for ownership certificates, an element of competition is introduced into the new share market, but since the funds have to be authorized to operate, the market for shares is managed and regulated by the state.

Another feature of the Slovenian model of privatization is the compulsory transfer of a part of the shares to the Development Fund. The Development Fund sells its shares to the authorized investment funds either for cash or in exchange for ownership certificates which they in turn have obtained from the population. The money raised by the Development Fund from the sale of its shares is used for various economic and social purposes, including rehabilitation of companies, stimulation of exports, technological and development projects and investments and the development of small businesses.

More than 90 per cent of the privatization plans submitted to the Privatization Agency proposed using internal buy-out, frequently combined with the exchange of shares for employees' ownership certificates as the principal method of privatization. Only 120 companies proposed using the method of public offering of shares. The consequence is that the privatization process in Slovenia will result in the creation of a large number of employee-owned enterprises.

Case Study: The Development Fund

The Development Fund was itself transformed into a public limited company in 1992, with a founding capital of one billion Slovenian tolars. Its functions are now threefold. In addition to the original function of corporate restructuring, it is now also responsible for assisting the ownership transformation of other companies undergoing privatization under the 1992 Law on the Transformation of Social Capital, and for providing financial assistance to private companies (SKLAD, 1995).

In its initial phase the Development Fund was the recipient of the shares of companies which voluntarily put themselves under its ambit in order to facilitate a process of restructuring. These companies were mainly ones which were in any case in financial difficulties and were at risk of bankruptcy. Altogether some 98 companies were taken over by the Fund for restructuring. The restructuring process itself involved introducing new management and financial systems, and laying off redundant workers. It often also involved splitting up large conglomerate enterprises into more manageable small or medium-sized units. For example, the Metalna company of Maribor, which produces agricultural machinery and construction equipment and is especially successful in producing cranes, was taken over by the Fund in 1992. It was converted into a holding company and the production units were established as ten separate subsidiaries, employing between 130 and 981 workers each.

The most successful of the firms owned by the Fund were sold off. By 1 January 1993, the Fund had sold 32 companies. Of the remaining 66 companies, 41 were wholly owned by the Fund. In 12 companies the Fund owned 75 per cent or more of the shares. In a further 12, the Fund had majority ownership. There was only one company in which the Fund owned less than 50 per cent of the shares. During 1993, 30 of the remaining companies improved their business results, 21 remained in the same condition and 12 operated at a loss (SKLAD, 1994). By May 1995, more companies had been successfully restructured and sold off, and the Fund had only 50 of the original 98 companies left under its management. In all, although many lay-offs have taken place, the Fund estimates that it has managed to save 34 000 jobs that would otherwise have been lost through the failure of loss-making firms.

The third function of the Fund is making available long-term investment finance to private and privatized companies on favourable terms. Using the revenues collected from the sale of restructured companies, the Fund is in a position to assist the development of other privatized firms. The Fund under-takes cofinancing of companies that have already been transformed, and private and mixed companies that have passed the initial stage of develop-ment, and which are profitable, or at least not loss makers. These loans are made at favourable rates of interest, although standard financial assessments are first made to decide whether a company is eligible for a loan. When the Long Term Financing Unit of the Fund advertised these loans it received 48 responses from companies wishing to apply for them. By the end of 1994, four of these applications had been approved, and 14 were still being proc-essed. In May 1995, the Fund entered into a joint venture with the EBRD, setting up a new financial institution to channel the EBRD loans for industrial investment. A similar joint venture has also been set up with a regional investment fund in Koper, called FINOR. This is a specifically regional institution which was set up before the Fund was established to develop the local economy of the lucrative tourist region on the coast of Slovenia. Together these financial institutions represent a powerful force for the im-plementation of industrial policy in Slovenia, and give the state a mechanism for directing low-cost loans to strategic industries.

By the end of 1994, the privatization process was well under way in Slovenia, and nearly all social sector companies had prepared privatization plans and had submitted them to the Privatization Agency for approval. In all, the Agency had received plans from 1211 companies, representing 90 per cent of all socially owned companies in Slovenia, and covering 89 per cent of all employees in the social sector. In 1994, the Agency had approved 428 privatization plans and 233 companies had been privatized. Most of these companies had opted for privatization by means of employee buy-outs. Table 11.1. shows the dominant role of employee ownership in the privatization plans of these companies.

Amongst enterprises whose privatization plans had been approved, the great majority (82 per cent) will emerge from privatization with 60 per cent of the shares held by employees, and in a further 4 per cent of enterprises employees will hold between 50 per cent and 60 per cent of the shares. However, the diffusion of employee shareholding is less extensive when one considers the size of the enterprises involved: 349 enterprises with 60 per cent employee share ownership will account for only 44 per cent of total

Table 11.1   Employee shareholding in approved privatization plans,
Slovenia

Employee shareholding (percentages)	Number of enterprises	Percentage of companies	Percentage of assets
60 and above	349	82	44
50–60	17	4	6
25–50	48	11	24
up to 25	14	3	26
Total	428	100	100

Source: Rop (1995).

assets of the enterprises involved. Clearly, employee share ownership will be concentrated amongst the smaller and medium-sized enterprises undergoing privatization: larger enterprises have put forward privatization plans based upon the open sale of shares rather than on internal employee buy-outs. This is not surprising considering the limited purchasing power of potential insider buyers, even with generous discounts available.

Table 11.2. shows that there has been a rapid increase in the number of firms in Slovenia since the deregulation of private enterprise at the start of the decade. Most of the dynamics of growth has come from the rapid increase in the number of new limited liability companies, which by 1993 accounted for over 80 per cent of all enterprises in Slovenia. Alongside the enterprise sector are a further 35 000 firms which have been registered under the long-standing laws on craft workshops. Although they have increased in number since 1990, these firms have not seen a rapid growth equivalent to that in the number of limited liability companies. The doubling in the total number of firms in Slovenia has come about mainly through the entry of new enterprises with limited liability. As can be seen from Table 11.2, by 1993, this new sector accounted for over half of all firms in Slovenia.

The development of the small-scale private sector through the entry of new private businesses has proceeded much more rapidly than the formal privatization of the relatively large-scale social ownership sector. A dual economy is emerging comprising, on the one hand, the remnants of the former self-management enterprises, now largely operating under employee share ownership, and, on the other hand, a large and growing small-firms sector under predominantly private ownership. However, as in Croatia and Macedonia FRY, there are also a number of small firms which have been set up as wholly owned subsidiaries of the employee-owned firms.

Table 11.2   Ownership structure of enterprises, Slovenia, 1993

Ownership form	Enterprises
Social	3 053
Limited liability	42 746
Cooperative	360
Mixed	1 575
Craft	35 911
Total	83 645

Source: *Statistical Yearbook of Slovenia*, 1994, Tables 19.1 and 3.3.

CONCLUSIONS

The recent post-independence reform programmes in the successor states have emphasized the abolition of the institutions of the self-management system and their replacement by a deregulated market, restructuring of the banking system, monetary stability, the creation of well defined property rights and the promotion of the entry of new private businesses. The emphasis on employee and management buy-outs in the practical outcome of the privatization process is likely to give rise to a dual economy in which an employee ownership sector coexists with an emerging small-scale private sector. It remains to be seen how effective the employee ownership sector will be, and a key question will be the extent to which employee ownership improves productivity and competitive performance, or whether it leads to renewed insider pressure for job stability and unjustified wage increases, and discourages foreign direct investment.

The issue is complicated by the variety of forms of market relations which exist between the new privatized large employee-owned firms and the new small firms entrants which have been established either under independent private ownership or as wholly owned subsidiaries of the large employee-owned firms. Where the employee-owned firms and the private firms are competing with each other for market share, the relative productivity performance of the two types of ownership may lead to a Darwinian struggle for survival. Where employee-owned firms and private firms are linked together in a network relationship, the two forms of ownership and enterprise governance may continue to coexist in an ecologically stable equilibrium. This possibility may be enhanced in cases such as that of TETEKS, where the small firms are set up as subsidiaries of the large parent firm. In such a case, as long as the parent firm retains a set of management objectives influenced by a substantial employee stockholding, there may be a continuing interest in the welfare and survival of the offspring subsidiary. In such a case it can be expected that the large firm will desist from overexploiting the small firm and indeed assist its development, growth and survival. Of course, a large number of potential outcomes are possible in such network relationships and, as we have seen, there is great pressure upon management of employee-owned firms to try to obtain a controlling interest for themselves. In this case the system would probably begin to evolve towards a form of ownership and economic patterns of behaviour much more similar to that found in western market economies with all the familiar problems of short termism and low levels of employee motivation which are key concerns of policy makers in the west.

ACKNOWLEDGEMENTS

The research was carried out under an ACE research fellowship at the University of Ljubljana, during May–June 1995; under an ODA project on economic reconstruction in war affected areas of Croatia, beginning in April 1996; and an ODA project on SME and regional development in Macedonia FRY, beginning in May 1996.

REFERENCES

Bartlett, W. (1991), 'Economic Change in Yugoslavia: From Crisis to Reform', in O. Sjoberg and M. Wyzan (eds), *Economic Change in the Balkan States: Albania, Bulgaria, Romania and Yugoslavia*, London: Pinter Publishers, pp. 32–46.

Bartlett, W. (1996), 'From Reform to Crisis: Economic Impacts of Secession, War and Sanctions in the former Yugoslavia', in I. Jeffries (ed.), *Problems of Economic and Political Transformation in the Balkans*, London: Pinter, pp. 151–72.

Bartlett, W. and J. Prasnikar (1995), 'Small Firms and Economic Transformation in Slovenia', *Communist Economies and Economic Transformation*, 7, (1), 83–103.

Bartlett, W. and M. Uvalić (1992), 'Economic Transition, Unemployment and Policy Response in the former Yugoslavia in the 1980s', *CMS Occasional Paper, No. 6*, Bristol: Centre for Mediterranean Studies.

Bateman, M. (ed.) (1996), *Business Cultures in Eastern Europe*, Oxford: Butterworth-Heinemann.

Bićanić, I. (1993), 'Privatization in Croatia', *East European Politics and Societies*, 1, (3).

Čučković, N. (1993), 'Privatization in Croatia: What Went Wrong?', *History of European Ideas*, 17, (6).

Furubotn, P. and S. Pejovich (1970), 'Property Rights and the Behaviour of the Yugoslav Firm in a Socialist State: The Example of Yugoslavia', *Zeitschrift für Nationaloekonomie*, 30, (3–4), 431–54.

Hafner, D.F. (1992), 'Political Modernisation in Slovenia in the 1980s and Early 1990s', *The Journal of Communist Studies*, 8, (4), 210–26.

Korze, U. and M. Simoneti (1992), 'Privatization in Slovenia – 1992', in A. Bohm and M. Simoneti (eds), *Privatization in Central and Eastern Europe*, Ljubljana: CEEPN Academy.

Lydall, H. (1989), *Yugoslavia in Crisis*, Oxford: Clarendon Press.

Mađar, Lj. (1992), 'The Economy of Yugoslavia: Structure, Growth Record and Institutional Framework', in J.B. Allcock, J.J. Horton and M. Milivojevic (eds), *Yugoslavia in Transition: Choices and Constraints*, Oxford: Berg.

Ramet, S.P. (1993), 'Slovenia's Road to Democracy', *Europe–Asia Studies*, **45**, (5), 869–86.

Rop, A. (1995), *Privatization in Slovenia: General Framework for Privatization in Slovenia*, Ljubljana: CEEPN Academy.

SKLAD (1994), *1993 Annual Report*, Ljubljana: Development Fund of the Republic of Slovenia.

SKLAD (1995) *Privatization in Slovenia*, Ljubljana: Development Fund of the Republic of Slovenia.

Stanovnik, T. and S. Kukar (1995), 'The Pension System in Slovenia: Past Developments and Future Prospects', *International Social Security Review*, **48**, (1), 35–43.

Uvalić, M. (1992), *Investment and Property Rights in Yugoslavia: The Long Transition to a Market Economy*, Cambridge: Cambridge University Press.

Uvalić, M. (1996), 'Employee Ownership in the Successor States of the Former Yugoslavia', paper presented at a conference on Employee Ownership in Central and Eastern Europe, Ukraine and the Baltic States, Florence, April.

12. Restructuring of the banks in Albania

Shkelqim Cani

In 1990, after the collapse of the then prevailing socioeconomic system, Albania was immediately faced with a mass exodus of young people from the country, bankruptcy of the national treasury, stand-still production units, failure of legal and political structure and chaotic conditions of normal life. Thanks to western economic aid and the emergence of a political democracy, the country has stood up to the challenge. Albania has emerged as a potential area for direct international investments, a European country with the fastest rate of growth of GNP in the 1990s. It has been turned into a vast construction site. The country has so far managed relatively well with macroeconomic aggregates by providing the basic necessary economic stability in the system, thus building confidence in the future of the country (Cani, 1995b).

In 1990, Albania inherited a backward, centralized and government-controlled system of banking and finance. At the end of 1991, there were four state-owned banks in operation. The State Bank of Albania performed the functions of both the central as well as the commercial bank. Following the enactment of banking laws, a two-tier banking system was created. The Bank of Albania (BOA), established in April 1992, was declared as the central bank of the country and the remaining three state-owned banks were allowed to function officially as commercial banks. In practice, the banking system continues to be characterized by market segmentation and specialization. Hence, by the first quarter of 1995, the Savings Bank (SB) held 80 per cent of households' savings deposits and around 19 per cent of total loans, while the National Commercial Bank (NCB) held 85 per cent of enterprise deposits and 39 per cent of all loans. The Rural Commercial Bank (RCB) continues to enjoy a monopoly in deposits and loans to the agricultural sector.

The first private bank in Albania was established in late 1993, as a 50 per cent joint venture between the National Commercial Bank and the Italian Banca di Roma. Soon afterwards, another joint venture bank, the Arab-Albanian Islamic Bank (AIB), and a wholly private bank were established. All these private banks are relatively small and their activities are limited mainly to fee-based businesses executing foreign transactions.

So far, the financial and banking systems have lagged behind the overall pace of development, thus hindering economic reforms. The financial market is not properly understood. It lacks synchronization and the secondary market is non-existent. Banking reforms are the key to the successful strategies of economic transformation. If privatization is to succeed, there should be a properly functioning capital market which in turn cannot be created unless a thorough reform of the banking system is enacted. Accordingly, privatization and the reform of the banking system must go hand in hand.

In principle, the BOA has been designed as a central bank. Obviously, to some extent, it is thanks to the BOA's policies that there is an improvement in the macrofinancial indicators. The BOA, following an example of foreign banks, has taken steps towards its reorganization, monetary and interest rate policy, and efficient supervision, drafting of guidelines to license the establishment of new banks and the classification of the credits according to international standards.

Simultaneously, access to the new computerized accounting systems is being worked out. Tenders of Treasury bills are frequently held. The monetary policy has relied mainly on the direct instruments of monetary control. The amount of credit since 1992 is being supervised through bank-by-bank ceilings on net credit to the non-governmental sector. In order to provide some flexibility and encourage the banks to start inter-bank operations, the ceilings are allowed to be tradable. Nevertheless, BOA is currently applying some other important instruments of indirect control, including window, reserve and liquidity requirements, as well as Treasury bills on the primary market.

Commercial bank services are poor, especially for depositors, who frequently waste a lot of time, ranging from one hour to one day, just completing simple bank operations such as a withdrawal.[1] Most transactions remain cash-based. Despite some improvements in the existing credit structure, the actual banking system has become a serious bottleneck to country's economic growth as credit demand for investment goods is growing following the privatization of most state enterprises. Table 12.1 shows the credit structure of Albanian banks as per April 1995.

The general inability of banks to respond to growing credit demand by the new private sector could be considered from several standpoints. Table 12.2 indicates the visible differences between the interest rates applied to loans granted by banks and by the private market. The interests applicable by the private market are estimated to be three and a half to four times higher than those of the banks.

The limit of credit granted to the commercial banks from BOA has been lower than the real needs and capabilities of the Albanian economy. However, at the end of the first half of 1995, this limit was utilized only by 53 per cent.

Table 12.1   Credit structure of Albanian banks, April 1995

	NCB	RCB	SB	AIB	DB	All banks
Total credits ($ million)	37.5	40.5	18.9	2.0	1.8	100.7
of which (per cent)						
short term	53.0	63.3	33.5	100.0	100.0	55.2
long term	47.0	36.7	66.5	0.0	0.0	44.8
of which (per cent)						
private sector	56.2	99.3	55.2	100.0	100.0	75.0
public sector	43.8	0.7	44.8	0.0	0.0	25.0

Note: NCB = National Commercial Bank; RCB = Rural Commercial Bank; SB = Saving Banks; AIB = Arab Islamic Bank; DB = Development Bank.

Source: Bank of Albania Statistics.

This leads to some serious consequences for the future economic development of the country.

One of the biggest problems that the state banks confront today is the rapid growth of new, non-performing credits, whose share in total new credit outstanding was 27 per cent at the end of 1994[2] and 32 per cent in June 1995, of which 87 per cent belongs to the private sector. The proportion of non-performing credits considered lost or bad debts rose from 29 per cent at the beginning of 1994 to 39 per cent by the end of the year. Therefore, as most Albanians place their funds in time deposits at the state-owned Savings Bank, this bank in turn, along with the other banks, uses a good part of this money to fund the public deficit and non-performing credits.

Table 12.2   Structure of interest rates in Albania (per cent per annum)

	Jan. '94 to July '94		July '94 onwards	
	Banks*	Private**	Banks*	Private**
12 months maturity	26	—	20	—
6 months maturity	22	—	17	—
3 months maturity	17	85–100	14	70–85

Note: * Published guideline rates; ** unofficial spot market rates.

Source: Bank of Albania Statistics.

Private-sector financial activity works in a shadow economy. The activity is almost entirely non-licensed, very suspicious and of considerable importance. Taking into account our indirect and approximate calculations, this private-sector financial activity has currently amassed some US$200–300 million from the population. There is a risk that a large amount of funds may be withdrawn from the state banks in the near future and go in search of more lucrative rates in the shadow economy. It is likely that this activity will continue to play an important role until the formal banking system increases the efficiency of its operations and is able to provide good services in most areas of the country. In spite of some amendments made during 1995, the weak legal system does not as yet permit a secure banking arrangement. Repayment is partially dependent upon the good standing of the individuals.

The fully liberalized street market has made cash foreign exchange transactions efficient and competitive. Foreign exchange transactions through the banking system, especially for foreign trade, continue to be difficult and costly. The foreign exchange bureau is limited to cash transactions only. Unfortunately, it has not been given a free hand to operate actively as the BOA is afraid of its getting out of control.

Despite an annual inflation rate of about 15–20 per cent, during 1994–96, the lek has held steady, but has been overvalued against foreign currencies, leading to a decline in local competitiveness and massive imports, which compete with the existing domestic production. This policy has been changed from the second half of 1994, permitting a slight depreciation of the lek. Over the short term, Albania may face two potential financial challenges (Cani, 1995a):

1. Inflation may rise as a result of currency resources related to donors' funds, remissions from abroad, export of goods, in which chromium represents 20 per cent total exports, and smuggling activities.
2. Past inflation will effect pressure to devaluate the lek. Since this phenomenon has not occurred so far, mainly for political reasons, expectations are that it will still take some time before it happens. Albania's export competitiveness will continue to erode, while imports will be further promoted, even though the nation's salary base is lower than that of other European countries.

RESTRUCTURING OF COMMERCIAL BANKS

The policy of the restructuring of existing banks has not been properly studied so far. What has been attained so far is a lot of drawbacks, and failure. Two examples may be cited. First, on 1 January 1993, NBA

(National Bank for Agriculture) merged with ACB (Agricultural Credit Bank) to form the Rural Commercial Bank (RCB).[3] This merging was completely mechanical and did not come out as a well studied or well argued organic need. Consequently, ACB, as a quality leading bank in Albania composed of bankers highly trained abroad and which might well have served as a nucleus to establish an up-to-date bank, was suffocated. The fusing of the two banks' accounts without conducting any preliminary auditing caused discrepancies.

The second case is that of the Bank for Agriculture and Development (BAD). In October 1993, the BAD was restructured, with the good assets and deposits transferred to the new NCB and the non-performing assets left in BAD, pending a comprehensive restructuring of the banking system and resolution of old bad debts. The intention of RCB was to meet the needs of private farmers and businessmen on commercial banking principles. Upon the creation of the bank, with the assistance of foreign specialists, a comprehensive programme was initiated and some progress was made in the accounting and credit areas. From 1994 onwards, this system did not work at all, as the result of both poor management and corporate governance and inadequate and inefficient commitment of foreign experts appointed to provide technical banking assistance in the bank. From October 1993 to September 1995, these experts were paid up to US$2.2 million for their assistance to the RCB. The losses indicated in the RCB balance sheet have resulted because of the high amount of non-duly-performed credits and non-handling of old credits inherited by the BAD, etc, which reflects upon the positive effect of the progress achieved by the RCB through accounting and financial reporting system, credit manual and supervision, staff training, etc.

PRIVATIZATION OF BANKS

Banks now face the need for radical change to be converted into independent decision makers and efficient bodies, very much like their western and some eastern homologues. Banks are in great need of staff training, outside technical assistance, and the reorganization and implementation of modern banking facilities and techniques. The process of establishing new private banks has also been delayed. In October 1995, the government introduced a scheme of bank restructuring for approval by Parliament, but this still contains inaccuracies and requires amendments. It only visualizes the privatization of the existing state banks within a very short period of time. The bank privatization scheme in Albania has its drawbacks. It should be implemented keeping in mind the following (Cani, 1995a):

1. The legal and semi-legal acts administering the banking activity in Albania are minimal. The two principal acts, The Banking System Act and The Bank of Albania Act enacted in April 1992, should have been entirely revised by now, starting with their imprecise definitions of what a bank and banking activity are. The same applies to the definitions stipulated in the Civil Code approved on 27 September 1994 regarding the banking contracts, which are apparently not explicit, leading to failure to implement them in practice. It is regarded as an unjustified lack of laws regulating the marketable securities and stock of exchange, foreign exchange, monetary and payment instruments and so on. In addition, the absence of administrative and account courts delays the process of handling and solving civil suits for entire months.

2. The issue of implementing a banking system independent of executive power is still pending to meet the expectations provided by law. Recently, the BOA is obliged to issue banknotes in order to finance the increasing budgetary deficit. It is not rare to hear of cases where loans are granted on political considerations. Loans are now mostly dispensed in dubious circumstances, while the government often charges the banks with tasks outside their usual activities. A positive reaction was the enactment of a law in 1994 forbidding the government to extend public guarantees on state bank loans to public enterprises any longer. In this framework, the privatization process will close the paths to governmental interventions.

3. Stopping the economically unsound lending practises and repaying of old inherited credits should be executed with more personal responsibility assumed by credit officers. These officers must maintain closer contacts with clients, but a certain fee based on the amount of credits collected should be paid to motivate them. We are fully convinced that applying a fee of 0.03–0.05 per cent on the credit collection will reduce the amount of duly non-performed credits (loans that are not being paid on time) by half, and even those classified as lost. This commission is trivial compared to the total bank cost or even credit cost, when the difference between credit and deposit interest rate levels for the same period is actually around 5 per cent. A positive impact would also be achieved by the replacement of some corrupt credit officers. The need for qualified experts to evaluate buildings, land and other real estate according to the market value is of essential importance. Unlike the situation in other countries, where the banks and the governments have been unwilling to push for bank failure – for the banks fear the financial impact on their balance sheets and the governments fear unemployment consequences – in Albania this has never been the case in the past, because the main law on bankruptcy only came into being in September 1996.

4. The commercial state-owned bank operations are generally characterized by passivity and a lack of initiative. The old concept that since 'clients need us, they should come to us and accept us as we are' still prevails among the majority of bank employees. But like every market, the financial market also has its own 'king-clients', and they have to be served.

5. The privatization of the existing banks has reached a critical point. The question is whether privatization will be successfully implemented. Among the most discussed alternatives to bank privatization, voucher privatization, through partial liquidation, sale to strategic investors or an international tender, was considered to be the best option. But taking into account the evident shortfalls of the principal liquid capital of the banks, a compromise version of the above alternative might have been more logical and desirable. The final results of the existing commercial banks' privatization will be largely influenced the following:

    ● Which schemes of savings and deposits and to what extent will these be secured, so that the depositors will not shy away and withdraw their deposits?
    ● Will the auditing of foreign experts be fully realized, up to the processing of financial results and balance sheets for each bank branch, prior to privatization, because the existing balance sheets are imprecise and based on old methods?
    ● Will the government be able to issue a full guideline stipulating in detail the procedure for privatization, define the procedure of bank assets' evaluation, depreciation rates, intangible assets such as goodwill and so on, in order to avoid the painful experiences of past privatization cases in other industries?
    ● Replacing the non-interest-bearing assets through productive and secure assets.
    ● Possibly relieving the banks of the loan portfolio of some worst performing branches.
    ● Relieving the banks of lost loans.
    ● As the restructuring of the banking system will undoubtedly be costly, the authorities need to monitor costs carefully and seek financing sources.

    Such technical problems are pressing and solutions to them could be found by taking advantage of the best experience available. This would contribute significantly to making bank privatization genuinely efficient, avoiding the routine of frequent ownership changes. Not all banks should be privatized at the same time; privatization should be staggered, so that the last of the chain to be privatized should profit from the best experience gained.

In the next four to five years, the new banks are supposed to play a leading role in the Albanian banking chain. Albanian businessmen, according to a survey recently conducted, see the creation of a private bank as a necessity, but there are a number of reasons why they are still hesitating and are not fully committed to undertaking such a big step: other businesses make huge profits; banking activity is conceived as rather difficult; the tradition of a joint-stock company has never been known; a minimum required investment of US$3 million is relatively high and unaffordable for the majority of Albanian businessmen;[4] the laws are still unstable and involve a lot of loopholes; the prevailing fear of potential shareholders of any counteraction from political parties and official authorities.

Despite these problems, it is very likely that new private banks will be opened by the beginning of 1997. In this respect, the new bank licensing regulations issued in June 1995 are a significant step in facilitating the process. Furthermore, the Albanian–American Enterprise Fund is expected to start lending activities and to create a new private bank for SME as well as equity participation. An initiative by the German Bank KfW to establish a lending institution for SMEs by 1996 was approved by the Albanian Parliament.

The government has always had a positive attitude towards the establishment of new private banks, but, in order to support this process effectively it must shift to the policy of promotion and cooperation. In this respect one of the possible suggested patterns could be the involvement of the state through the purchase of 10–30 per cent of shares in initial capital – as a passive shareholder entitled to sell its own share to public over a certain period of time. Perhaps the Albanian-American Enterprise Fund will cooperate with the Albanian investors to set up a joint stock bank.

Owing to the weak legal structure in Albania, the EBRD has rejected a plan to establish an onshore investment bank in favour of an offshore facility. In fact, the EBRD should have taken the advantage of the fact that population of Albanian descent possesses estimated some US$2 billion in deposit accounts abroad. Creation of such a facility could have easily mobilized these resources for investment in Albania. The question is no longer whether to create these private banks or not, but how efficiently this money will be administered.

NOTES

1. Referring to a personal survey conducted in November 1994 on the ease of banking operation handling, the following is the time required for a single money transaction: (a) same bank, same branch, two hours and twenty minutes; (b) same bank, different branches, three to 14 days; (c) different banks and branches, from seven to 21 days.

2. According to a public statement by the owner of the biggest Albanian company, his equity amounts to some US$300 million. Total deposits placed in state banks in April 1995 were US$1.8 billion.
3. By that time the executive staff of ACB had introduced a scheme along with economic arguments supporting the idea of bank privatization, which might have been the optimal solution.
4. According to the new bank licensing regulations issued on June 1995, the minimum required capital for Albanians is US$1 million, while it is US$ 2 million for foreigners.

REFERENCES

Cani, S. (1995a), 'Financial Reforms in Albania', in *Restruktriranje gospodarstva u tranziciji*, Zagreb: Ekonomski fakultet (International Conference, 8–11 November 1995 – Papers and Proceedings).

Cani, S. (1995b), *Future Investment: Prospects in Albania*, Proceedings of the International Conference, 28–30 June, Tirana: Government of Albania G-24 European Commission.

13. Company restructuring and business analysis

Janko Tintor

Transition and restructuring is a multidimensional process of moving over to a market-oriented business. Accordingly, a number of changes – political, social, legal and economic – are taking place in Central and East European countries. Like any other process of change, transition to a market economy means introducing a certain degree of instability and crisis on the macro and micro level. The scope and intensity of changes in the economic environment can be illustrated by company restructuring, as well as by changes that are taking place in ownership, labour relations, internal organization, investment and the volume of business conducted.

To illustrate these changes, let us take the example of Croatia, where the process of change in ownership, namely privatization, started in 1992. By 1 September 1994, this had happened in 2364 companies. Over 47.5 per cent of the large companies were privatized in full. The state privatization agency held majority shares in 15.9 per cent and minority shares in 36.6 per cent of the companies. At the same time, medium-sized and small companies were totally privatized. Such structured privatization is reflected in the structure of the total value of capital. The share of the state was then estimated at DM10.722 million. With such a change, particularly with new business entries, the share of small and medium-sized businesses was increased and the long-existing gap between self-employed companies and large conglomerates was filled. But such extensive state ownership has helped the state to continue to exercise significant influence.

Alongside privatization, some other changes have taken place. For example, the abandoning of the automatic system of refinancing bank loans, the introduction of the money market and other institutions of the financial system (such as creating a primitive share market). All these changes have taken place in rather unfavourable conditions created by the loss of the former Yugoslav market, a long-lasting civil war, the burden of refugees, and so forth, which have resulted in the decline of private-sector activities. The gross domestic product during 1991–3 was reduced by 25 per cent, the unemployment rate shot up to 17 per cent and war damages were incurred roughly to the tune of US$15 billion (Jurković and Škreb, 1994).

Similar changes have been witnessed in other former socialist countries. According to statistics published at the beginning of 1995, some 897 000 small and medium-sized companies in Russia, employing over 8.5 million people, were in operation. In the Czech Republic the registered number of private firms was 1 058 784. Some 76.5 per cent of the industrial enterprises had fewer than 500 employees. In the Ukraine, at the end of 1995, the share of small and medium-sized companies was 16 per cent in overall industry, 15 per cent in construction activity along and 45 per cent in trade and commerce. Apart from diversification of activities, small and medium-sized companies in transitional economies have other characteristics in common, such as a relatively small number of employees and a relatively low share in the gross domestic product. These developments have an impact on the overall economic situation in the country. Furthermore, it is symptomatic that in all these countries companies operate under similar market conditions, such as slowed down economic activity, high rates of inflation, unusually high rates of interest on bank loans, and so on.

Evidently, the conclusion is simple: conditions under which transition and the process of restructuring is taking place in most of these countries are more or less identical. In other words, the process is going on under unfavourable market conditions. For the purpose of analysis, the uniformity of the process of restructuring and the conditions under which it is taking place, the companies of these countries – the transitional firms – can be considered as homogeneous subjects.

CONDITIONS OF RESTRUCTURING

A firm is an organized system of transforming resources. Taking time and location into consideration as factors, it transforms the resource input (labour, ideas, capital, raw material and so on) into output (product, services and so on). It is understood that the market value of the input thus transformed exceeds its original value (costs), otherwise there will be no production. Owing to this very fact, it is natural to expect that a firm will economize resources as they are vital for its survival and growth. Each enterprise has its implicit and explicit strategy for establishing itself within a given environment so as to achieve its goals and maximize a positive exchange value between output and input in time (Hinterhuber, 1989, p.160).

Our definition of a company/firm contains two elementary facts. First, an enterprise is an organized system of production in which a number of elements are conditioned, and certain connecting principles regulate these elements to knit them into a single whole, that is a functional purpose. Second, an enterprise exists in time, implying growth and development of all its characteristic features.

The content of restructuring is based on the first mentioned characteristic feature. Seen as a system, the firm is a single entity by nature. It is possible to disaggregate it according to its individual features (Kajzer, 1993). Some economists distinguish among firms according to the following characteristics: management, information system, production, marketing and company finance. It should be noted that it is not possible to restructure each element in isolation, but the company as a whole. In other words, company restructuring involves changes, not only in the manner of conducting business in a market environment, but also in all the above-mentioned elements.

The manner and problems of restructuring are based on the second characteristic feature. The company can survive only if it grows. Many theories claim to govern this aspect. The most accepted and commonly used theory is the life cycle theory (Gloeckner-Holme, 1988 p. 61). According to Nagel, six different factors (strategy, organization, associates, governance system, information system and attitude towards the customer) and five different phases (start, expansion, consolidation, growth and integration) are essential for a company's growth and development. In each phase, different factors have different content and a different form of influence (Nagel, 1988). The growth of a company is measured by the growth of its potential, volume of production, income and profits, and by the number of employees in the company. The development of the company is indicated by an increased degree of efficiency and effectiveness. Both the growth and development of a company are determined by the above-mentioned factors. In each phase of the life cycle the company must adjust to changes as required by the environment. Without a proper governance system, change in organization, changes in attitude towards the customers and so on, it is difficult to understand the environment and create any business strategy, so that a company is likely to land in a crisis. Parallel to such an explanation, the life cycle theory differentiates between two types of orientations which serve as the basis for the operational orientation of the strategy for growth and development. The first orientation is towards internal forces (technology, cost reduction, high profit-yielding product, rationalization, increased efficiency and so on). Companies having such orientation are those in a lower phase of development. The alternative is outward orientation, and companies opting for such solutions are evidently in higher phases of development. They look for solutions in customers and market, product and service quality, innovations and competition.

The companies in transitional economies have only been able to reach the second and third phase of development. They were introvert in approach.

Their management, organization and information system were designed to cope with an underdeveloped market. For this very reason, these companies are not yet prepared for transition to higher phases of development. In fact, an enterprise is an economic (as well as a social) and national (naturally global in an open economy) subject – thus a subsystem. The conditions of restructuring are generated within this subsystem as well as in the surrounding environment. Naturally, there is turbulence which is, by definition, irregular non-linear and erratic in behaviour. In such circumstances, it is logical to conclude that specific events will alter the entire configuration of the whole economic system. Thus there is an increasing conflict between fundamental trends in the economy, which push towards integration, and trends in world polity. An integrated world economy and a splintered world polity can coexist only in tension, conflict and mutual misunderstanding (Drucker, 1981). Behind this change lie changes in world population. An analysis of world population and labour forces shows relative changes.[1] This difference in the growth rate of the labour force is a matter of restructuring (Johnston, 1991). The differences also stretch to age and sex structure. This calls for an overall restructuring of the international system.[2] The population growth rates in transitional economies are not high, but the structure of the population is almost the same as those in developing countries. Here we have an educated and highly skilled population with high production and consumption potential, but, in view of the company's orientations, the manner of functioning of the economic system and so on, these countries have an excess labour supply and thus very much resemble developing countries.

The limited possibilities for such a change will lead to economic integration. This integration will be of a far different nature from that in the past. The practice of production sharing will perhaps be the most important phase of economic integration. In such an integration, the resources of developing countries, for example labour for the traditional jobs, are combined with the resources of developed countries (management, technology, educated people, markets, purchasing power and so on). In such an integration there is no relocation of the production process or moving one factor closer to the other production factors. It involves location of production and the relevant factors in the same place (Drucker, 1981, pp. 95, 105).

Evidently, the general process of functionally and structurally reconstituting the world economic and political system has brought greater complexity to economic, political and other environments in which contemporary enterprises have to conduct their businesses. The transition process in which these changes are taking place in Eastern Europe only emphasizes the complexities and turbulence. In strategic terms, every company and its management are faced by the task of creating potentials for survival, growth and development. In operational terms, they have to find the most rational use for existing facilities. Therefore an enterprise needs adequate management potential which can respond to its contemporary chaotic environment.

As far as restructuring is concerned,

- it is a general process equally important to developed, developing and transitional economies;
- it takes place in conflicting circumstances of economic integration and disintegration of the world political system;
- it continues under conditions of unequally available potentials in developed, transitional and developing countries; and
- it grows under turbulent conditions in which the behaviour of the firm is unpredictable.

All these elements necessarily create the new characteristics of a modern firm. The old multinational corporations based on capital and financial control are being replaced by transnational confederations based on production sharing and on the controlling ability to adapt quickly – in production, design and marketing. Managing and marketing organizations are crucial and will primarily organize production and distribution. The cohesion of an enterprise will lie more in controlling marketing than in controlling capital. Subsidiaries of multinational corporations are being turned into subcontractors, independently carrying out a whole range of production but only on the local or national market. At the same time, they produce a part of the product range for the whole corporation. This requires a new structure. Instead of the present high pyramid in which all departments are under the command of top management, future top management will have a new role of integrative force. It will control through marketing, rather than through its legal authority. It will be like the conductor of an orchestra rather than the general of an army. Transnational confederation requires simultaneous tight control of top management over the entire entity and more freedom and responsibility of its individual parts. There is an increased need for system organization.[3]

Restructuring and transition combined into a single process of development in Central and Eastern Europe involves restructuring of companies by the size and extent of their growth. Again, it depends, to a certain extent, upon the general level of economic development in these countries. The differences in the levels of development of companies can be best explained by the previously mentioned life cycle theory of firms. Bleicher differentiates six phases of growth of which three, pioneering, opening of the market and diversification, are based on the internal growth of the company; two phases, acquisition and cooperation, are based on external growth of the company. The sixth phase is based on a combination of internal and external factors and is called restructuring. In this advanced phase, highly developed corporations (companies) reorganize themselves. This is a crisis phase for these companies. The collapse of the socialist system in transitional economies meant an intensification of the internal causes of such a crisis (Bleicher, 1995, pp. 347–78).

Types of crises in enterprises can be differentiated (Hauschildt, 1988). Within this context, Croatia, unfortunately, has very limited research regarding the state of health of domestic companies. What is characteristically true for a limited and small number of firms is valid for other companies, too. The crisis of firms in transitional economies is in direct relationship to a combined force of action of heterogeneous factors, so that the state of crisis in these firms is not sufficiently clear. For the same reason one could identify only some of the causes, as mentioned below.

1. *In production*: obsolete technology; excess or undercapacity; single product orientation; a limited production programme; regional and local orientation; a primitive system of division into production units and the preservation of an outmoded style of management; inadequate product quality control.
2. *In the field of supplies procurement*: disrupted supply channels with scant possibilities for renewal or orientation towards new ones; political risks; financial risk in the procurement of raw materials due to foreign exchange rate fluctuations; the inability to adapt to substitute materials; irrationally high quantities of stocks, and so on.
3. *In the domain of sales*: loss of market and buyers; the necessity for new orientation but the inability of firms to create a new market portfolio; lack of innovation in product and sale channels; a cost-oriented, high price policy.
4. *Finance*: a disproportionate structure of ownership and capital; an undeveloped financial market; limited and constrained financing with borrowed capital and lack of possibilities of a financial anchor; high costs of borrowed capital; lack of circulating capital; and so on.
5. *Financial discipline*: deficiencies and discrepancies in cost accounting and balance sheets; lack of expertise in identifying successful products, buyer groups, markets, branches, departments and so on; dependence on short-term successes; relying on a short-term budget and the neglect of a serious business analysis; overreliance and obsession with the strategy of maintaining the status quo, or survival.
6. *Organization and management*: too much dependence on the proprietor or the new owner; nepotism; patriarchal style of management; lack of professionalism; attempts at superficial control, frequent conflicts with associates and subordinates, centralized and ambiguous assignment of duties and responsibilities; inability to adapt to the needs of potential businesses.

As evidence suggests, in all transitional economies, the state continues to hold a major share of capital and, thereby, control over major economic events. The state still holds the status of 'the only institution of political power at home and abroad' in which political theory and constitutional law recognize nothing else but the individual sovereign state. Creation of some transitional economies as sovereign states with enhanced power at home, with impact of ownership structure on economic events is the new legal and political reality of restructuring in Central and Eastern Europe. Each transitional state today is basically faced by the task of defining its own legal status as the bearer of political and economic power.[4] These states will have to decide, on the one hand, what part of their economy they wish to restructure and integrate into the global system and, on the other, how to use their power and influence to help available human, spatial and other resources to integrate with outside technology, capital, marketing potentials and so on. Accordingly, in transitional economies, where the state is the main agent of restructuring, a well defined strategy needs to be introduced in which the role and place of the firm will be clearly defined.

BUSINESS ANALYSIS: AN INSTRUMENT OF RESTRUCTURING

In the earlier sections we highlighted some of the negative features of firms in a transitional economy which have been inherited from the past. The state of affairs in which the companies find themselves today is basically a result of their inadequate knowledge of their own position – their strengths and weaknesses. Such a situation can be explained by the firms' position in lower phases of development and growth according to the life cycle theory in which these transitional firms currently find themselves. In the closed economy with socialized risks and non-market behaviour in which these firms found themselves, the success of the firms was supposed to be based on the rational use of available resources and on the creation of new products. Efficiency-based competitiveness was not considered at all important and thus was not developed.

For decision making, the management requires information and business analysis from the comptrollers. There are two basic objectives to business analysis. One is to prepare the company in a planned manner for the best and most rational conduct of business. The other is to create a foundation for those long-term business decisions which aim at restructuring the financial and internal organization of the company and its personnel. Controlling, as a system of information, consists of three subsystems: business analysis, planning and information, and coordination. Results of a defective business analysis are transmitted to other subsystems and reflect on the ability to manage.

In transitional countries, there are two types of causes which determine the state of business analysis. In the first category, reasons relate to the lower life cycle stage of companies, because of which business analysis was oriented only towards the day-to-day functioning of the company. Basically, it dealt with the analysis of plan targets and achievements. Objectively speaking, in its content, instruments, organization, sources of data and so on it was suited to lower levels of management. In decision making there was a problem of improvement in the quality of work. Cross-sections and comparative analyses were the main instruments of such analysis. The analysis of the causes of a certain state were of subsidiary importance. The analysis of current and future potentials, from a strategic policy point of view, was considered irrelevant. The second category of causes concerns the manner in which decisions concerning a company's growth and development are made. The size and allocation of investment were outside the scope of the companies and were primarily based upon macroeconomic trends. The socialization of risk and losses made it possible for companies to exist without any analysis of strategic position and potential. In other words, the state of business analysis and planning and management based on this in transitional firms was institutionally and instrumentally developed for operational purposes. A slight difference was notable in former Yugoslavia. A relatively open economy, the existence of a rudimentary market, a decentralized style of management and so on helped develop business analysis in a company's strategic orientation. But the civil war, change in the ownership structure, reduction of markets and matters of survival pushed companies into relying on short-term strategy. The consequences for business analysis were twofold. On the one hand, the surveys conducted pointed out that either there was no drawn-up and publicly known company strategy or, if there was, it was inadequately determined. On the other hand, under the influence of general economic conditions, which are the result of the current process of transition, the existing, so-called 'plan and analysis' department in companies reverted to the use of operational accounting statements.

Restructuring, as a process and method of integration into the world economy, presupposes a clear and well-defined strategy which combines existing domestic and foreign potentials. Naturally, a clear picture of the same is a presupposition for future strategy. This primarily implies the assessment of the firm's position according to criteria of pre-industrial, industrial or post-industrial society (Bea and Haas, 1995). Secondly, the existing structure of man, material and spatial potentials with which technology, capital and market demands can be integrated needs to be expanded. Finally, to fully understand the company's portfolio, one part of the analysis will have to cover those aspects where the state can help influence an efficient and effective integration process, while the other part will have to take the integration model of 'product sharing' into account and become part of a new class of interested transnational economic confederations.

For this objective to be achieved, not only an adequate understanding of restructuring process from an institutional, functional, organizational and development aspect of business analysis is required but also operative analysis which must include a strategic business analysis. In other words, it is essential to institutionalize business analysis as a permanent instrument of information for company governance.

Unfortunately, so far, companies in transitional economies have not reached the higher stages of their life cycle and thus have not yet created their 'clearing houses'. In a majority of cases, the problem posed is how procedurally and structurally to institutionalize 'business analysis'. In our opinion, assessing the reality of the situation, for example, in Croatia, but also in other countries, there are two directions and two ways to do this. While one direction is the institutionalization and strengthening of operational planning, internal analysis and control within the company, the other direction stresses the importance of institutionalization of the process and structural formation of strategic analysis and planning that is controlling for the purpose of creating presuppositions which will enable the decision makers to learn from events and surroundings.

Depending upon the manner of integeration of companies into the national and global economy strategic analysis, planning and control can be implemented in two ways: firstly, those sectors of the national economy which will enter the international competition game will have to depend upon those institutions which specialize in studying various aspects of the world economy. Such as orientation depends upon infrastructural facilities. Secondly, different solution is offered for those companies or sector which will become subcontractors and cooperators or parts of the transnational confederations. In future, the principal task of management will be confined only to the task of educating people and enabling them to read in between the lines and convert available information into sound and rational business decisions.

Strategic business analysis is an underdeveloped field in transitional economies. It is therefore essential to establish a comprehensive business analysis as a tool for implementing and attaining the restructuring of companies in general.

NOTES

1. The expected growth of 1.6 per cent in the labour force is not evenly distributed. While in OECD countries it is expected to be 0.5 per cent, in developing economies it is expected to be 2.1 per cent.
2. In this context it is worth quoting P. Drucker, 'In the twenty first century, population structure and populations dynamics may well again be stable, if not static. But in the last decade of the twentieth century, population structures will be the least stable and most drastically changing element in economics, society, and world politics, and perhaps the single most important cause of turbulence' (Drucker, 1981, p. 76).
3. It might seem useful to adopt the Japanese business practice in which production and marketing in many activities are organized in two separate companies, and a third one is set up for design and world marketing of products, while manufacturing is organized as a series of successive processes. These processes need not be located at the same place, or in a single company, and are not necessarily in the same country.
4. On the other hand, in the last forty years the importance of the sovereign national state as the only institution of power has been reduced. In internal politics, western democracies which are composed of various institutions are developing. In contact with other countries they achieve certain tasks through transnational associations. The task for the national states will not be a simple one as they will soon have to share power with other institutions and power bearers (Bodin, quoted by Drucker, 1993).

REFERENCES

Bea, F. and J. Haas (1995), *Strategisches Management*, Stuttgart/Jena: Fischer Verlag.

Bleicher, K. (1995), *Das Konzept des Integriertes Management*, Frankfurt/New York: Campus Verlag.

Drucker, P. (1981), *Managing in Turbulent Times*, London: Pan Books.

Drucker, P. (1993), *Die postkapitalistische Gesellschaft*, Düsseldorf: Econ Verlag.

Gloeckner-Holme, I. (1988), *Betriebsformen-Marketing im Einzelhandel*, Augsburg: FGM.

Hauschildt, J. (1988), *Krisendyagnose durch Bilanzanalyse*, Cologne: O. Schmidt Verlag.

Hinterhuber, H. (1989), *Strategische Unternehmensfuerung*, Berlin: Der Gruyter Verlag.

Johnston, W. (1991), 'Global Work Force: The New York Labor Market', *Harvard Business Review*, **69**, (2), pp. 115–27.

Jurković, P. and M. Škreb (1994), 'Financijska reforma u Hrvatskoj', *Ekonomija*, (1–3).

Kajzer, Š. (1993), 'Management', in J. Belak, (ed), *Podjetnistvo, politika podjetja in management*, Maribor: Obzorje.

Nagel, K. (1988), *Die 6 Erfolgsfaktoren des Unternehmen*, Landesberg/Lech: Modern Industrie Verlag.

14. Banking sector reforms in Croatia: problems and prospects

Marko Škreb

Croatia became an independent country in 1991. Its experience in creating and managing a sovereign financial system is rather limited. The National Bank of Croatia, formerly a branch of the National Bank of Yugoslavia, started to act as an independent central bank only at the end of 1991; the Croatian dinar (HRD) was introduced as a transitional currency on 25 December 1991. Thus the National Bank of Croatia (NBC) became the monetary authority of Croatia. The National Bank of Croatia Act and other statutory laws define legal framework for its activities. A new currency – the kuna (HRK) – was introduced at the end of May 1994.

Unfortunately, with independence, the aggression on Croatian territory started. Mainly as a result of the war and disintegration of former Yugoslavia, major macroeconomic imbalances emerged. The most visible consequence was that the Croatian economy suffered from very high inflation, keeping in mind that inflation was very high in former Yugoslavia as well. On average during the first ten months of 1993, the monthly inflation rate was 28 per cent. This prompted the NBC and the Croatian government to launch in October 1993 a Stabilization Programme (Anušić *et al.*, 1995). Its immediate aim was to slow down the inflation rate swiftly. It worked remarkably well. In 1994, 1995 and the first eight months of 1996 (last available data) average yearly inflation in Croatia was 1 per cent. The Programme is proceeding in three, overlapping phases. The first one, aimed at achieving rapid disinflation, is over. The second phase comprises structural changes in the economy. They include speeding up of the privatization process, demonopolization of the economy, restructuring of loss-making industries (such as shipbuilding), rehabilitation of the banking sector and so on. The last phase should build up sound foundations for reconstruction of the Croatian economy and start upon a sustained economic growth path. High economic growth rates are expected from 1997 onwards.

Banks are operating in a not very favourable environment. War damages are estimated at about US$22 billion. With the total GDP in 1996 not exceeding US$20 billion, it does look impressive. Owing to the war and disintegration of Yugoslavia, an enormous supply shock caused GDP to decline by one third in the 1989–93 period and unemployment rose to a high level (13 per cent). As in other former socialist countries (see Bićanić and Škreb, 1992) in Croatia the service sector is not adequately developed, especially the financial sector. Financial markets are narrow and shallow. With the long history of high inflation and a socialist system, this is no surprise. A stock exchange exists in Zagreb, but trading is very limited. There are just a few stocks and bonds traded. According to available data, non-bank financial institutions do not play an important role (with the possible exception of very short – less than one month – lending). By mid-1996, there were 21 savings banks, about 80 other savings institutions (credit cooperatives, credit unions and so on) and 14 insurance companies. Taken together, they are rather small intermediaries. Out of total assets of financial institutions, the share of savings banks and other financial institutions is probably less than 10 per cent. The Pension Fund, whose assets have increased with the privatization process, does not play an active role in intermediation of resources. Total revenues of the Pension Fund are forecast at more than 12 per cent of the 1996 GDP and those of the Health Fund at 8 per cent. Thus, with the central government share of one-third of the GDP in 1996, the total fiscal burden is more than 50 per cent.

THE BANKING SYSTEM

In Croatia the monobanking system was abolished much earlier than in other socialist countries. Only during the first five year plan (1947–52) was the 'classical' central planning system effective, including the typical passive financial accommodation of physical production. In the early 1950s a set of reforms was enacted that gradually introduced self-management. Although all economic history of Croatia is marked by a set of economic reforms (see Bićanić and Škreb, 1994), important reforms in the economy at large and the financial system took place in the early 1960s. The two-tier banking system was introduced in the mid-1960s, but as a result of a process of reforms, not one radical reform. Banks were severely limited in their activities, basically collecting deposits and extending credits.

The Banking Act from 1989 introduced fundamental changes. It can be argued that it permitted the onset of commercial banking reform in Croatia (see Martić and Škreb, 1993). All banks were transformed into either public limited liability companies (most of them) or private ones. Founders of those banks were actually transformed into 'shareholders'. But borrowing enterprises were still influential in the credit decisions of the banks. Until then, all banks operated only in the interest of their major debtors: mainly large socially owned and often loss-making enterprises. The new Banking law of 1993 introduced a lot of changes and was much more compatible with the usual environment of a predominantly privately owned market economy. It permitted private ownership, introduced prudential regulation, licensing of banks was made easier, and so on. The political events of 1990 and later (namely the disintegration of Yugoslavia) preclude a full evaluation of the effects of this reform.

Today, banks in Croatia are of a universal type, as in most other European countries. To operate in Croatia all banks must obtain a licence from the National Bank of Croatia. By the end of 1994, 53 banks were operating in Croatia.[1] One of them is a development bank (HBOR, or Croatian Bank for Reconstruction and Development); 42 banks were licensed for international operations. Given the small size of the economy, this might seem a large enough number for a competitive banking industry. However, banking in Croatia is concentrated. It is true that the Banking Law of 1993 has eased new entry into banking in an effort to spur competition. Indeed, the NBC issued a large number of licences, but large 'old' banks still dominate the market. Numbers clearly confirm this (see Table 14.1).

Table 14.1   Total gross capital of Croation banks, 31 December 1993–5 (percentage share)

	1993	1994	1995
Two largest banks	40	44	41
Four largest banks (CR4)	46	57	57
Herfindahl index	0.120	0.116	0.105

Source: Computed by the author.

Measured in terms of total assets disbursed, the degree of concentration is even higher. This can be seen in Table 14.2. The very high value of the Herfindahl index confirms the hypothesis of an oligopolistic structure of Croatian banking industry, but it has to be noted from Table 14.2 that, in the three years indicated, the concentration has been slightly declining. It is probable that an analysis of regional distribution of banks would show a greater degree of concentration in some regions of Croatia. Former so-called 'regional banks' (whose role in the socialist system was to develop or invest within a region) remained very influential in some areas. So any effort to increase competition in the banking industry must be a permanent one.

Table 14.2   Total assets disbursed by Croation banks, 31 December 1993–5 (percentage share)

	1993	1994	1995
Two largest banks	55	54	54
Four largest banks (CR4)	74	71	68
Herfindahl index	0.177	0.167	0.159

Source: Computed by the author.

OWNERSHIP AND REGULATION OF BANKS

The conditions for ownership of banks in Croatia have changed only recently. Before 1989, no bank could be privately owned. Owing to the predominant 'social ownership' in the economy, there was no clear owner of banks. They were actually 'owned' by their founders, usually enterprises. The Banks and Savings Banks Act (1993) removed limitations on private and foreign owner-ship of banks.

A large part of banks' equity capital is still owned by companies which were not completely privatized. It is important to stress that the privatization process is not complete, so that by their share ownership companies are either fully private, majority private, partly state-owned or fully state-owned. The state-owned shares are held by the Pension Fund, Health Fund or by the Croatian Privatization Fund (CPF). Thus, by implication, the same is true of banks. CPF is a newly established institution in charge of overseeing and managing the privatization and enterprise restructuring. At the end of 1995, out of 53 banks, 39 (or 74 per cent) are predominantly private banks. Private banks control 45 per cent of the total balance sheet. Following some large privatisations in banking, it may be inferred that by the end of 1996 this percentage will be significantly more than 50 per cent.

The Banks and Savings Banks Act emphasizes the principles of free entry and exit. The main goal is to increase competition and in particular to break the existing regional monopolies. Easy entry has to have very strict rules for prudential supervision, which will be described in more detail below. Banks are independent in their business activities from the state and the National Bank of Croatia. As they are joint stock companies, their management is responsible to the shareholders. Banks may be established by only one legal or natural person, resident or non-resident. The minimum equity capital requirement is set at the counter value of about DM5 million in domestic currency. Banks dealing in foreign exchange need three times that amount.

A minimum equity capital for a savings bank is set at the counter value of DM1 million in HRK, but the activity of a savings banks is limited compared to that of a bank. For example, according to the regulations, savings banks cannot take foreign exchange deposits or enterprise deposits in the national currency. Both banks and savings banks must obtain a licence from the National Bank of Croatia which, being in charge of supervising banks (including savings banks), has issued regulations for that purpose. The capital adequacy ratio is set at a minimum of 8 per cent, in accordance with European Union directives. Banks must provide security of their operations, and therefore are required to set aside reserves. On top of specific reserves for covering identified potential loan losses, banks must set aside general reserves against potential losses from risky investment and corresponding off-balance items. The annual report of the bank must be checked and evaluated by an authorized external auditor.

PERFORMANCE OF BANKS

Banking business is risky. Thus commercial banks must analyse and take risks. How successful are Croatian banks at this? During 1995, according to aggregate data, Croatian banks had a total profit of about HRK548 million (about US$100 million). Bearing in mind that in 1993 banks recorded a net loss, and in 1994 only a slight profit, this is a very positive trend, but in general there is a lot of room for increased efficiency and profitability of commercial banks. This should be achieved both by more prudent asset management and by cutting cost techniques (slimming down).

Credit decisions in some (especially large and medium-sized, state-controlled) banks are still influenced by banks' debtors – enterprises or regional politicians. Political and social motives sometimes outweigh profit-maximizing criteria in bank management. Croatian banks are on average overstaffed and their management should concentrate on reducing staff numbers if they are to be competitive on the market.

The performance of banks has been affected by changes in monetary policy since independence. The main changes in monetary policy since monetary independence are as follows (Škreb, 1995).

1. At the beginning of 1992, credits from central to commercial banks was limited; it was abolished altogether in 1993.
2. Domestic credit to central government has been legally restricted to 5 per cent of budgetary revenues. The government can take only short-term (so called 'bridging') loans which have to be repaid by the end of the fiscal year; thus they do not finance the budget deficit.

3. A lot of effort has been put into increasing the financial discipline of commercial banks, but the overall financial discipline of the economy in general, including some banks, can still be considered too soft. Obviously, increasing financial discipline is a lengthy process, and cannot be achieved overnight (Kornai, 1993).
4. National Bank of Croatia is actively engaged in developing financial markets and new financial instruments. Thus it has introduced the so-called 'NBC bills', whose main aim is to sterilize monetary effects of interventions on the foreign exchange markets.
5. During the last couple of years, the main instrument of monetary policy has been interventions of the National Bank on the foreign exchange markets. Throughout the period from 1993 to 1996, more than 97 per cent of the increase in the monetary base has been caused by monetary effects of foreign exchange transactions of monetary authorities.

According to end of May 1996 data, claims on central government represent about 23 per cent and claims on other domestic sectors 53 per cent of total assets. Claims on enterprises are 86 per cent of claims on other domestic sectors. Compared to 1993, claims on enterprises have risen, which is a good indication that banks are lending more to business-related activity.

PROBLEMS OF CROATIAN BANKS

Since independence, the Croatian government has undertaken serious efforts to recapitalize and rehabilitate banks in Croatia. The banking sector has benefited from two support operations. The first is known as Frozen Foreign Exchange Savings Deposits and the other as the Big Bonds Scheme. For many years Croatian residents were allowed to keep their savings in foreign currency-denominated deposits. Bearing in mind that Croatia has always had a tourist industry and that there is a large number of Croatian guest workers in western countries, this was a natural reaction on the part of the monetary authorities. But commercial banks in Croatia surrendered those foreign exchange deposits to the National Bank of Yugoslavia. The banks were given dinars (Yugoslav dinars at that time) and the right to buy foreign exchange from federal authorities. On their assets side, banks extended credits in national currency. Their liabilities towards depositors were (of course) in foreign exchange. Lending interest rates were negative in real terms. Because of depreciation of the national currency and revaluation, liabilities towards depositors increased steeply. Political influence in the allocation of resources, combined with negative interest rates, resulted in the accumulation of non-performing loans and banks' liquidity was in danger.

With the disintegration of Yugoslavia, about US$3.2 billion of foreign currency-denominated deposits from Croatia remained in Belgrade. The option to buy them has become a fiction. Before disintegration there was an explicit guarantee of the Yugoslav Federation for foreign currency-denominated deposits. The new Croatian government explicitly took over that guarantee but, to avoid a run on banks and a collapse of the banking system, withdrawals were limited. *De facto*, those deposits were frozen: hence the name of the rescue operation. After that, the government allowed these frozen deposits to be used for various purposes (privatization of enterprises and socially owned apartments). Later on these deposits were transformed into a public debt. This debt is being repaid in 20 instalments and interest is paid twice a year; it is of ten years' maturity, starting in mid-1995. The principal is indexed to the Deutschmark (regardless of the original deposit currency) and the annual interest rate is 5 per cent. By the end of June 1996, it is clear that this is a very heavy burden for the central budget and that a different (more gradual) scheme for repayment will have to be adopted in the near future.

The second big effort of Croatian government to recapitalize and support banks – the Big Bonds Scheme – is based on the following idea. The Croatian government issued bonds, at that time to the value of 24.5 billion HRD (worth roughly US$1 billion). These bonds were given to enterprises which had great financial difficulties (having actually defaulted on their bank debts). In exchange, the government got additional equity in those enterprises (the enterprises were recapitalized). To be eligible, enterprises had to submit a rehabilitation programme. Enterprises used the bonds to pay off their debts to banks. The amount used for this purpose was less than the value of issued bonds and amounted to roughly US$750 million. By reducing their debts, enterprises become profitable. On the other hand, banks in their portfolios held government bonds instead of bad (non-performing) loans and became solvent. Big bonds are of 20 years' maturity and their principal is indexed to producer prices.

Through this scheme the capital–asset ratio in banks changed dramatically, but, as a result of the war, a radical clean-up of the banks' balance sheet was not done. Unfortunately, it seems that no one supervised the implementation of the rehabilitation programme of the enterprises, so most of them remained financially troubled and accumulated new debts. Big Bonds can be considered only a partial success. The balance sheet of banks looks 'much nicer', and the same is true of enterprises that got these bonds, but those banks were not obliged to write off part of their capital because of non-performing loans (which would be normal in a rehabilitation procedure for a bank). The ownership structure of banks remained the same. On top of this, as enterprises were not restructured, new bad loans have accumulated.

Having in mind the heavy burden on the budget, there will be no more attempts to recapitalize the whole of Croatian banks. The Big Bonds Scheme has clearly shown that there is a serious 'moral hazard' problem in Croatian banks. Rehabilitation of some banks has started on a case-by-case approach. A new Law on Rehabilitation and Restructuring of Banks was adopted in July 1994. Banks whose potential losses amount to more than 50 per cent of liability capital are subject to rehabilitation and restructuring.

On the basis of end of 1993 data, four banks were chosen as immediate candidates for rehabilitation and restructuring. Rehabilitation of three of them has either been completed or is well under way. The decision on the last one on the list will not be taken until the end of 1996. But, without a clear picture on rehabilitation and restructuring of their main customers (debtors to be more precise), there is no point in unconditional recapitalization of those banks. On the other hand, rehabilitation of some banks is considered a crucial step in further implementation of the stabilization programme. This is a lengthy process indeed. Within future plans for bank rehabilitation or recapitalization the know-how will be supplied by the National Bank of Croatia and funds will be obtained from the central budget (Agency for Deposit Insurance and Restructuring of Banks).

Obviously, the state does play a major role in rehabilitation of banks in Croatia. This is an additional burden on the already overworked state. One should bear in mind that this can be dangerous, as state failures can be even more devastating than market failures, especially so in transitional economies (Bićanić and Škreb, 1992). It is expected that international financial organizations (like the World Bank group and EBRD) will help in restructuring and recapitalizing Croatian banks in the near future.

Further reforms, aimed at changing the behaviour in banks and in the economy by imposing stringent budget constraints (increasing financial discipline) and optimizing resource allocation, especially in large loss-making still state-controlled enterprises, are urgently needed. It is amazing to see how vested interests are deeply rooted. Microeconomic restructuring is something that we have to confront on the winding road of transformation to a market economy. To achieve this goal, organizing an efficient payment system, necessary for good financial intermediation, is a prerequisite.

Bank rehabilitation is a very tricky business, for various reasons, and thus such decisions are often delayed. Without any attempt to be exhaustive, three groups of reasons are given here for rehabilitation being so slow. First, there is lack of funds. Bank rehabilitation is costly. In 1996 alone, about HRK 450 million (1.4 per cent of total budgetary expenditures) was given in liquid assets to commercial banks in the process of rehabilitation. If the problem of bank rehabilitation is viewed as a redistributional issue, it is important to address the question of who will be worse off. Additional funds are difficult to find, especially in stagnating economies. Foreign capital is reluctant to come, especially because of high country risk. Thus the problem of bank recapitalization (which usually follows the process of rehabilitation) is tackled by government-issued securities. Following this, the problem of servicing the public debt becomes increasingly important.

The problem of bank rehabilitation cannot be separated from the question of enterprise restructuring (Borish *et al.*, 1995). In spite of difficult conditions, the Croatian government has taken firm steps in both enterprise and bank rehabilitation. Of course, this is just a first step on a multi-year exercise in fundamental restructuring of the Croatian economy.

The second reason concerns long-term macroeconomic stability. To finance long-term growth, banks need long-term funds, and those funds are usually lacking. Owing to low credibility of the banking system (allegedly) large amounts of household savings are still deposited in neighbouring countries whose financial systems are considered stable (Austria, Germany and Italy, for example). Thus it is essential for the government to sell the message that it aims to conduct a stable policy and to pursue financial discipline. It seems safe to assume that, without an increase in credibility (decrease of risk) of the country in general and the banking system in particular, there will be no long-term source of funds and no long-term financing by the banks. When speaking about credible long-term policies, financial discipline deserves special attention. It must be maintained and strengthened constantly. The government's role in this is crucial. If it does not set an example, this may undermine all efforts on other parts of transition reform. The moral of the story is that, without financial discipline of the government (in meeting its obligations and forcing other agents to do so), there will be no confidence and problems of financial intermediation may arise.

One of the facets of lack of trust in the banking system (besides high real interest rates) is financial disintermediation and the already mentioned very short-term financing (or the conspicuous lack of long-term financing). With long-term credibility it is much easier to foresee the new entry of foreign banks and their possible takeover of a troubled domestic bank. Needless to say, without macroeconomic stability financial intermediation is severely distorted and the process of bank rehabilitation cannot take place, or will be severely undermined (Škreb, 1995).

The third reason for the slowness of rehabilitation is to do with political willingness and strength to pursue restructuring. Political economy considerations cannot be neglected within the framework of systemic bank restructuring. This is especially true for all economic policy in transitional economies (see, for example, Rodrik, 1966). Without clear political support for reforms, they cannot take place. Resolving systemic banking problem is a practical exercise in multiple enterprise restructuring. This, as we have pointed out already, means substantial redistribution. Therefore some interests groups will be worse off than before restructuring. Micro reforms have their names and social security numbers on them; that is, they hurt real people. Besides this, they need a number of people working on case-by-case restructuring plans. This is usually not the case with macroeconomic stabilization programmes, which are more glamorous (seeking to achieve a dramatic drop in inflation) and affect society as a whole.

As, by definition, 'bad' banks need restructuring, it might be inferred that banks need restructuring (in transition economies) because their loans were disbursed on the basis of political considerations (not adequately measuring the risk) and not sound banking practices (otherwise they would not have turned sour in such a high percentage of cases). These banks are usually state-controlled, because in such banks politicians can influence decisions. From this it is not difficult to conclude that such banks are managed by influential people or, to be more precise, they were influential at the time of their appointment, as otherwise they would not have been appointed. This means at least two things:

1. People managing those banks were appointed by the then political elite. If this elite has not changed, their power may remain and it may be difficult to change the management of a bank in the process of restructuring, possibly creating a future moral hazard problem. (If I was rescued by the state once and nothing happened, why not try again?)
2. Bank managers have vested interests (so do managers of enterprises who received soft loans) in the existing power structure (which caused systemic bank problems) and will strongly oppose any structural change if this may mean the loss of their existing powers. They may go along with rehabilitation plans if they bear no consequences for previous behaviour, but then again we are faced with a serious moral hazard. The same is true for politicians who, without the influence over banks (which might extend credit to an enterprise whose workers are on strike), have substantially less power.

Therefore one should expect strong resistance to banking reforms from interest groups. Strong political consensus on the necessity of bank restructuring is needed. Without this the whole process cannot take place. Besides, governments rarely act quickly and necessary decisions are often delayed for various reasons (government failures, for example). Thus at least two additional problems may arise:

1. when the government announces bank rehabilitation but cannot pursue this with adequate measures immediately (because of lack of funds and/ or political impotence, as described above);

2. when measures undertaken to rehabilitate banks are not radical enough, this may enforce a moral hazard problem (as we have seen above) for the future.

Arguably, the only thing that is worse for the economy as a whole than doing nothing on warranted rehabilitation (and increasing the risk of the collapse of the financial system) is improper rehabilitation because it substantially decreases credibility (through the moral hazard problem) and increases costs of future (necessary) bank rehabilitations.

As in other transitional economies, the banking sector represents the bulk of financial markets in Croatia. Therefore the role of the banking industry is vital in financial intermediation and sustained economic growth. Needless to say, within the framework of non-rehabilitated banks, its goal cannot be performed efficiently. Immediately following macroeconomic stabilization, the problem of the banking industry must be high on the agenda. Unfortunately, bank rehabilitation is a complex exercise in microeconomic restructuring, hurting groups of people who will, most probably, strongly resist pressures to change their behaviour. On the other hand, bank rehabilitation is a costly business, which means that substantial funds must be provided for it.

Bank rehabilitation cannot be separated from enterprise restructuring, making the exercise even more complicated. Thus it comes as no surprise that the process of bank rehabilitation is slower than is both expected and warranted in Croatia. It can only be pointed out that the banking sector is very sensitive and systemic bank risk cannot be avoided, but this risk must be carefully monitored and minimized. If it is not, there is a genuine risk that macroeconomic stability may be endangered in the near future.

Creating sound finance in transitional economies is definitely a long-term project, not a once and for all activity. For example, bank rehabilitation is a 'new' activity for almost all transitional economies whose skills (including institutions and professionals alike) cannot be learned overnight. There is an obvious learning-by-doing element in this process, but this is a very costly activity indeed. Bearing in mind that commercial banks in Croatia can be considered the main financial intermediaries, both human and financial capital must be found. The same is true of political willingness. In the end, sound economic policy is always good politics as well. Of course, the pros and cons of bank restructuring (speed and extent) must be closely balanced, as in economics we cannot have what we want, we can only have what is possible. Thus the fate of transition depends very much on the overall economic and political evaluation as well as budgetary and human resources devoted to the banking sector in Croatia.

NOTE

1. If not otherwise stated, the source of all the data in the text is from National Bank of Croatia *Monthly Bulletin* or the 'Analysis of the Banking Sector in Croatia', National Bank of Croatia (mimeo).

REFERENCES

Anušić, Z., Ž. Rohatinski and V. Šonje (eds) (1995), *A Road to Low Inflation*, Zgreb: Government of Croatia.
Bićanić, I. and M. Škreb (1992), 'A Paradox of Transition to a Market Economy: How will the Role of the State Change?', in F. Targetti (ed.), *Privatization in Europe: West and East European Experiences*, Aldershot: Dartmouth.
Bićanić, I. and M. Škreb (1994), 'The Yugoslav Economy from Amalgamation to Disintegration: Failed Efforts at Moulding a New Economic Space, 1919–1993', in D. Good (ed.), *Economic Transformation in Central and Eastern Europe: Lessons and Legacies from the Past*, London: Routledge.
Borish, M., M. Long and M. Noel (1995), 'Restructuring Banks and Enterprises', *World Bank Discussion Paper No. 279*, Washington, DC.
Kornai, J. (1993), 'The Evolution of Financial Discipline Under the Postsocialist System', *Kyklos*, **46**, (3), 315–36.
Martić, R. and M. Škreb (1993), 'The Present State and Future Developments of the Financial System in Croatia', *Razvoj/Development – International*, (7), 273–86.
Rodrik, D. (1996), 'Understanding Economic Policy Reform', *Journal of Economic Literature*, 19–41.
Škreb, M. (1995), 'Monetary Independence as a Precondition for Macroeconomic Stability – The Case of Croatia', *Development and International Co-operation*, **XI**, (20–21), 159–82.

Index